THE CINEMA OF GLOBALIZATION ▬▬▬▬

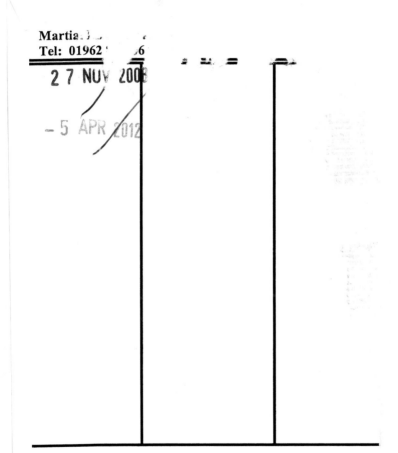

THE CINEMA OF GLOBALIZATION

*A Guide
to Films about the
New Economic Order*

TOM ZANIELLO

ILR Press
An imprint of
Cornell University Press
Ithaca and London

First published 2007 by Cornell University Press
First printing, Cornell Paperbacks, 2007

Printed in the United States of America

Library of Congress Cataloging-in-Publication Data

Zaniello, Tom, 1943–
    The cinema of globalization : a guide to films about the new economic order / Tom Zaniello.
        p.   cm.
    Includes bibliographical references and index.
    ISBN-13: 978-0-8014-4492-0 (cloth : alk. paper)
    ISBN-13: 978-0-8014-7306-7 (pbk. : alk. paper)
1. Globalization in motion pictures.   I. Title.
    PN1995.9.G59Z36 2007
    791.43'655—dc22

                                                                        2006036019

Cornell University Press strives to use environmentally responsible suppliers and materials to the fullest extent possible in the publishing of its books. Such materials include vegetable-based, low-VOC inks and acid-free papers that are recycled, totally chlorine-free, or partly composed of nonwood fibers. For further information, visit our website at www.cornellpress.cornell.edu.

Cloth printing   10 9 8 7 6 5 4 3 2 1
Paperback printing   10 9 8 7 6 5 4 3 2 1

For my AFS family

Yvonne, Alois, and Sibylle Ambauen (Switzerland)

Maria Antlitzhofer (Austria)

Valentina Brusati (Italy)

Elisabetta and Enrico Franciosi (Italy)

Helga and Kuno Hones (Germany)

Eva and Dario Meraviglia (Germany and Italy)

Anna Lordes Breve Romero (Honduras)

Johannes Voegele (Germany)

The law locks up the man or woman
Who steals the goose from the common,
But lets the greater felon loose
Who steals the common from the goose

—British folk lyric,
early nineteenth century

There is no Jade Emperor in heaven.
There is no Dragon King on earth.
I am the Jade Emperor.
I am the Dragon King.
Make way for me
You hills and mountains,
I'm coming.

—Chinese peasant song, 1958

CONTENTS ▤▤▤

ACKNOWLEDGMENTS ≡≡≡≡

Both Northern Kentucky University and the National Labor College have provided me with ideal teaching environments in which many of the films and ideas in this book could be tested in classrooms and in conversations with faculty, students, and staff.

I am fortunate to work with a wonderful team of faculty and staff in the Honors Program at Northern Kentucky University whom I cannot thank enough for their dedication and good humor: Jodi Ferner, Ron Hoffman, Dave Kime, Kelli Sittason, Aaron Zlatkin, and Belle Zembrodt. Honors students Crystal Day and Laura Teeter have been our very helpful student assistants.

Administrators at Northern Kentucky University over the years have been supportive of my research and teaching interests; this group includes but by all means is not limited to Gail Wells, Mary Ryan, and Mike Klembara.

Many individuals, distributors, and organizations have been generous in loaning films and in some cases photo stills for reproduction: Larry Adelman, Sue Barker, Ellen Brière, Larry Duncan, Judith Helfand, Ken Eisen, Marty Otanez, David Redmon, Sarah Reynolds, Ronit Ridberg, Stephanie Saxe, Gregg Spotts, Bullfrog Films, California Newsreel, Documentary Educational Resources, Filmakers Library, Films Media Group, First Run/Icarus Films, Klein Lewis Productions, Labor Beat, Media Education Foundation, New Day Films, Ruth Diskin Films, Shadow Distribution, Snitow/Kaufman Productions, Whispered Media, and Women Make Movies. Without their help, this volume would be incomplete.

I am indebted to Sherry Linkon and John Russo of the Youngstown Center for Working Class Studies and Michael Zweig of the Stony Brook Center for the Study of Working Class Life for facilitating conferences at which I tried out some of the ideas in this book.

Thanks to Chris Garlock, Katherine Isaac, and the dedicated workers and volunteers of the Debs-Jones-Douglass Institute who sponsor the annual DC Labor FilmFest at AFI's Silver Theater in Silver Spring, Maryland, where I have seen many excellent films, a number of which I discuss in this volume.

The National Film Theater and the annual London Film Festival of the British Film Institute always earn my gratitude by presenting a wonderful variety of films from around the world, some of which are included here.

This book is dedicated to my extended AFS (www.afs.org) foreign exchange family who helped me to learn about the world many years ago and continues to teach me to this day. My immediate family (Fran, Sarah and Dan, and Ben and Marion), either AFSers themselves or experienced travelers, have also taught me much about the world (and they have opinions about films, too). Likewise a big thanks and transatlantic hug to friends in London (Anna, Mike, Becca, and Lara Faulkner) who helped me to begin and sustain quite a few crosscultural and cinematic experiences over the years.

I am (as always) indebted to Fran Benson of Cornell University Press, whose support of my work continues to mean so much to me.

I look forward to hearing from readers about their experience with this book. As there are other films I could have included and some that certainly will be available after publication, I also welcome readers' suggestions. Contact me at tzaniello@nku.edu.

THE CINEMA OF GLOBALIZATION

INTRODUCTION ≣≣≣

What Is Globalization?

It begins, at breakfast, with the label on a bottle of Dole's 100% Apple Juice: "Contains concentrate from Germany, Austria, Italy, Hungary, Argentina, Chile, China, Turkey, Brazil, and the United States." How can this be? Globalization, of course.

Globalization is an economic and political phenomenon involving the transnational creation of goods and services by multinational corporations at the lowest cost and for maximum profit. To achieve this, these corporations, led and to a certain extent controlled by transnational organizations such as the World Bank (WB), the World Trade Organization (WTO), and the International Monetary Fund (IMF), exploit raw materials, labor, and the unimpeded flow of capital, in disregard of national borders.

If this working definition sounds like a description of traditional colonialism or even neocolonialism, it is perhaps because the transnational organizations are dominated by the former colonial powers, now gathered as the Group of 8 or the G-8 (Canada, France, Germany, Italy, Japan, Russia, the United Kingdom, and the United States). The reality on the ground is of course more complicated. China (the favored trading partner of multinational corporations), on the one hand, is an Asian economic tiger despite its vast peasant population because of the massive internal migration of workers from the farm to the city and aggressive entrepreneurial capitalism, both key indicators of globalization. A former neocolonial outpost like Venezuela, on the other hand, struggles to maintain control of its oil supply in the face of relentless global pressure from G-8 countries to secure scarce resources for themselves. Similarly, Bolivia, in part because of its election of Evo Morales (an Aymara Indian) as president in 2003, has resisted IMF, World Bank, and other outside capitalist pressure and returned its water supply to public control and nationalized its oil and natural gas fields.

Globalization has supplanted neocolonialism as the dominant paradigm of the relationship between labor and capital in the world. The debate about its positive or negative effects is ongoing: perhaps readers of this book and viewers of the more than two hundred films discussed will not be surprised that those films which take a labor perspective find that globalization often exploits labor, and those films which offer the perspective of business or transnational organizations tend to be overly confident about their successes.

This book offers readers and viewers the opportunity to explore globalization through films both about and from the world. I have used as broad a net as possible to gather titles (see "How Films Were Selected for This Guide" below.) Readers will not find a history of globalization here but a guide to films that have depicted the processes of globalization, its origins, its relationship with colonialism and neocolonialism, and movements to counter or protest its adverse effects.

What makes globalization so dominant today is the convergence in the last twenty-five years of political initiatives, neoliberal economics, new technologies, transportation options, and the digitalization of logistics and financial systems, all part of what I define below in the indicators of globalization. Although much of what we see in globalization today—imbalances in trading relationships, sweatshops, migratory labor, and the exploitation of Third World resources—existed before, the current era is characterized by some new features, among which we might include the leadership of transnational organizations such as the World Bank, digitalization, outsourcing and offshoring, and containerized shipping. Without these indicators, globalization in its current form would not exist.

The Indicators of Globalization

INDICATORS AT A GLANCE

transnational organizations
global labor
global capital
digitalization
changes in the workplace
outsourcing and offshoring
deregulation and privatization
oil
scarce resources
intellectual property rights
China
containerized shipping
export processing zones
anti-globalization

KEY TERMS

Banking and Global Financing
History of Globalization
Neocolonialism

Below I discuss each of the indicators and recommend resources not cited in the specific entries. For some indicators, I also give related key terms; films concerning those key terms are listed in the topical index. The detailed discussions of the films are of course in the individual film entries.

Transnational Organizations

Global economic and political control is now funneled through transnational organizations, such as the World Bank, the World Trade Organization, and the International Monetary Fund, rather than through direct colonial and neocolonial exploitation. The WB, WTO, and IMF represent the public face of globalization and for good reason: they are staffed and led by political deal makers, international brokers, investors, and trade negotiators for much of the world's business. The current president of the World Bank is, after all, Paul Wolfowitz, neoconservative political scientist and former U.S. deputy secretary of defense.

Such leadership may argue for a purely economic motivation, but part of the agenda of these organizations has been to aid the developing world and reduce world poverty. Consequently, no movement of billions of dollars or the goods and services those sums of money represent can operate outside the political context.

The World Bank, formally known as the International Bank for Reconstruction and Development, began after World War II as a mechanism for rebuilding the devastated countries where the war was fought. It has become known for its loans to developing nations and the "structural adjustment" (typically, reduction in government support for social welfare programs and privatization of public utilities) it requires.

The International Monetary Fund has among other functions the regulatory power over currency regulations and arrangements as a means of assuring worldwide financial stability.

The World Trade Organization, formerly the General Agreement on Tariffs and Trade (GATT), concentrates on reducing trade barriers and fostering tariff-free trading policies. The labor, environmental, and public health policies of individual nations are sometimes defined as impediments to free trade and are subject to revision or abolition.

So influential and powerful are these three organizations that some commentators refer to them as supranational bodies. In any case, they have both attracted a significant share of the cinema of globalization and generated protests about its policies worldwide.

Recommended Readings

DeLillo, Don. *Cosmopolis*. New York: Scribner, 2003. A comic exposé of a billionaire assets manager who has a fatal date with the declining value of the yen and this prophesy: "How will we know when the global era officially ends? When stretch limousines begin to disappear from the streets of Manhattan."

Garson, Barbara. *Money Makes the World Go Around*. New York: Penguin, 2001. The author follows her local bank deposit of $29,500 (the advance on royalties she received for the book) as it moves through the world's banking systems.

Harford, Tim. *The Undercover Economist*. New York: Oxford University Press, 2006. A World Bank consultant does not discuss the "trade of goods and services," the "migration of people," and the "exchange of technical knowledge," because "they are not what people think of when they talk about globalization." Instead he discusses "direct foreign investment" and "cross border investments" in this defense of globalization as environmentally friendly and conducive to good jobs in sweatshops.

Perkins, John. *Confessions of an Economic Hit Man*. San Francisco: Berret-Koehler Publishers, 2004. Best-selling exposé by a covert operative of the U.S. National Security Agency who bought and sold leaders of government and business all over the world.

Global Labor

KEY TERMS

Labor History
Migrant Labor (Other Than the United States)
Migrant Labor (United States)
Sex Work/Trafficking
Taxi Drivers
Women Workers and Child Labor

The global labor force has been significantly transformed by migratory labor—both within a number of countries and across their national borders—and by the exploitation of women and child workers: Turkish guest workers in Germany, Afghan refugees seeking work in Iraq, Eastern European carpenters on building sites in London—the list is endless. Millions of Chinese move from their rural homes to factory centers where local authorities barely tolerate them. Besides the Mexicans who come to the United States both legally and illegally, people from Central America, India, China, and the Middle East all pass through Mexico to come to the United States. This situation brings Michael Flynn of the International Relations Center to the conclusion that the United States' "southern border is no longer just a border with Mexico; it is a global frontier separating an idealized north from an increasingly impoverished south" (31 December 2005, online at www.americas.irc-online.org).

The documentation of migratory labor to and within the United States is considerable: numerous entries in this volume explore this topic as if it were an American obsession (see the topical index). Other filmmakers have looked at the status and conditions of migratory labor beyond U.S. borders, and if the statistics are to be believed such migration has consequences not only for the United States but the world. One of the leading analysts of globalization, Mike Davis, has argued in *Planet of Slums* (London: Verso Books, 2006), that the "emergence of polycentric urban systems without clear rural/urban boundaries"—that is, megacities of slums—are a direct result of the indicators of globalization, especially the restructuring of Third World economies by the IMF that resulted in the curtailment of social services and the loss of rural livelihoods. This disruption has led to the migration of literally millions of workers to these slums.

Some analysts such as Kim Moody see international labor as a resilient force, taking the challenges of globalization head on, as films about recuperated factories under workers' control in Argentina demonstrate: capital may be withdrawn, but the workforce sometimes fights back. Harvard economist Richard Freeman (see "Recommended Readings" below), on the other hand, argues that globalization maintains an unchanged supply of capital while doubling its workforce as China, India, and former Soviet states enter the labor market. The result is a labor pool facing ever decreasing wages.

The variety of labor in this indicator includes not only women and child workers who are employed in factories and sweatshops worldwide but also those women and (usually) teenage girls who are recruited, tricked, or kidnapped to work in brothels or in the porn industry. Human trafficking, in addition to the illegal exploitation of workers in sweatshops and factories and attacks on migratory labor, are uniquely global crimes in that they happen everywhere.

The spectrum between voluntary sex work and human trafficking (illegal by definition) may be narrow to some, but both terms are in widespread and, I would say, controversial use. Selecting one or the other is a political choice. Article 3 of the *Protocol to Prevent, Suppress and Punish Trafficking in Persons, Especially Women and Children*, which supplements the United Nations Convention against Transnational Organized Crime, defines "trafficking in persons" as the "the exploitation of the prostitution of others or other forms of sexual exploitation, forced labor or services, slavery or practices similar to slavery, servitude or the removal of organs." This remarkable statement serves as a framework for numerous films in these subcategories of global labor.

Recommended Readings

Ehrenreich, Barbara, and Arlie Russell Hochschild, eds. *Global Women: Nannies, Maids, and Sex Workers in the New Economy.* New York: Henry Holt, 2002. A collection of essays analyzing the occupations mentioned in the subtitle as well as their common origin in the economic pressure on the Third World women to care for or service First World children and men.

Freeman, Richard. "China, India, and the Doubling of the Global Labor Force: Who Pays the Price of Globalization?" *The Globalist,* 3 June 2005 (online at www.japanfocus.org/article.asp?id=377). Explains how "a decline in the global capital/labor ratio shifts the balance of power in markets away from wages paid to workers and toward capital, as more workers compete for working with that capital."

Kempadoo, Kamilla, and Jo Doezema, eds. *Global Sex Workers: Rights, Resistance, and Redefinition.* New York: Routledge, 1998. Collection of essays in support of the movement to define all aspects of prostitution as gainful labor.

Moody, Kim. *Workers in a Lean World: Unions in the International Economy.* London: Verso Books, 1997. Moody argues the opposite of what many commentators have taken for granted: labor militancy worldwide remains high, either in conjunction with or despite union leadership.

Stalker, Peter. *Workers without Frontiers: The Impact of Globalization on International Migration.* London: Lynne Rienner, 2000. Argues that the "capitalist penetration of rich economies . . . destroys traditional sources of income and simultaneously creates a pool of mobile labor, part of which is driven to migrate internationally," aided by the very "communication and transport links" created by the entry of international capital.

Tekin, Latife. *Berji Kristen: Tales from the Garbage Hills.* Trans. Ruth Christie and Saliha Paker. London: Marion Boyers, 2004. Stories of the people who live and work in Istanbul's massive garbage dump, so similar to slums across the megacities of the world.

Global Capital

KEY TERMS

Enron
Wal-Mart

Global capital is now characterized by the free movement of investment by multinational corporations and financial institutions across national borders. Enron, with its exploitation of real and virtual markets, and Wal-Mart, with its supply-chain efficiency, reliance on China, and ruthless drive for low wages, are paradigmatic corporations of the global era and have received the most attention in the cinema of globalization: the former a powerful company that went bankrupt as the latter became even more dominant.

Enron was the seventh largest corporation in the world at its zenith in the 1990s. Like most corporations it used stock options worth millions of dollars for executive pay packages, but this largesse did not appear on their financial statements (indeed even today it would earn at most a footnote). In the context of the deregulation of energy companies, Enron transformed itself from an energy provider to an energy trader, pioneering the development of derivative trading (contracts whose value depends on changes in prices of a related or underlying "product" or instrument), off-the-books partnerships (to reduce debt), and accounting maneuvers such as mark-to-marketing or gain-on-sale marketing (logging profits before they were earned). The trial and conviction of Enron's chief executives in 2006 returned the company to the news, and its effects on the economic norms of the United States are still being explored in numerous films.

Few subjects in this book have directly generated as many films as Wal-Mart. It is now apparent, as a conference on Wal-Mart at Santa Barbara predicted in 2003 (see Nelson Lichtenstein's edition of the conferees in "Recommended Readings"), that Wal-Mart is the paradigmatic corporation of the twenty-first century, just as the Pennsylvania railroad was in the nineteenth century, General Motors was in the first half of the twentieth, and Microsoft in the second half.

The films in this group date from 2003 to 2006 and attempt to take stock of Wal-Mart's impact on work in America and China (the source of 80–90 percent of Wal-Mart's products), especially the company's virulent anti-union policy, its depressed wage scale, its cut-throat competitiveness, and its domination of retail business in all the markets it penetrates.

Virtually all the films suggest that Wal-Mart's manipulation of class issues is part of its success: it recruits from an enormous pool of needy workers (mostly women), it targets its sales pitch to workers and the working poor, and it dismisses the environmental and anti-sprawl activists as hopelessly middle class. The films usually concede certain aspects of savvy business strategy that propelled Wal-Mart to the head of its class, such as its data analysis at the checkout counter, its product supply lines, its alliance with the Chinese business community, and its promotion of nonuniversity trained managers.

The average wage at Wal-Mart is between $7.50 and $8.50 per hour for a 28-hour week, with an annual employee turnover as high as 50 percent. The annual income of the CEO, Lee Scott, is about $30 million, and five heirs of Sam Walton, the founder of Wal-Mart, have fortunes worth $20 billion each. Wal-Mart is the number one corporate target for lawsuits, including those for racial and sexual discrimination (the largest class-action suit in U.S. history was on behalf of Wal-Mart's 1.6 million women workers), refusal to pay overtime, locking in workers overnight, and working off the clock. No North American Wal-Mart store or facility is unionized, but German, Chinese, and Japanese Wal-Marts are (variously) unionized, usually because Wal-Mart acquired an already unionized chain of stores.

Recommended Readings

Biody, Dan. *The Iron Triangle: Inside the Secret World of the Carlyle Group.* Hoboken: John Wiley & Sons, 2003. Microanalysis of the multinational corporation that is the epitome of the military-industrial (and political) complex of military contractors and global investment companies most people never hear of.

Hutton, Will, and Anthony Giddens, eds. *Global Capitalism.* New York: New Press, 2000. A wide-ranging and intriguing collection of essays written by such diverse hands as ecologist Vandana Shiva and former U.S. Federal Reserve chairman Paul F. Volcker.

Lichtenstein, Nelson, ed. *Wal-Mart: The Face of Twenty-First Century Capitalism.* New York: New Press, 2006. Jim Hoopes's essay, "Growth Through Knowledge: Wal-Mart, High Technology, and the Ever Less Visible Hand of the Manager," argues that "the exploitation of the working poor is now central to the business strategy favored by America's most powerful and, by some criteria, most successful corporation."

Poovey, Mary. "Can Numbers Ensure Honesty? Unrealistic Expectations and the U.S. Accounting Scandal." *Notices of the American Mathematical Society* 50, no. 1 (January 2003): 27–35. The best short essay on Enronics.

Tillman, Robert H., and Michael L. Indergaard. *Pump and Dump: The Rancid Rules of the New Economy.* New Brunswick: Rutgers University Press, 2005. Detailed analysis of the unregulated economic system that created Enron and continues to support so-called free-market chicanery.

Digitalization

Digitalization has enabled, through the development of the World Wide Web, the distribution of the world's raw materials and goods and created new forms of global media and communications. Globalization in its present stage could not exist without digitalization. Although neocolonialism and capitalism both succeeded within their own parameters for many years without it, and practices such as outsourcing can exist without it, digitalization accelerated the changes of globalization. Wal-Mart's success, according to most commentators, lies in their innovations in supply-chain logistics, using bar coding, for example, as a means for not only keeping inventory but ordering directly from their suppliers (in China in the vast majority of cases).

Beyond the mass distribution of DVDs (and home burning of disks from broadcast television, cable, or the Web), digitalization is also the foundation of new media and distribution methods (see "What Is the Cinema of Globalization?" below).

The ease of distributing, circulating, and manipulating digital film has complicated the traditions of documentary film, especially cinema verité, which developed in part to provide a self-evident document of unedited reality on celluloid film. Corporate and political organizations offer video footage for broadcast as news ("Report Faults Video Reports Shown as News," *New York Times*, 6 April 2006), while alternative media organizations (like Guerilla News Network or Indymedia) compete with both films that exist only in cyberspace (*The Diamond Life*) or pooled video footage transmitted by satellite and webcast (*Showdown in Seattle*).

Recommended Readings

Gregory, Sam, et al., eds. *Video for Change: A Guide for Advocacy and Activism.* London: Pluto Press, 2005. Especially strong on explaining how to use new and old media for agit-prop and investigative filmmaking.

Hyde, Gene. "Independent Media Centers: Cyber-Subversion and the Alternative Press." *First Monday*, 25 March 2002 (online at www.firstmonday.org/issues/issue7_4/hyde/). Surveys the origins and work of Indymedia (Independent Media Centers), a confederation of journalists and videographers who provide an "online alternative to corporate media" worldwide.

Changes in the Workplace

Changes in the workplace have significantly altered the lives of both blue- and white-collar workers, as well as contributed to the banning or marginalization of unions or attacks on them. This indicator defies brief categorization, since changes on the factory floor, farm or food processing site, and in the front office are complex and numerous. I have been even more selective than usual in choosing entries for this topic, concentrating on a number of films that are representative of particular trends. Even so, the range of topics within this indicator is very wide: thus *The Inheritance* (Denmark) points to a shift from family-owned business to multinational control, while *Waydowntown* (Canada) suggests a relationship between a globalized urban architecture and office culture. *Fear and Trembling* (set in Japan) attempts an understanding of a national business culture, while the *Grupo Alavio Films* (Argentina) suggest how a politically charged working-class movement (active in recuperating factories to make them worker-run) can radically change how businesses function.

> **KEY TERMS**
>
> Changes in the Workplace: Europe
> Changes in the Workplace: North America
> Changes in the Workplace: Worldwide

Recommended Reading

Ritzer, George. *The McDonaldization of Society.* 4th ed. Thousand Oaks: Pine Forge Press, 2004. The drive toward the "rationalization" of work has taken the creativity out of work and led to greater efficiency and massive sameness not only in the workplace but in the landscape (big box stores).

Outsourcing and Offshoring

Both outsourcing (contracting jobs to other companies, preferably in low-wage countries) and offshoring (moving an operation to another location but keeping ownership within the company) were developed by multinational companies who could afford dramatic changes in doing business. The implications of these moves are immense: changes in migratory patterns of labor in the developing countries that host these operations and usually drastic reductions in the original home country workforce, for example. In Third World countries outsourcing and offshoring have meant new jobs in both high-tech assembly plants and sweatshops, but in the scramble to provide cheap goods for export developed countries may lose jobs or face wage depression. At first these operations were centered on manufacturing, but with digitalization and the development of the World Wide Web, outsourcing of what might be called purely communications and computing operations has become routine, especially to India, and led to the massive development of their call centers.

Recommended Readings

Dobbs, Lou. *Exporting America: Why Corporate Greed Is Shipping American Jobs Overseas.* New York: Warner Business Books, 2004. The popular CNN host, hardcore Republican, and opponent of free trade offers his critique of offshoring. He caused a hullabaloo by attacking American corporations on his show (*Lou Dobbs Tonight*).

Starke, Linda, ed. *State of the World 2006.* New York: W. W. Norton, 2006. Jennifer L. Rurner and Lu Zhi's essay in this volume, "Building a Green Civil Society in China," discusses China's attempt to reduce the environmental impact of all its new factories: "The decentralization of economic power has considerably lessened the central government's ability to enforce environmental laws."

Vashistha, Atul, and Avinash. *The Offshore Nation: Strategies for Success in Global Outsourcing and Offshoring.* New York: McGraw Hill, 2006. Two consultants to *Standard & Poor's 500* companies offer advice to corporate planners on how to succeed abroad.

Deregulation and Privatization

KEY TERMS

Reaganomics
Thatcherism

In the 1980s the United States and the United Kingdom shared a number of economic and public policy developments, but few were as politically energizing to the right and catastrophic to the left as the deregulation of industries and utilities and the privatization of publicly held companies. What accompanied these processes was a corresponding reduction in the power of labor unions. Two charismatic figures, Prime Minister Maggie Thatcher and President Ronald Reagan, dominate most of the films that fall under this indicator.

Margaret Thatcher became leader of the Conservative Party in 1975 and prime minister in 1979. Nicknamed the Iron Lady for her resolute and dogged determination to take the Tories and her country sharply to the right, her leadership through 1990 created what even some of her closest allies (such as Nigel Lawson, chancellor of the Exchequer from 1983 to 1989) called Thatcherism.

Thatcherism was half economic policy, half pure right-wing politics, and 100 percent nervy. For the economic ledger, Thatcher championed free markets, fiscal restraint, tax cuts, privatization, and union busting. Politically her administration pioneered the militaristic deployment of police forces on a national scale and crackdown on perceived working-class militancy (such as the time-honored power of picketing). In many instances she embodied the paradox found in Western conservative parties: Peter Clarke ("The Rise and Fall of Thatcherism," *London Review of Books*, 10 December 1998) argued that the more libertarian her proposals sounded and the more they celebrated less government, the more likely they were to be "centralist solutions" filled with "moral authoritarianism."

What could have been her Waterloo—the miners' strike of 1984–85—instead became her crowning achievement. Tory Nicholas Ridley outlined a strategy in 1974 (leaked in *The Economist* in 1978) to defeat the unions in the power sector by stockpiling coal and to develop a national police strike force to defeat mass picketing—a strategy that was eventually carried out. British cinema has been obsessed with this strike ever since.

The Professional Air Traffic Controllers Organization (PATCO) strike was the equivalent watershed for Ronald Reagan's presidency (1980–88). Asserting an executive authority and pressing his belief that unionism was inimical to his program of shrinking big government by expanding corporate power, Reagan fired all of the strikers and welcomed scabs (military and government air controllers) into the towers. John Gray, once a leading Thatcherite and the author of *False Dawn* (see below), summarized this process as condoning "economic inequality" and producing "a business culture in which the social costs of enterprise could be ignored in good conscience." Reaganomics, he argued, valorized "the freedoms of corporate executives in a deregulated economy."

Besides downsizing government and supply-side economics, what Reaganomics and Thatcherism had in common was the triumph of the free market capitalism espoused by Friedrich von Hayek, a 1974 winner of the Nobel Prize in economics. Von Hayek believed that when the wealthy became even wealthier they were not indulging (in John Gray's words) in "special privileges and bonuses granted within a peculiar variant of capitalism. They were the exercise of inalienable human rights."

Numerous films have taken the measure of not only these historic figures but their successors as well. Like the members of Tony Blair's New Labour Party, Clintonian Democrats followed in Republican footsteps in certain arenas, such as welfare reform, and entered into a devil's wager to stop the spread of Republicanism by adopting some of their priorities, including the expansion of free trade by the NAFTA agreement and the loosening of regulatory standards in accounting (led by the Democratic senators from Connecticut, Joseph Lieberman and Christopher Dodd). The latter developments are a major theme of the films about Enron.

Recommended Readings

"Appomattox or Civil War?" *The Economist,* 27 May 1978, 21–22. A summary of the Ridley Report, the Thatcherite blueprint for remaking the British economy.

Friedman, Lester. *Fires Were Started: British Cinema and Thatcherism.* Minneapolis: University of Minnesota Press, 1993. Excellent collection of essays, including Leonard Quart's very helpful "The Religion of the Market: Thatcherite Politics and the British Film of the 1980s."

Gray, John. *False Dawn: The Delusion of Global Capitalism.* New York: New Press, 1998. An ideal book for comparing the political implications of Thatcherism and Reaganomics.

Hayward, Steven F. *The Age of Reagan, 1964–1980: The Fall of the Old Liberal Order.* New York: Prima Lifestyles (Crown), 2001. This unabashed celebration of Reaganomics, written by a conservative who makes clear that progressive ("liberal") social programs failed because of film critics like the late Pauline Kael of *The New Yorker,* not to mention President LBJ's War on Poverty.

Osler, David. *Labour Party PLC: New Labour as a Party of Business.* Edinburgh: Mainstream Pub-

lishing 2002. Argues for the continuity of political and economic policies from Thatcher's Tories through Tony Blair's New Labour Party.

Young, Hugo. *The Iron Lady: A Biography of Margaret Thatcher*. New York: Farrar, Straus and Giroux, 1989. A detailed political biography known in the United Kingdom by its clubby title, "One of Us."

Oil

In his 2006 State of the Union address, George Bush II announced that "America is addicted to oil, which is often imported from unstable parts of the world." This conclusion, from a member of the ruling class whose political career and economic fortunes are founded on oil, comes as no surprise to students of globalization, many of whom argue that the competition for oil is the single most volatile indicator of globalization—and, one might add, the source of immense profit for multinational corporations such as Exxon, which netted profits of $36 billion in 2005.

Oil runs a close second to Wal-Mart as the leading subject of the cinema of globalization. Oil has been one of the defining issues in debates about American foreign policy for many years, but as countries such as China accelerate their movement into advanced manufacturing and urban development, the competition for oil increases. Although no film can cover this topic completely, quite a few entries in this book offer both comprehensive and speculative perspectives on the matter. Unlike the lists of films for most of the other indicators, there are as many feature films as documentaries under the heading of oil.

Recommended Readings

Abdelrahman, Munif. *Cities of Salt*. Vol. 1, *Cities of Salt*; vol. 2, *The Trench*; vol. 3, *Variation on Night and Day*. Trans. Peter Theroux. New York: Vintage, 1991. Three of the five original novels in Arabic that chart the transformation of an unnamed Gulf country (Saudi Arabia) from a relatively sleepy Bedouin desert territory into an American and British dominated oil sheikdom. The author, who lost his Saudi citizenship for political reasons, worked for many years as a crude oil marketer for a Syrian oil company. His expertise in matters of oil and his understanding of the region make this the preeminent novel of the most important raw material of globalization.

Alvarez, A. *Offshore: A North Sea Journey*. Boston: Houghton Mifflin, 1986. A revealing look inside the surreal world of offshore oil rigs.

Klare, Michael T. *Resource Wars: The New Landscape of Global Conflict*. New York: Henry Holt, 2001. Commentary from a leading expert on the proposition that "the wars of the future will largely be fought over the possession and control of vital economic goods—especially resources needed for the functioning of modern industrial societies." In addition to oil and natural gas, Klare surveys the struggles over water, diamonds, other minerals, and timber.

Roberts, Paul. *The End of Oil*. Boston: Houghton Mifflin, 2004. Comprehensive introduction to "the edge of a perilous new world" represented by limited oil supplies.

Scarce Resources

The label on a bottle of Dasani water from the Coca-Cola Company says that its water is "filtered through a state-of-the-art purification system and enhanced with minerals for a pure clean taste that can't be beat." Dasani water is therefore tap water slightly transformed into imitation spring water. Why?

Water traditionally has been part of "the commons" or shared public resources, but it joins an ever-widening pool of resources—besides oil—that private enterprise endeavors to capture for profit. That diamonds, gold and silver mining, and other precious metals and minerals (coltan used for digital products, for example) have always enjoyed high prices because of scarcity and monopolistic practice is not news, but the list of scarce resources has grown today to include timber and fish.

Recommended Readings

Aldiss, Brian. *Earthworks*. London: Faber & Faber, 1965. Futuristic novel involving a cargo ship of plain (but now rare) earth that is part of the worldwide drive to replenish regions under extreme environmental distress.

Clover, Charles. *The End of the Line*. London: Ebury Press, 2004. Documents "how over-fishing is changing the world and what we eat" and includes detailed lists of which fish to choose and which to avoid on the basis of their sustainable populations.

Dean, Cornelia. "Scientists Warn Fewer Kinds of Fish are Swimming the Ocean." *New York Times*, 29 July 2005. Based on research in fishing data records, scientists see a great loss of fish species diversity, as much as 50 percent since the 1950s.

Klein, Naomi. "Reclaiming the Commons." *New Left Review*, May–June 2001, 81–89. Develops the quest of the title as an important component of the anti-globalization movement (see below).

Pearce, Fred. *When the Rivers Run Dry: Water—The Defining Crisis of the Twenty-First Century*. Boston: Beacon Press, 2006. Argues persuasively that future catastrophes will result from a shortage of water rather than oil.

Intellectual Property Rights

Intellectual property rights involve not only the copyright of creative and intellectual work but literally the stuff of life: the DNA of genetically modified organisms. The development and control of drugs worldwide and issues of food production now fall under the purview of the WTO TRIP (Trade Related Intellectual Property Rights) rule book, which enables corporations to patent living matter—not only genetically modified organisms but their very DNA and seed cultures. Much of the research on GMOs focuses on crops for First World consumption rather than the crops that matter to poor farmers—cassava, bananas, beans, and yams, according to Geoffrey C. Hawtin of the International Plant Genetic Resources Institute.

Marcia Angell, a former *New England Journal of Medicine* editor, points to Reaganomics as the reason for the drug companies' rise to economic power and control of key aspects of intellectual property rights. Besides the obvious Republican campaign promise to support business and end what right-wingers call over-regulation, the Bayle-Dole Act in 1980 gave drug companies the right to patent any discovery made by government-funded research; previously, Angell writes in *The Truth about Drug Companies*, "taxpayer-financed discoveries were in the public domain." Congress passed another boon to drug companies with the Hatch-Waxman Act in 1984, which extended the monopoly rights for brand-name drugs. Exclusive rights to important drugs means that generic drugs cannot be developed for more than fourteen years after a breakthrough for which taxpayers in most cases sponsored the research.

Recommended Readings

Angell, Marcia. *The Truth about Drug Companies: How They Deceive Us and What to Do about It*. New York: Random House, 2004. Detailed history of the topic.

Tokar, Brian, ed. *Gene Traders: Biotechnology, World Trade, and the Globalization of Hunger*. Burlington: Toward Freedom, 2004. A collection of essays on the interaction of agribusiness sponsoring genetically modified organisms and powerful organizations such as the World Bank.

China

With a low cost for manufactured goods, a seemingly endless supply of cheap labor, controlled and docile unions, and aggressive entrepreneurs, China has become the world's favored trading partner. It has reached this status despite its communist heritage: its peasant masses have become migratory labor, most of its factories are no longer state-owned or collectively run, its sweatshops cater to American and other multinational demands, and even without the demands of a World Bank its social services are being curtailed. We have almost reached the point where no film about international trade and multinational business could exist without considering China.

China's tremendous economic growth has trumped all previous Western political distrust and paranoia: in the past when we spoke of "Made in China" we of course meant Taiwan or Hong Kong. China has moved from the status of Red Menace to Favored Trading Partner and from the daring diplomatic target of President Nixon to the World Bank partner of President Clinton. And in the final triumph of globalization, China and Wal-Mart have virtual equal status as trading partners (see "Transnational Organizations" above).

Recommended Readings

McGregor, James. *One Billion Customers: Lessons from the Front Line of Doing Business in China.* New York: Wall Street Journal Books, 2005. Detailed case studies of how companies attempt to penetrate the Chinese market.

Starke, Linda, ed. *State of the World 2006.* New York: W. W. Norton, 2006. A comprehensive collection of essays from the Worldwatch Institute on "progress toward a sustainable society" with a special focus on China and India.

Containerized Shipping

Containerized shipping provides the literal means of transportation for the world's raw materials and finished goods. For this indicator we should imagine the global fleet as consisting not only of ships that transport a container anywhere from 20 to 53 feet long, which is then delivered inland by train or truck—the triumph of globalized shipping, in fact—but also the tankers that move crude oil around the world and the fish factory ships that can raise more fish in one day than some Third World villages harvest in a year. In short the fleet of ships operating on every ocean in the world with global appetites for scarce resources and raw materials and finished goods.

What began as a novel way to deliver materiel to American troops during the Vietnam War has developed into the key logistics tool of globalization. And while giant oil tankers have had serious accidents worldwide, container ships have a longevity that ceases only when they are beached at the wrecking yards of India and Pakistan and dismantled (see *Workingman's Death*).

The elimination of dockworkers and their militant unions is also part of this development: not only are fewer hands needed to load and unload ships, but the docks have become deregulated and privatized, encouraging practices (such as casualisation in the United Kingdom) that foster a workforce of part-time and inexperienced employees.

Recommended Readings
Barboza, David. "A New Port in Shanghai, 20 Miles Out to Sea." *New York Times*, 12 December 2005. China aims to move from number 3 in the list of the world's largest container shipping ports (behind Hong Kong and Singapore) to number 1, building a port to handle twenty million containers by 2020.
Cudahy, Brian. *Box Boats: How Container Ships Changed the World*. New York: Fordham University Press, 2006. Traces the "box" from its first success in supplying U.S. troops in the Vietnam War to its essential role in the global exchange of raw materials and finished goods.

Export Processing Zones (EPZs)

The beauty of EPZs for multinational corporations is their disconnect to the national sovereignty whose geography they share. Thus free trade zones, special customs and warehouse zones, free ports, and maquiladoras all become a virtual corporate territory in which the taxes and laws of the host country are up for negotiation. In some cases container ships dock, offload materials to a nearby EPZ factory, have workers transform them into finished products, and ship them right out on yet another container ship.

China offers a special case. Collectively owned factories (called Township and Village Enterprises) were transformed into Special Economic Zones, which through privatization passed into the hands of local capitalists and officials and/or foreign investors. (See Gerard Greenfield's analyses of the changes in China's economy and discussion of the growing discontent among Chinese workers in the 1990s.)

Recommended Readings
Fischer, Ronald D., ed. *Latin America and the Global Economy: Export Trade and the Threat of Protection*. London: Palgrave Macmillan, 2001. Wide-ranging collection of essays, using case studies to illuminate EPZs and other aspects of globalized trade.
Goodman, Peter S., and Philip P. Pan. "Chinese Workers Pay for Wal-Mart's Low Prices." *Washington Post,* 8 February 2004. Wal-Mart is ideal for China because it is "the world's greatest facilitator of capitalist production, beckoning multinational giants with tax-free zones and harsh punishment for anyone with designs on organizing a labor movement."
Greenfield, Gerard. "China's Communist Capitalism: The Real World of Market Socialism." In *Ruthless Criticism of All that Exists: Socialist Register 1997*, ed. Leo Panitch, 96–122. London: Merlin Press, 1997. Argues that privatization in China reduces the labor force as it lowers wages and suspends traditional workers' rights in a system as much "neo-authoritarian" as it is neo-liberal.

Anti-globalization

KEY TERMS

Earth as Colony
Global Catastrophes

Although three major demonstrations against the WTO—in Seattle in 1999, Washington, D.C., in 2000, and Genoa in 2001—are the most public manifestations of the anti-globalization movement, numerous other aspects of anti-globalization activism are important: the antisweatshop movement, pure food activists, and open land and fishing rights organizations all represent alternative political visions, and all of them have generated a significant number of films. The most comprehensive anti-globalization activists are Naomi Klein, author of *No Logo* (see below), and Charles Kernaghan, leader of the National Labor Committee (in part supported by unions such as Unite!). Both strive to uncover political and corporate ties among the ruling elite in the United States and elsewhere and attempt to rally opposition through extensive demonstrations, media campaigns, and films.

There are, however, two other kinds of anti-globalization cinema that have received less critical attention: catastrophe and science fiction films. The plots of many of these films are similar: because of some activity in the financial or political sphere, chaos is let loose, usually in cities such as London, Tokyo, or New York. First the banking system falls apart and then the whole economy. In some cases the catastrophe is environmental or biological (through genetically modified organisms), as in two science fiction classics (neither in this volume) whose effects never become global, *Mimic* (1997) and *Andromeda Strain* (1971): in the former scientists create a mutant roach, while in the latter the mutating virus is from outer space.

Like the earlier scare about the SARS virus that originated in China in 2003, the avian flu virus first began to infect humans in 2006 who—although they contracted the virus from birds—generated fears that the virus could mutate into a form humans could pass on to each other not in isolated instances but as a contagion. *Fatal Contact: Bird Flu in America* (2006), the first major film to offer the doomsday speculation of a mutating avian virus spread through human contact, dramatized one controversial factor in a potential pandemic: transmission of the virus by migrating wild fowl. Mike Davis in *The Monster at Our Door: The Global Threat of Avian Flu* (New York: New Press, 2005) does not downgrade that factor's importance but emphasizes instead how avian flu transmission is a feature of migratory labor: internal migrants in countries such as China crowd into slums to be near new factories and by rural tradition keep fowl as either pets or food sources.

Science fiction films do not always speculate what workers will still be necessary in the technological future to build and run all the cool machines and mine new planets for scarce resources. A few glances in this direction are evident: in *Alien* (1979) the crew are really cargo workers, in *Screamers* (1995) the setting is an abandoned mine, and in the television series *Babylon 5* (season 1 [1994], episode "By Any Means Necessary") the spaceships's dockworkers actually go on strike because of speedup and safety issues.

This book includes science fiction films in which the earth becomes the colony of an alien civilization: visiting aliens (usually cleverly disguised as humans) seize control of economic or corporate power and literally suck the earth dry of its resources, treating the planet, therefore, as a Third World colony ripe for extraterrestrial exploitation. The films *They Live* and *Save the Green Planet* portray the aliens' economic control as neocolonial rulers.

David Korten's *When Corporations Rule the World* offers a critique of corporate power that epitomizes a number of these cinematic genres: "As corporations gain in autonomous institutional power and become more detached from people and place, the human interest and the corporate interest inevitably diverge. It is almost as though we were being invaded by alien beings intent on colonizing our planet, reducing us to serfs, and then excluding as many of us as possible."

Recommended Readings

Cazdyn, Eric. *The Flash of Capital: Film and Geopolitics in Japan.* Durham: Duke University Press, 2002. An extraordinary analysis of Japanese film, including science fiction and anime, which discusses globalization as a "transformed configuration of the world system" in which national capitalisms give way to transnational capitalism "while preserving the [nation-state's] ideological usefulness."

Klein, Naomi. *No Logo: Taking Aim at the Brand Bullies* (New York: Picador, 2000). The pioneering critique of corporate branding and its role in global marketing.

Korten, David C. *The Great Turning: From Empire to Earth Community*. San Francisco: Berrett-Koehler, 2006. Expands his critique of multinational corporations (in *When Corporations Rule the World* [Bloomfield, Conn.: Kumarian Press, 2001]) to the widespread corrosive effects of chauvinism of whatever source (race, religion, etc.) and offers an alternative, the Earth Charter, a decentralized proclamation of community.

McGrath, John. *Hyperlynx*. London: Oberon Books, 2002. One-woman play about a British intelligence agent who is having a crisis of conscience as she is placed in charge of infiltrating and watching anti-globalization organizations in London.

Newman, Robert. *The Fountain at the Center of the World*. Brooklyn: Soft Skull Press, 2004. Heralded (inaccurately) as the first novel of globalization, Newman's complicated plot takes us all over the world, through the experiences of a Mexican migrant to the United States and a corporate communications flunky ("It is easier and less costly to change the way people think about reality than to change reality") who turn out to be brothers, finally converging on the 1999 WTO protests in Seattle. (A BBC film *Scribbling* [2002] featured Newman and the writing of the novel.)

Roy, Arundhati, and David Barsamian. *The Checkbook and the Cruise Missile*. Boston: South End Press, 2004. After her success with the novel *The God of Small Things* (New York: Random House, 1997), Arundhati Roy became internationally known not only as a spokesperson for the detrimental effects of globalization in India (specifically her campaign against the Narmada River Dam) but also as a campaigner against the excessive use of American power. This collection of essays, originally titled *The Globalization of Dissent,* continues her polemics against globalization.

Although there is little widespread consensus across the political spectrum about what constitutes globalization, my list of indicators accords with most of the literature on the subject, and there is strong agreement on at least five of the indicators (transnational organizations, digitalization, outsourcing and offshoring, deregulation and privatization, and containerized shipping) as the sine qua non of globalization. Three representative voices from the political center, right, and left have written about many of the same aspects of globalization I have identified.

Thomas L. Friedman's two books about globalization, *The Lexus and the Olive Tree* (New York: Farrar, Straus and Giroux, 1999; revised, 2000) and *The World is Flat* (New York: Farrar, Straus and Giroux, 2005) would be considered by many to be politically centrist, although his discussion of labor worldwide is limited mainly to whether jobs can be outsourced: of the millions of workers in worldwide migratory patterns, for example, his analysis is minimal. The strength of his books lies in his extended discussions of digitalization, changes in the workplace, and outsourcing and offshoring. He situates the sea change in digitalization caused by the arrival of Netscape and the fiber optic network and discusses changes in work flow through internal communications (what he calls insourcing).

Philippe Legrain, a former advisor to the director general of the World Bank and an enthusiastic supporter of the beneficial effects of globalization, has what I would call a rightist view. His book, *Open World: The Truth about Globalization* (New York: Ivan Dee, 2004), stresses the success of foreign investment and global communications and notes that factories and sweatshops are usually locally owned and hence beneficial to the countries in which they are located. He concludes that "the evidence that globalization helps alleviate poverty is overwhelming." His remark, if true, would erase much of the footage of many of the films in this book.

From the left Susan George's blistering critique of globalization and its corrosive effect on First World economies, *The Debt Boomerang* (London: Pluto Press, 1992), offers a provocative thesis about globalization (especially in regard to transnational organizations, global labor, global capital, and changes in the workplace): the West (in some other commentaries, the North) actually loses so many jobs and markets and has to contend with controversies over such issues as immigration policy, higher taxes, and drug traffic that globalization may be an endgame it should not always be playing. Add the increasing number of wars and conflicts over oil and scarce resources accompanied by environmental destruction and the title of her book becomes clear. Her conclusion that "globalization is a political order made by and for transnational corporations" is supported by many but not all of the films in this volume.

What Is the Cinema of Globalization?

The digitalization and online delivery of moving images that do not exist in any traditional medium have challenged us to define *cinema* in the broadest possible way. The art of moving pictures now encompasses traditional celluloid film (both 16mm and 35mm), videotape, and many other options possible only because of digitalization.

Although the costs of digital production and distribution are relatively low and the rate of digital production has accelerated, the industry of cable television and made-for-TV films and the broadcast and satellite transmission of films regardless of origin has not significantly decreased. Furthermore filmmakers have turned to animation, CGI (computer generated imagery), and gallery or other onsite installations using video or digital projection as other means of developing their visions of globalization. Filmmakers combine animation and live action photography routinely as well as digitally altered images recorded by various means.

DVD has become an important mass medium in its own right: it serves as a vehicle for both digital and traditional films, for commercial releases and home movies, and for original releases as well as second runs. Although DVDs exist because of digitalization, digitalization also delivers films that do not exist outside of a Web site: two entries in this volume, for example, *Outsource This!* and *Why Cybraceros?*, both tongue-in-cheek dramatizations of labor migration, are what I would call Web-based cinema: they are narratives, involve filmed actions, but are digitally manipulated and occupy only cyberspace. Another similar entry in this volume, *Unknown Quantity* (on global catastrophes), however, has never been distributed or exhibited outside of gallery installations.

The rise of video capabilities in cell phones and iPods will continue the trend toward digitalization through full downloads of streaming and flash video. Short films with content other than entertainment are already a feature of political, investigative, and news websites, and there is every reason to expect that longer films about globalization made in these new media will begin to be available.

The primary criteria for inclusion of films in this guide, however, are not predicated on the method of production of the moving images but on the subject matter of the films. Nonetheless, it is important to realize that one of the indicators of globalization—digitalization—is in fact the reason the cinema of globalization can be such an elastic rubric.

How Films Were Selected for This Guide

Films, regardless of medium, therefore, were selected for this volume based on the following criteria:

1. films about global labor and labor unions affected by globalization;
2. films about global capital and multinational corporations;
3. films about the transnational organizations (WB, IMF, WTO) most closely identified with globalization and global capital;
4. films about labor history and the daily life of working-class people as they relate to the development of globalization;
5. films about the environment directly related to changes in labor or capital;
6. films about changes in both the workplace and the corporate office in the era of multinational corporations;
7. films specifically tracking the indicators and key terms from the list above.

The origins of the 213 films covered in the 201 entries (a few entries have multiple films) are varied, although the majority (143) are from English-language film industries (101 from the United States and 42 from the United Kingdom, Australia, Canada, and Ireland). The remaining 70 films are from Europe (32) Asia (14), Latin America (12), Africa (8), and the Middle East (4). (Some of the films have multiple countries of origin, but I used the primary or first country listed in the production credits for this survey.)

How to Read the Entries

General Information

There are two ways to access the films in this volume: alphabetically by title or by the topical index, which is organized by indicator (e.g., transnational organizations), key term (e.g., neocolonialism), or other topic (e.g., Africa).

In each entry the title of the film is followed by an alternative or foreign title (if one exists) and the indicator or key term of globalization. Essential information about the film follows: date of release, length in minutes, country of origin, language of film (if not in English), director's name, and distributor (see below). If there is an MPAA rating (R, PG-13, or PG) or the film is in black and white (B & W), I have so noted. I follow American usage generally, with the exception of the spelling of the United Kingdom's Labour Party.

A significantly more challenging issue of terminology is the widespread use of the term "Third World" to denote undeveloped and underdeveloped countries; "Global South" is the term usually preferred by anti-globalization critics and activists. In film studies the term "Third Cinema"—Hollywood is First Cinema and European art or auteur-centered filmmaking is Second—gained popularity for a time to describe the films of mostly former imperialist colonies. It has never really caught on, despite Mike Wayne's *Political Film: The Dialectics of Third Cinema* (London: Pluto Press, 2001), which argues (convincingly) for its continued relevance to denote anticolonial and politically progressive films, many of which target the national bourgeoisie of former colonies. For the most part I have retained

"Third World" because of its continued widespread usage, although if a film or resource uses Global South I follow their lead in context.

When an entry is a documentary or related form, I have included the type (see "Documentaries and Related Genres" below). In some instances, entries have designations from other genres—an animated film or a television series (with multiple episodes or shows)—but if there is no specific designation the entry is a feature or short (fiction) film (see "Traditional Feature and Other Fiction Films" below.)

This is the third in my series of volumes on labor films; the first was *Working Stiffs, Union Maids, Reds, and Riffraff: An Organized Guide to Films about Labor* (1997) and the second was a revised edition of *Working Stiffs*, subtitled *An Expanded Guide to Films about Labor* (2003), both published by ILR/Cornell University Press. I have included here (with revisions) twelve films from the latter because they represent important issues in the cinema of globalization:

Collision Course

Controlling Interest

Le Franc

H-2 Worker

Hyenas

Life and Debt

The Little Girl Who Sold the Sun

Mickey Mouse Goes to Haiti

The Navigators

The New Rulers of the World

Taxi Dreams

Wall Street

The length of the entries varies, usually depending on the length or complexity of the film. Each entry offers a summary of the main issues in the film and their relationship to globalization, sometimes a reference to the film's place in a director's work or tradition of cinema, and usually an assessment/opinion of the film's strengths and weaknesses. I have not avoided a critical comment or two when I felt it was justified.

When an entry includes a cross-reference to another film in the book, a "see" or "q.v." reference is used. Films that were included in *Working Stiffs* (without an entry in this book) are so noted, but other films are simply identified by year of release.

All of the entries are followed by one or more selected resources, which may be a critical review of the film, background reference material, or further information about globalization. I include more reviews from the *New York Times* (various critics) and the *Chicago Sun-Times* (Roger Ebert) than from other media because I usually find them quite helpful and they are readily accessed on the Web (especially through www.imdb.com or www.rottentomatoes.com or www.metacritics.com). Many other reviews are available at these sites if my choices are not as helpful as I intend.

Because of the ease of use of major search engines, I only on occasion include a Web address, usually when I feel the entry is not as readily available. If no website is listed it is because the entry is easy to locate. If the Web address given is no longer functional, first try a search engine. If it is still not available it is possible to pursue it among the 55 billion web pages archived (as of 2005) in the Internet Archive (online at www.archive.org/web/web .php) using their Wayback Machine search.

Documentaries and Related Genres

Although many viewers identify the documentary as the primary genre for the exploration of social and economic issues, most likely they are thinking of those produced for public television stations and commercial television. These are usually traditional documentaries that attempt a balance of viewpoints on a topic or television news documentaries that feature a correspondent or reporter who remains on camera for a significant period of time.

In truth there is a much wider range of documentaries, as well as semirelated fictional forms:

1. *Social Realist Documentaries*. The films in this category illuminate a social problem or argue for a massive change in public priorities. They typically use an authoritative voice-of-God narrator, black-and-white contemporary footage, and informational titles and maps. Recommended: *New Earth*.

2. *Traditional Documentaries*. These films are derived in spirit from the social realist documentaries of the 1930s in their focus on social problems and historical events. They use a mixture of interviews, archival footage, news or newsreel footage, photo stills, and text (informational titles), linked by an obvious chronology and/or location or by a central theme, conveyed by a strong, often objective-sounding narrator, and in some cases with either actual or commentative music and sound. Recommended: *The Corporation*.

3. *Cinema Verité*. With the introduction in the 1960s of portable and lightweight cameras with synchronized sound, these documentaries rely on extended long takes of actions, conversations, or interviews, filmed somewhat spontaneously with minimal or no lighting, and with minimal or no presence of the investigative reporter or narrator; they tend to have no musical track and no other interpretative or framing devices. Stephen Mamber's classic definition—filming "real people in undirected situations"—is succinct and accurate. Recommended: *Choropampa*.

4. *TV Documentaries*. Intended for broadcast television, they now are often available online or on DVD. They may have the strong narrator and singleness of purpose of a traditional documentary, but they are often introduced or narrated by a star or celebrity reporter (who may even appear in the film); *Frontline*, for example, calls its narrator a "correspondent," but the brief is investigative. They use location shooting as if reporting a news event and rely on numerous interviews, either in the field or in the studio. Recommended: *Bigger Than Enron*.

5. *Agit-Prop Documentaries*. Drawing on the techniques of traditional and television documentary styles, these films are often sponsored by political groups or unions to convey a strong political message or call to arms. They are specifically

designed to organize workers or mobilize community support and boycotts or expose an injustice. Agit-prop films differ from other documentaries because they do not take a long view of history, they do not deliberately challenge the form of the documentary itself, nor do they offer a balanced journalistic report. Recommended: *Mickey Mouse Goes to Haiti*.

6. *Postmodern Documentaries*. These hybrid films draw freely on the other documentary varieties and intercut scripted or fictional scenes as well as sequences from other films (sometimes Hollywood films, sometimes deliberately campy or absurd footage) and often star the filmmaker as an essential part of the action. Recommended: *From the Other Side*.

7. *Structuralist Documentaries*. Originally and especially in the 1970s, structural or structuralist cinema meant avant-garde or experimental films that used "the shaping of film's material—"light, time, and process" as "a new form of aesthetic pleasure, free of symbolism or narrative," according to A. L. Rees, *A History of Experimental Film and Video* (London: British Film Institute Publishing, 1999). Subsequently filmmakers used the form to explore imagery, landscape, and action as primarily visual (and aural) experiences with minimal or no narrative or conceptual framework. The structuralist documentaries in this book have more narrative coherence than their avant-garde predecessors, although they do, as Nicky Hamlyn (*Film Art Phenomena* [London: British Film Institute Publishing, 2003]) suggests, tend "to explore a location" rather than use landscape, as mainstream films tend to, "as a backdrop for drama." Recommended: *Under the Tower*; *El Valley Central*.

8. *Ethnographic Fictions*. Although anthropologist and cinema-verité pioneer Jean Rouch is the filmmaker most identified with ethnographic fictions, a variation on ethnographic filmmaking, other directors have used the concept on occasion. The essence of the approach is to use nonprofessionals to mimic an activity as if they were doing it "in real life." Thus the subject of the film approximates what Karl G. Heider, another anthropologist and filmmaker, contends is the essence of ethnographic film—filming "whole bodies, whole people, and whole acts" (*Ethnographic Film* [Austin: University of Texas Press, 1976])—but with a scenario that is sometimes scripted in collaboration with the subjects of the film. Recommended: *The Jaguar Quartet*; *Divine Carcasse*.

9. *Mock Documentaries*. These pseudodocumentaries have the form of traditional (or other types of) documentaries but use professional and nonprofessional actors in scripted or semiscripted action. Successful ones convince (or even fool) viewers into believing that what they are seeing "actually" happened and was being filmed as it occurred in real life (as opposed to scripted). Recommended: *The Battle of Orgreave*.

Traditional Feature and Other Fiction Films

The American feature-length (fiction) films in this guide originate in Hollywood and television studios from both commercial and cable producers and from independent filmmakers. Films from other national cinemas may be independent or state-subsidized. I discuss a film's origin whenever it makes a difference in understanding or assessing the film. The genres of these films vary, although social realism, comedy, and romantic drama are well represented. Perhaps readers will also discover some unexpected genres, such as political thrillers (even a virtual subgenre, the petro-thriller, about corporate and governmental conspiracies to secure oil), catastrophe films (the end of the world), and science fiction films (alternative or future realities). Although these last two genres are reasonably well known, their specific relevance to globalization has been discussed above.

Other fictional forms, such as episodic television series, animated films, and short films, are discussed within the entries themselves. Mock documentaries and ethnographic fictions are hybrids of fiction and documentary and are discussed for convenience in the documentary section above.

Film Availability and Distributors

Most of the films in this volume are available online or on DVD (and occasionally still only in VHS); in some instances I saw a film at a film festival, in a theater, or other venue and its distribution has been delayed for some reason. And of course some films enter or leave distribution channels all the time. Use of a good Web search engine is the best avenue of up-to-date availability and distribution information.

Nevertheless most of the films in this volume are available for sale or rental from the big-volume Web sales outlets such as Amazon.com or DeepDiscountDVD.com or Moviesunlimited.com (and quite a few others), mixed sales and rental groups such as Facets.org, and purely rental outlets such as Netflix.com. If these do not have the films you are interested in, use your favorite search engine. A few films are simply not available in any format.

For a significant number of documentaries distributed by specialty outlets, I have included the website (if it relates to only one film in this volume) or the name of one of the following distributors in the heading of the entry (if more than one film in this book is available from the same distributor):

> Bullfrog Films, www.bullfrogfilms.com
>
> California Newsreel, www.newsreel.org
>
> Documentary Educational Resources, www.der.org
>
> Filmakers Library, www.filmakers.com
>
> First Run/Icarus Films, www.frif.com
>
> Media Education Foundation, www.mediaed.org
>
> New Day Films, www.newday.com
>
> NLC (National Labor Committee), www.nlcnet.org
>
> PBS, www.shop.pbs.org
>
> Ruth Diskin Films, www.ruthfilms.com
>
> Whispered Media, www.whisperedmedia.org

≡ THE FILMS ≡

▶▶▶
Afro@digital

DIGITALIZATION

2003, 52 mins., Congo/France, in English,
  French, Yoruba, and Jula with English
  subtitles
Director: Balufu Bakupa-Kanyinda
Traditional Documentary
Distributor: California Newsreel

Until the rise of cell phone usage in Africa, telecommunications were expensive and unreliable, especially in rural areas. Since a letter took up to twenty days to be delivered in Burkina-Faso, for example, digitalization clearly facilitated simple communications, but it has brought other benefits as well. Urban cybercafes, long a mainstay for youth in the First World, have become for select African countries educational centers for learning and research. In rural communities savvy leaders have organized visits of a cyberbus, whose deployment of a large screen and a projector meant the internet was open to the entire community. When Web commerce began to take hold, some African banks developed new methods of online account transfers for customers without credit cards.

Afro@digital argues that digitalization in Africa does not have to be a continuation of neocolonialism if the African people can participate in a global community of users and can produce their own content about their lives. One way for Africans to control their own digital content is through the use of video forums and teleconferencing linking students and educators across the continent in distance-learning centers. In the film, a musician notes that only after access to digitalization was he able to successfully record and reproduce the indigenous music of pygmies that had not been loud enough for the patterns in their harmonies to be perceived.

A fascinating piece of neocolonial history may overlap this self-conscious pursuit of a digital culture: filmmaker Georges Kamanayo discusses the oldest mathematical artifact ever discovered, the Ishango Bone from the eastern Congo, an object twenty thousand years old that was most likely a calculating tool. Its surface looks like a bar code of prime numbers, and it has a counting function using base 12 for its numerical system. Although the artifact was discovered by Belgian explorers in the 1950s and warehoused in Brussels, only recently has it become available to Africans for study. Kamanayo plans to use it—like the plinth in Stanley Kubrick's *2001: A Space Odyssey* (1968)—as an ancient object symbolizing Africa's digital future.

Recommended Reading
  Clancy, Jim. "Inside Africa." CNN International (edition.cnn.com), 12 August 2000. Short news report on the Ishango Bone and Kamanayo's film.

▶▶▶
Alambrista

The Jumper
The Illegal

MIGRANT LABOR (UNITED STATES)

1977 and 2004, 110 mins., United States, in
  English and Spanish with English
  subtitles
Director: Robert M. Young
Screenplay: Robert M. Young

This early film about migrant laborers from Mexico was originally released in 1977, but despite a Caméra d'Or award at the Cannes Film Festival the following year, it was rarely seen or appreciated for its insights. The director released a new cut in 2004, with new scenes and soundtrack and with a new score by Dr. Loco and Sus Tiburones del Norte (Jose Cuellar's band).

The film does not allow its protagonist, Roberto, to flourish, despite his successful entry into the United States. He is burdened by his guilt over the wife and child he has left behind and the relationship he has begun with a gringo woman. Roberto's own father crossed over a number of years earlier and never returned. And, like the African American hero of Robert Young's *Nothing But a*

Man (in *Working Stiffs*), Roberto is in danger of repeating his father's transgression. Roberto soon retraces the steps of thousands of undocumented workers before him and moves from field labor to desperate day labor jobs.

"Alambrista" literally means an acrobat on the high wire; it has come to mean, simply enough, an illegal immigrant. In many ways Roberto is a composite character, created from a number of probably similar experiences of illegal immigrants. Young nonetheless makes him a convincing representative of the many workers who, with just a false step or two, can fall from their precarious spot.

The DVD also contains an early documentary by Young, *Children of the Fields* (1973), about child workers as migrant laborers ("An American Family in Arizona" is the subtitle of the film). It covers similar disturbing ground as *Dateline*'s 1997 television documentary, *Children of the Harvest* (see *Working Stiffs*).

Recommended Readings

Cull, Nicholas J., and David Carrasco. *Alambrista and the U.S.-Mexico Border*. Albuquerque: University of New Mexico Press, 2004. This volume has numerous essays about the film and a DVD of the film itself.

Maslin, Janet. "Robert M. Young's *Alambrista*." *New York Times*, 23 September 1979. "A small, gentle, beautifully made film about a subject that might, in more conventional hands, have received either harsher or more histrionic treatment."

▶▶▶

All for One

ANTI-GLOBALIZATION
CONTAINERIZED SHIPPING

1997, 21 mins., United States
Director: Larry Duncan
Agit-Prop Documentary
Distributor: Labor Beat (www.laborbeat
  .org)

To contest one of the major changes in servicing the docks—reducing the unionized workforce—dockworkers have resorted to slowdowns, wildcat strikes, and walkouts. But in some cases, especially in England, they were sometimes blindsided by management decisions.

Videographers from around the world—Liverpool, San Francisco, Stockholm, and Tokyo—pooled their footage of a single day, January 20, 1997, when protests and port work-stoppages took place to support five hundred Liverpool dockworkers fired in a dispute over the use of "casual"—that is, nonunion, temporary—labor. The biggest contributor to the one-day solidarity strike was the American West Coast dockworkers' union, the International Longshore and Warehouse Union (ILWU), which shut down operations from Los Angeles to Seattle. Footage of the stoppage on the Tokyo docks stressed the ship owners' globalization agenda: deregulate the ports, privatize the docks, and rely on casual labor.

This is a quiet film enlivened in the Liverpool sequences by a traffic blockade by sympathetic taxi drivers and demonstrators perched atop the cranes that load and unload the container ships. The San Francisco footage features the working-class poet Jack Hirschhorn, who rhymes: "Privatize will blind your eyes." The pooling of the footage represents an attempt at alternative news programming, similar to *Showdown in Seattle* and *This Is What Democracy Looks Like* (both q.v.).

Recommended Reading

Hain, Peter. *Political Strikes*. Harmondsworth: Penguin, 1986. A history and analysis of British trade union strikes, including the dockworkers', arguing that the "nature of strikes is determined by the political climate and not simply the role of unions and employers."

▶▶▶

American Daylight

OUTSOURCING AND OFFSHORING

2004, 98 mins., India, in English
Director: Roger Christian
Screenplay: Farrukh Dhondy

It's daytime in America, night in India, so Indian call centers serving transnational businesses are staffed by workers selected—or coached—for what might pass for an American accent. Sujata (played by Koel Puri), nicknamed Sue, speaks unaccented English. She is too trusting and is seduced by the voice, confident manner, and apparent dilemma of an American millionaire, Lawrence (played by Nick Moran), who says his estranged wife is emptying his bank account. On the surface this could be the material for a comedy—"Sleepless in Bangalore"—but Sue's supervisor, Pat (played by Vijay Raaz), is jealous and well aware that she has bent the rules to help Lawrence.

When Lawrence wants to meet Sue, not realizing who or where she is, the potential farce turns tragic. Outsourcing manufacturing is no longer news in the First World, and offshoring financial arrangements have been extensively exposed by the collapse of Enron. But the film brings to life a virtually invisible phenomenon of everyday life: the voice *of* a corporate office is no longer *at* a corporate workplace.

This is a rare (fictional) look inside a call center, using an actual workplace in Bangalore for filming, a location whose absence in the visual media is inversely proportional to its size as an industry: hundreds of call centers service major American and British companies, especially computer, airline, banking, and credit card operations, with American Express, Dell, Microsoft, L.L. Bean, and Bell South as some of the pioneers (see www.siliconindia.com).

Recommended Readings

Kalita, S. Mitra. "Hope and Toil at India's Call Centers." *Washington Post*, 27 December 2005. Stories from the all-night workforce, including a possible "cultural backlash, as the country's young hip BPO [business process outsourcing] workers run up against the traditions of the older generations."

Landler, Mark. "Hi, I'm in Bangalore (But I Dare Not Tell)." *New York Times*, 21 March 2001. Workers for an American telecommunications company create fictional personas to pass as Americans: Nishara, a confident Bangalorean

worker who identifies herself as Naomi from Perth Amboy, N.J., is amused when Americans say "No way, José," because "there is no José."

⋈⋈⋈

American Jobs

OUTSOURCING AND OFFSHORING

2005, 60 mins., United States
Director: Greg Spotts
Traditional Documentary
Distributor: American Jobs (www.americanjobsfilm.com)

One of the few documentaries concerned almost exclusively with outsourcing, Gregg Spotts's *American Jobs* is really about the end of American jobs in such industries as computer programming, airplane manufacturing, and clothing. After visiting fifteen American cities and interviewing scores of displaced workers, Spotts also began campaigning against CAFTA, the Central American Free Trade Agreement, arguing that the failure of NAFTA to develop American jobs—or build consumers for American products—will just be repeated.

His interviews uncovered situations that should embarrass any company but are significant variations on the usual outsourcing formulas. Myra Bronstein, a Seattle-area tech worker at WatchMark, trained her Indian replacement in exchange for severance benefits. Siemens computer programmers saw desks gradually began to fill up with Indian guest workers with L-1 visas, intracompany transfers from overseas. A Boeing machinist explains that his milling machines were sold to the state-owned Turkish military aircraft company, who will now do the work he had been doing.

Spotts tries to maintain a nonpartisan stance in his film: after all, Bill Clinton was the great salesman for NAFTA and there is not a Republican-Democratic split on the later agreements, such as CAFTA. Spotts believes that the hype for free trade includes doctoring statistics about outsourcing: "There are no official figures on job loss due to white-collar tech outsourcing because it's not in [the Labor Department's] interest to keep track" (see Gard).

And on the topic of Washington looking out for American jobs, Spotts cites the manufacture of American army berets by a Chinese company and of uniforms for the Department of Homeland Security by a Mexican company. I'm sure these items were inspected at the border or at the container shipping facilities.

Spotts is especially strong on the role of L-1B temporary visa workers, a cousin of the H-1B (formerly H-2 visa). Workers with L-1B visas were supposed to be transfers from within a company, and therefore the law set no limits on their numbers or visa duration. What may have begun as a scheme to bring overseas managers to the United States for specialized training soon turned into a insourcing maneuver that used foreign workers to replace American workers, first on American soil, and then—as they would eventually return home—as means for offshoring (keeping them within the company) or outsourcing (placing them in another company). In one example Spotts offers involving Siemens tech workers in Orlando, Indian workers were brought in who were already contract workers for another company (The Tata Group) "temporarily" working for Siemens. A global shell game was in operation.

Recommended Readings

Gard, Lauren. "The Story of *American Jobs.*" *Business Week,* 19 September 2004. Interview with Spotts emphasizing why he chose the topic of (mainly) white-collar outsourcing.

Spotts, Greg. *CAFTA and Free Trade: What Every American Should Know.* New York: The Disinformation Company, 2005. Spotts continues his campaign against outsourcing in this critique of NAFTA's offspring for Central America.

Tata, Ratan. "A World to Win." Tata Group website (www.tata.com), 27 April 2005. The chairman of Tata argues that "one of the major drivers of going international is to reduce our vulnerability to a single economy" and the need to blend in a foreign culture: "If we are going to China, we should have a Chinese face, and not an Indian face in China."

ᕮᕮᕮ

Another World Is Possible

Un altro mondo è possible

ANTI-GLOBALIZATION

2001, 60 or 120 mins., Italy, in Italian with English subtitles
Directors: Francesco Maselli (lead director), with Marco Bellocchio, Francesca and Christina Comencini, Mario Monicelli, Gillo Pontecorvo, Ettore Scola, Paolo and Vittorio Taviani, and more than twenty other Italian directors
Cinema-Verité Documentary
Distributor: See search engines

This remarkable collaboration may be unique for the number of filmmakers alone. Organized by Francesco Maselli, whose films are not well known outside of Italy, the collective was named Il Cinema Italiana and was affiliated with the Genoa Social Forum, the umbrella group of groups protesting the 2001 G-8 meeting held in Genoa, where one of the demonstrators was killed by the police. Maselli has his own way of making sense of the demonstrators by delineating the different constituent groups as *pacifisti, anarchici, missionary, and riformisti economica* (see Calhoun).

The older filmmakers had deep experience in either the resistance against the fascists in World War II, the postwar explosion of neorealism (a movement with a number of labor masterpieces, the most famous being *The Bicycle Thief,* in *Working Stiffs*), and other films that explored the social and political movements of workers, the poor, and the urban dispossessed. These films often featured nonprofessionals, even if it was scripted.

The filming of the Genoa G-8 demonstrations in July 2001 of course featured the ultimate use of nonprofessionals—hundreds of thousands of protestors. Their struggle and the attacks by police and carabinieri (the national paramilitary force) were documented by hundreds of film crews.

Another World is Possible, using original

music by noted composer Ennio Morricone, was presold to the Italian media because of the reputation of the filmmakers. Two other documentaries (also not currently available) emphasizing police brutality were made by directors in the collective: both Francesca Comencini's *Carlo Giuliani, Ragazzo* and Roberto Torelli's *Bella Ciao* used footage from Rai 2 (the Italian state television network), but the final films were banned from Italian television.

Recommended Reading

Calhoun, David. "Lights, Camera, Protest . . ." *Observer Review* (London), 29 July 2001, 8. Discusses how the collective of directors filmed the demonstrations.

⊢⊢⊢

The Apprentice

CHANGES IN THE WORKPLACE: NORTH AMERICA

2003–6, 4 seasons, 15–18 episodes per season, 60–90 mins. each, United States
Producer: Mark Burnett
TV Documentary Series

Memo #1 to *Apprentice* audition staff: "Lose the clueless and obnoxious candidates." Reply: "Smart and nice don't play well on TV." Memo #2: "Do all women contestants have to wear miniskirts?" The fact that this exchange of memos likely did not happen explains the serious deterioration in the quality of this faux-capitalism reality TV series developed by and featuring real estate mogul and charming egomaniac Donald Trump. Season one was intriguing, two was barely passable, three was insufferable, and four was notable for high-achieving women dissing each other. A parallel season in 2005, with ex-con Martha Stewart, may be beyond comment, but The Donald waited until it was over to announce that Martha Stewart knew nothing about running a television show. This remark came when Trump and two of his children spent too much air-time refereeing the constant bickering of his own contestants.

The format of the show pit two teams of as-piring "apprentices" to the Master. Sometimes divided by gender, sometimes by education (college versus street smarts), each team received a task—rent out an apartment or stage a sports charity event—and they scurry about like frat brothers or sisters in search of a good price on a keg. After they carry out their task—under time pressure inevitably—they are evaluated either by their sales figures, Trump's executive assistants, or experts in the relevant field of endeavor. The teams reassemble in the boardroom in Trump Tower. (A set? Or is a real Trump boardroom already by definition a set?) Through self-inflicted bitchery and occasional praise from both within and outside of the team, two or three contestants face Trump at the end and one is told, "You're fired!" He or she takes the equivalent of a perp walk out of the suite and into a taxi, swallowed up by the beautifully photographed nighttime streets of the Big Apple. (For some of us the real star of the show is Manhattan—photographed lovingly from every angle at every time of day; these shots are used as transitions throughout the show.)

No one seriously believes that the tasks set for the contestants are appropriate qualifying tests for aspiring capitalists. But is golf? Squash? And, for Silicon Valley, triathlons? Thus we have to conclude that something else is going on in this once popular television series. Despite its label, reality TV is really the bastard child of cinema verité and guerilla TV: it captures people in situations sometimes spontaneously and sometimes provoked but always heavily edited from many hours of untelevised footage.

We might conclude then that this is the face of capitalism our global partners are supposed to believe in—that American remains a meritocracy, that talent, looks, and street smarts are the mark of a successful entrepreneur. Maybe. But as most analysts of rich people tell us the best way to become rich is to have rich parents. There is no question that Trump respects the bottom line: teams that don't earn enough money doing some inane task lose a member.

If this is an advertisement for American capitalism and culture then how well did other versions play around the world? Most of the moguls in other countries told their failed apprentices that they were fired (or dismissed) à la the Master, but the Scandinavians were characteristically welfare-statist: Inger Ellen Nicolaisen, the founder of a chain of sixty-four hair salons, adjusted the exit line to "Sorry, but you're fired," while Norway's Jari Sarasvuo, a global marketer, said, "You're free to leave" ("It's a Small Global Boardroom After All," *New York Times,* 15 May 2005).

One of the missed opportunities of the show is the O'Jays' theme song, "For the Love of Money," in which we learn that some people will "steal from their mother" and "rob their own brother," not to mention that "a women will sell her precious body." And although the O'Jays sing "don't let money rule you," this last crucial piece of advice is curiously missing from the soundtrack.

Recommended Readings

Stanley, Alessandra. "No Rookie Now: 'Apprentice' Feeds on Office Tension." *New York Times,* 18 December 2004. Best short commentary comparing first two seasons, concluding that its strength is its successful rendition of "workday tension."

Traub, James. "Trumpologies." *New York Times Magazine,* 12 September 2004, 34–39. Argues for Trump as a "populist plutocrat" who is "a zealot in the cult of fame."

⋈⋈⋈

Argentina: Hope in Hard Times

BANKING AND GLOBAL FINANCING
GLOBAL LABOR
TRANSNATIONAL ORGANIZATIONS

2004, 74 mins., United States
Directors: Mark Dworkin and Melissa
    Young
Agit-Prop Documentary
Distributor: Bullfrog Films

Argentina in the twentieth century had a relatively robust economy; today, a cabbie tells the filmmakers, Argentina's three classes—upper, middle, and working class—have dwindled to two, the rich and the poor. Furthermore, another interviewee says, when you fall out of the working class you are likely to become a *cartonero,* one of the legions of street people who scour the dumps and other garbage piles for material (especially paper, cardboard, glass) to sell to recycling plants for a few cents. (A documentary from Spain and Argentina, *The White Train* [2003], not currently available, surveys the *cartonero's* work in detail.)

At one point in the film Joseph Stiglitz, former chief economist for the World Bank and a Nobel Prize winner in economics in 2001, admits what became obvious: the policies of the WTO, the IMF, and the World Bank have failed Argentina. Other experts note that the privatization of public sector services has led to a volatile economy too dependent on the whims of investment capital. When the film was made in 2002 unemployment was at 40 percent and people coped by visiting weekly barter fairs.

When directors Mark Dworkin and Melissa Young visited Argentina in 2002, there were some signs of recovery at least in spirit, and they set out to document Argentinians who participated in rural coops, factory takeovers (*The Take,* q.v.), and neighborhood street fairs. By 2004 the economy had grown 8 percent two years in a row without, the film emphasizes, relying on the IMF.

The film celebrates a number of small victories. The *cartoneros,* for example, struggled with the city for a "white train," a metro service once a night with all its seats removed so that they could wheel their carts on board with ease. Workers at the Brukman clothing factory in Buenos Aires had tried to take over the factory in 2003 and were attacked by local police. They eventually prevailed. The Brukman workers explain their policy of equal pay for all workers, a remarkable labor experiment.

The film opens with what look like middle- and working-class Argentinians banging all kinds of things on the shuttered doors and windows of their failing banks. This provocative sequence settles down a bit into some traditional filmed interviews, as the filmmakers stress the optimism of those they interview.

Recommended Readings

Klein, Naomi. "How Argentina's New President Deals with the Occupied Factories Will Be Hugely Significant." *The Guardian,* 28 April 2003. In the heavily politicized atmosphere, "Brukman's workers are treated as if sewing a grey suit were a capital crime."

Lynn, Madeleine. "Conversation with Filmmakers Mark Dworkin and Melissa Young." *Carnegie Council on Ethics and International Affairs,* 11 May 2005 (online at www.cceia.org/viewMedia.php/prmID/5160). Extensive interview with the filmmakers, who also directed *Net Loss* (q.v.), on salmon fishing.

▶◀▶◀▶◀

Auf Wiedersehen, Pet

THATCHERISM
TRANSNATIONAL MIGRATION

TV series; 1983–1986, 26 episodes, 50 mins. each; 2002–2004, 14 episodes, 60 mins. each; United Kingdom
Directors: Roger Bamford, Anthony Garner, David Innes Edwards, Sandy Johnson, Baz Taylor, and Paul Seed
Screenplay: Ian La Frenais, Dick Clement, Stan Hey, Bernie Cooper, Francis Megahy, and Franc Roddam

Comedies about globalization are few and far between, especially those that involve white migrant labor leaving one First World country for another. Enduring the period from Margaret Thatcher to Tony Blair—from no jobs in the 1980s to employing their own migrant laborers in the new century—this gang of white working-class friends from Newcastle leave for jobs as "brickies" (bricklayers) in Düsseldorf. They continue the long-standing British tradition of rude and farcical humor, often involving working-class characters who never seem to quite get the handle on their jobs. Perhaps because the series is set in Germany, it doesn't quite descend to such dubious British fare as *Carry On at Your Convenience* (1971), about a union struggle in a toilet bowl factory.

The three friends soon join other *gastar-beiter* (guest workers) from England and other countries, but in keeping with the spirit of the series the real problems of the majority of guest workers in Germany, the Turks, are mostly finessed, except for the occasional bad joke at their expense (calling the Turkish cement haulers "ayatollahs"). The first series finds them working on a suburban construction site, trading remarks about the Brits bombing Germany and now rebuilding it, while the second series in the Thatcher years has them returning to England to restore a country manor house.

In the third and fourth series, the politics and patterns of international migration having gotten a bit more complicated, the men find themselves in Cuba rebuilding the British Embassy, which has been damaged by a hurricane. Then they're back in the United Kingdom working as gaffers or employers themselves, hiring laborers on both sides of the Yugoslavian civil war (Kosovans and Serbs) to dismantle the Middlesbrough Transporter Bridge (a famous landmark in Teeside) and sell it to a buyer in Malaysia.

Along the way the men learn some truths about themselves and their loved ones, understand real migrant laborers better (they are shocked when they discover that the former Yugoslavs are illegal immigrants living in filthy conditions, and try to have interesting sex with German women. They are globalized trotters on a mission rudely hatched from economic realities, singing "Deutschland über alles" and "Rule, Britannia" indiscriminately and foolishly.

Direct remarks about Thatcherism are infrequent but telling. One of the lads reminds his friends that they are among the three million unemployed back home and that it is foolish while in Germany to "become nationalistic for the country that won't employ them." When one of the men gets bounced for fighting, it is the German workers who threaten a strike if he is not reinstated, not his fellow Thatcherite exiles.

Recommended Reading

Broomby, Rob. "Germany's Guest Workers Mark 40 Years." *BBC News,* 30 October 2001 (online at news.bbc.co.uk). A survey of the history of the main guestworkers in Germany—the Turks, two million of whom live and work in Germany.

▶◀▶◀▶◀
Baked Alaska

OIL

2002, 26 mins., United Kingdom
Director: Franny Armstrong
Traditional Documentary
Distributor: Bullfrog Films

In addition to a delicious dessert, the term "Baked Alaska" refers to changes in Alaska's climate. Is it global warming? Alaska's average temperatures, one source argues, are rising at ten times the rate of the rest of the world. Fairbanks, the capital, near which the Trans-Alaska Pipeline passes, used to have minus-forty-degree winters; now only a couple of days bring minus thirty degrees. Complicating this trend is the Alaskan economy's dependence on oil and disagreements among the indigenous peoples about whether the great Arctic National Wildlife Preserve should be open to oil exploration and development. The Inupiat Eskimos of Kaktovik are for the drilling—they can use the jobs and money for schools—while the Gwich'in Indians are "caribou people" and fear the drilling will directly reduce the numbers of calves born each year, especially since the area for calving (few predators, good foraging) is in fact the proposed location of the new oil wells.

The film points to the gradually melting permafrost, currently about a half a mile thick, as a cause for concern. As the United States's dependence on fossil fuel continues and greater emissions result, global warming increases (so goes one argument) and Alaska starts to bake, that is, thaws more quickly. Although the director specializes in contentious topics—see her *McLibel*—with two sets of Native peoples disagreeing here it is hard to favor a simple solution. If anything the director leans toward an embargo on the drilling but lets the other side speak as well.

Recommended Readings
Adam, David. "Melting of Permafrost Threatens Homes and Roads, Scientists Warn." *The Guardian,* 21 December 2005. The environmental correspondent reviews global warming and tends to support the film's viewpoint that ironically it is the contested oil and its greenhouse effect that is melting Alaska.

Mayell, Hillary. "Is Warming Causing Alaska Meltdown?" *National Geographic News*, 18 December 2001 (online at news.nationalgeographic.com/news/2001/12/1217_alaskaglaciers.html). Argues that the jury is still out on whether natural or human processes are causing Alaska's undoubted warming.

▶◀▶◀▶◀
The Bank

BANKING AND GLOBAL FINANCING
GLOBAL CATASTROPHES

2001, 103 mins., Australia
Director: Robert Connolly
Screenplay: Robert Connolly

The Bank is one of the few films offering opening credits that even come close to those Saul Bass designed for Alfred Hitchcock's *Vertigo*. Brightly colored fractal patterns overlaid with streaming mathematical formulas and a score reminiscent of Hitchcock's favorite composer, Bernard Herrmann, are based (with the partial exception of the music) on Mandelbrot equations: each viral-like pattern generates an identical pattern from within and we see the fractal growing as if it were alive or a crystal reproducing itself. We learn that these patterns are the visual expression of a set of mathematical equations that Jim Doyle (played by David Wenham), a somewhat mysterious young man (in Australian slang, an "ocker" or country outsider), uses to convince Simon O'Reilly (played by Anthony LaPaglia), the CEO of CentaBank, a major Australian bank, that he can score amazing gains on international trading markets.

To reveal too much of Doyle's backstory would spoil the outcome of this global banking thriller, but it is one of three plot lines that converge by film's end. The second complication involves a couple who lost their small boating business when CentaBank flimflammed their loan, not disclosing that it was dependent on international currency investments.

The central story involves Doyle's work for CentaBank in Melbourne, where he is tutored by his boss, a Gordon Gekko–type who is beyond greed: "I'm like God," he announces, "with a better suit." The beauty of Doyle's system is that he can time investments and sales in the stock market based on his formulas, that is, he knows when the market is moving up or down and buys or sells appropriately. (It makes total sense when you see it, but don't try it at home.) Earlier in the film O'Reilly has been threatened by his board to continue to build profits or else; when he is ready for his big score, he turns the tables on them and makes them complicit in his probably illegal scheme by invoking the obligation to the stockholders to maximize profits. (Only one board member raises ethical objections and walks out; the others sign their pact with the devil.)

All thrillers are seductive by nature: as we are sucked into Doyle's scheme to beat the world's financial markets, we half want him to succeed. When we gradually realize Doyle is up to something, we are pulled up short by our complicity as viewers: "It's really quite simple," he says, "I just hate banks." Whether you do or not, you will find it hard not to watch what happens.

Recommended Reading

Holden, Stephen. "A Taste for Chaos Theory and Corporate Crime." *New York Times,* 25 October 2002. Although he finds the ending "as silly as it is satisfying," the film, which reached screens after the Enron and WorldCom scandals had broken, was "well timed to tap the public's disgust with financial institutions and the number crunchers who run them."

▶◀▶◀

Baran

MIGRANT LABOR (OTHER THAN THE UNITED STATES)

2001, 94 mins., Iran, in Dari and Persian (Farsi) with English subtitles

Director: Majid Majidi
Screenplay: Majid Majidi

In the globalized labor market inevitably affected by civil and other wars, migrant workers are sometimes trying to escape not only hard times back home but danger as well: thus in *Baran* illegal Afghan workers on a construction site in Teheran will do almost anything to escape the refugee camps resulting from the wars in which the Taliban, the Soviets, and the Americans have clashed for more than thirty years. In fact, as a title explains at the opening of the film, 1.4 million Afghans were living in Iran at one point. That they are both illegal workers and a suspect minority makes the cry of "Run, Afghans, run!" uttered during a raid by labor inspectors especially poignant.

When Najaf (played by Gholam Ali Bakhshi), an Afghan worker, falls and breaks his leg, his son Rahmat (played by Zahra Bahrami) is sent to take his place. When it is clear that Rahmat cannot do any hard work, the site foreman, Memar (played by Mohammad Amir Naji), switches Rahmat's job with Lateef's (played by Hossein Abedini), who up to now has had the relatively jolly and busybody task of providing tea and snacks to the workers. Lateef, needless to say, is put out.

But his harassment of Rahmat turns to puppy love when he discovers that Rahmat is really a girl, whose name, we learn eventually, is Baran (which means "rain"). When the labor inspectors stage a surprise visit, all of the Afghans are eventually barred from the site and Baran goes back to a refugee camp, where she has to do some difficult work. Despite his love—or perhaps more accurately because of it—Lateef is the source of money that enables Baran's family to return to Afghanistan. Baran's and Lateef's brief farewell as he retrieves Baran's shoe from the mud is charged with both a sense of intense emotional contact and inevitable separation.

Migrants within Third World countries seem to contradict the usual model of global labor flowing from the poor South to the richer North. *Baran* is one of the small group of films that highlights the difficulties of what might be called lateral migration. Lateef and the foreman at the site are actually Iranian Azeris, a minority population as well, mostly blue-collar workers who compete with the Afghans for jobs.

Director Majid Majidi's *Color of Paradise* (1999), about a blind boy and his family's difficulties in accepting him, had been the most successful Iranian film ever released in the United States. He clearly understands the different ways children interact with a hostile world. The actress who plays Baran was taken to an Afghan refugee camp when she was two months old and was sixteen when the film was made: "I found myself living in a place called a camp. I didn't know what crime I had committed. Maybe being an Afghan was my crime" (see *Washington Post* article below). Majidi also made a documentary, *Barefoot to Herat* (2002), about his visits to refugee camps during and after the Taliban period.

Recommended Readings

"An Iranian Director's Tribute to Destitute Afghan Refugees." *Washington Post,* 18 January 2002. Discusses the director's experiences with the refugee camps.

Scott, A. O. "Iranian Boy, Afghan Girl and Love's Strange Magic." *New York Times,* 9 October 2001. Without "sentimentalizing" or "denying its brutality" the reality of the refugee experience has been transformed "into a lyrical and celebratory vision."

The Battle of Orgreave: Prime Minister Thatcher's government used national mobile police forces to break the 1984–85 miners' strike.

▶◀▶◀

The Battle of Orgreave

THATCHERISM

2001, 60 mins., United Kingdom
Director: Mike Figgis
Reenactment Director: Jeremy Deller
Mock Documentary

If the miners' strike of 1984–85 produced the defining campaign in Thatcherite England—the process by which the Conservative government exercised its final solution for labor unions—then the Battle of Orgreave on June 18, 1984, was the defining event of the strike itself. Breaking the strike was a

Tory priority, but deploying (and in a sense trying out) a national police force was also important: what became routine policy for First World globalization was now fixed at this point in Thatcherite England. For a BBC Channel 4 broadcast, performance artist Jeremy Deller led a collective of performance artists (Artangel) who staged part of the battle in 2001 using historical reenactment society members and local folk, including miners and others who had been present at the actual battle.

Deller, with five camera crews led by director Mike Figgis, handled the event in the manner pioneered by Peter Watkins, the director of *Culloden* and *La Commune* (q.v. *The Universal Clock*). The film crews wandered through the "battle" filming it as if they were there and occasionally stopping participants for an interview.

Like all battles, many details about the actual struggle are in dispute. Upwards of four thousand miners from many different mining communities and their supporters converged on the coke works at Orgreave in South Yorkshire to prevent coal from entering. Upwards of three thousand police likewise assembled to prevent the miners from succeeding and to attack them in the process.

The police forces were from at least ten different counties organized in almost two hundred Police Support Units (PSUs), each with their own level of riot training and gear. K-9 and mounted police units were also present. Many commentators note that this battle marked the decisive turn from defensive policing to attack or offensive policing, a shift consonant with Thatcherite ideology.

Many viewers will see the police forces as unnecessarily coercive and Thatcher's core strategy repugnant. Deller demonstrated another approach to onsite political art when he won the prestigious Turner Prize in 2004 for "Memory Bucket," his video/photographic installation documenting his travels to Texas and the site of the Branch Davidian siege in Waco and President Bush II's ranch in Crawford.

Recommended Reading

Deller, Jeremy. *The English Civil War: Part II.* Ed. Gerrie van Noord. Manchester: Artangel, 2001. Collection of essays, photos, and a CD with interviews with miners, all focusing on the Battle of Orgreave and the reenactment staged by Deller and Artangel.

⊢⊢⊢

The Bed You Sleep In

CHANGES IN THE WORKPLACE: NORTH
 AMERICA
HISTORY OF GLOBALIZATION

1993, 117 mins., United States
Director: Jon Jost
Screenplay: Jon Jost

Not many films end with a triple suicide and a philosophical quotation from Ralph Waldo Emerson. Jon Jost is the kind of independent filmmaker who writes, directs,

shoots, and edits his own projects. In this almost meditative drama set in a logging mill in the Northwest, the mill owner and CEO, Ray Weiss (played by Tom Blair), is beset by problems: the success of the environmentalists in protecting the spotted owl in his region has produced a shortage of lumber, and even though he has orders to fill he cannot get the raw timber. And in an early example of globalization from the Japanese end, orders are now going overseas rather than to his company.

But Tom has problems at home as well. Personal expenses are mounting up, but even worse is a letter that arrives out of the blue from his daughter, who, based on "recovered memories" surfacing in a campus woman's support group, accuses him of sexually abusing her when she was a young teenager. His second wife—not his daughter's mother—seems to believe the accusations and all hell breaks loose. Or, more precisely, all hell breaks out but more slowly than it should, because one of Tom's problems is his relatively low level of human or emotional affect. He is not a cold fish but barely a lukewarm one.

And, speaking of fish, his only pleasure is fly fishing. Ironically he seems not to realize that his natural allies, one would think, are the environmentalists. Jost films all of this in a slow, deliberative style, emphasizing the raw beauty of the mechanical claws and roaring saws that transform the logs into so many board feet of lumber before our eyes. He also notices that Toledo, Oregon, seems dangerously on its way to becoming a rust belt of sorts, despite its location in a setting of great natural beauty. At the end of the film, after most of Tom's life has fallen apart, we see a clearcut mountain and a quotation from one of Emerson's essays, "Prudence": "Every violation of truth is not only a sort of suicide in the liar, but it is a stab at the heart of human society."

The final message seems to match perfectly the complexity of Jost's view of the industry and the human drama he has created. We learn that the mill he used for his set in fact closed a year later because of the lack of raw timber, the environmental regulations to protect the marbled murrelet (a forest-nesting seabird), and Japanese competition.

Recommended Reading

Rosenbaum, Jonathan. Review on *Chicago Reader* website (onfilm.chicagoreader.com). Rave short review: "A tragic, beautiful, and mysterious film that alternates between all-American landscapes (many of them composed as diptychs) and an unraveling nuclear family, this is as evocative and apocalyptic as Jost's cinema gets—a film full of unanswered questions that will nag at you for days even as it makes fully understandable the sort of feelings about this country that drove Jost into European exile not long after it was completed."

▸▸▸

Beijing Bicycle

CHINA

2001, 113 mins., Taiwan/China, in Mandarin
  with English subtitles
Director: Xiaoshuai Wang
Screenplay: Peggy Chiao, Hsiao-ming, Hsu
  Danian Tang, and Xiao Shuai Wang

In *The Bicycle Thief* (see *Working Stiffs*), one of the most famous films of Italian neorealism, a poster hanger's bike is stolen: no bike, no job. In Wang's contemporary Chinese film, Guo (played by Lin Cui), a young country lad, secures a good job in the city as a bicycle courier, only to have his bicycle stolen just as he had almost earned enough in commissions to make the bike his own.

In the Italian film, the bicycle thief (or thieves) remained elusive, as if symbolizing a decayed city's indifference to a struggling worker's dilemma. It is clear, however, who the Beijing bicycle thief is: Jian (played by Bin Li), a somewhat more affluent schoolboy, roughly Guo's age, who steals the bike (or steals his father's money and buys the stolen bike) to impress a pretty classmate and ride with his own somewhat more entitled friends.

In the China of *Beijing Bicycle* a bicycle is a significant possession, and it takes on a life of its own as a symbol of rising consumerism as both boys battle—in vastly different ways—

for its possession. The bicycle courier business is a sign of increasing capitalist development and the migration of country youth to the city replicates a widespread Chinese pattern. Guo's frustration in losing his job points to a countrywide phenomenon—the disappearance of the traditional socialist safety net for its poor.

Wang's social realism is perhaps one of the quietest but most effective looks at the emotional as well as the economic costs of China's resolute but often conflicted contemporary social experiment.

Recommended Reading

Ingman, Marrit. "Beijing Bicycle." *Austin Chronicle*, 8 March 2002. The film is "quite upfront in depicting the thoroughgoing, frequently violent hostility between the locals and the desperate newcomers who've come to Beijing after failing to eke out a living in farming or construction."

▸▸▸

Bella Ciao

ANTI-GLOBALIZATION

2001, 113 mins., Italy, in Italian with English
  subtitles
Directors: Marco Giusti and Roberto Torelli
TV Documentary

Pooling video footage of demonstrations has emerged as the favorite mode of anti-globalization compilation films. *Bello Ciao* (or *Hello, Darling,* the literal translation of the title of a World War II resistance song) is based on the work of national and regional Italian television station (RAI) crews and independent filmmakers during the July 2001 anti-globalization demonstrations in Genoa. Although much of the widely publicized footage of the demonstrations features the killing of Carlo Giuliani and the attacks by police and carabinieri (the national paramilitary force) on various people, this film develops a chronological timeline of the different groups of demonstrators and examines them in detail.

For example, the first major demonstration by immigrant workers (the *migrantes*) in Italy was actually earlier than the climactic march two days later, on July 21, that resulted in Giuliani's death. The earlier march brought out 50,000 people: for a country still unable to accept its waves of immigrants, this was a remarkable moment indeed. The sequences covering the perhaps 250,000 marchers of the main demonstration also includes footage of the enigmatic and still-controversial Black Block, a group of masked protesters who would normally consist of risk-taking, vandalistic anarchists but which may have included Italian and other fascists or agents provocateurs (according to leftist reports "Italy after Genoa" and "Interview with Protestors Beaten by Italian Police" in the *Socialist Worker,* 4 August 2001). Whatever their makeup, the Black Block trashed cars and store windows at first seemingly unimpeded by the police, who then attacked the general mass of demonstrators allegedly because of the violence of the Black Block. And, finally, the police attack on media headquarters and sleeping halls of the Genoa Social Forum, the coalition of hundreds of anti-globalization groups, on the night of July 20–21, is also fully covered.

Trials of the police involved in the attacks began in February 2005. Mark Covell, an independent journalist who was mistaken for a member of the Black Block, reported on the police riot. Whatever the ultimate truth about the causes of the violence, the film makes clear who the main perpetrators of violence were.

Recommended Reading

Covell, Mark. "I Still Have Nightmares." *BBC News World Edition,* 6 February 2005 (online at news.bbc.co.uk/2/hi/europe/4229777 .stm). A journalist with Indymedia (an independent news and media organization, online at www.indymedia.org) reports being brutally beaten by policemen who called him a member of the Black Bloc.

⋈⋈⋈

Betrayed

CONTAINERIZED SHIPPING
DEREGULATION AND PRIVATIZATION
HISTORY OF GLOBALIZATION

2004, 56 mins., Canada
Director: Elaine Brière
Traditional Documentary
Distributor: Elaine Brière (www.elainebriere .ca)

Bordered by three oceans, Canada has always been a nation of seafarers and shipping companies. Subtitled "The Story of Canadian Merchant Seamen," this film examines the cu-

Betrayed: New Zealanders support the Canadian Seamen's Union on strike in 1949. Courtesy Ellen Brière.

rious history of the dismantling of the Canadian merchant marine and its leading union, the Canadian Seamen's Union (CSU), and the privatization of the merchant fleet in 1949, a half century before this key indicator of globalization became an household term.

Betrayed makes the compelling case that the privatization of the fleet in 1949 happened despite the merchant marine's successful trade record. Although the CSU won a successful strike in 1947 for an eight-hour day and established a reputation as a worldwide progressive force, just three years later the employers, supported by the government, destroyed the union and the fleet by bringing in an American union no less, the AFL-CIO affiliated the Seafarers' International Union (SIU), controlled by Hal C. Banks, an American thug. Banks, although not well known, is the subject of *Canada's Sweetheart: The Saga of Hal C. Banks* (see *Working Stiffs*), which explores the brutal rise to power of Banks and the SIU using McCarthyite smears and plain old dirty tricks.

Brìere concentrates on a detailed examination of the CSU's strengths and its eventual demise. The villain in her film is not so much Banks as the Canadian Steamship Lines, for its role on the 1949 strike and its participation in the process known as Flags of Convenience (FOC), which provides ship owners and corporations with ships that fly foreign flags to avoid taxes and the more progressive labor, safety, and environmental standards of North American and Western European countries. The CSL was owned by Paul Martin, the former Canadian finance minister who became elected prime minister in 2003, and it is still controlled by his family.

The power of red-baiting in the late 1940s trumped the war records of the returning veterans who had joined the CSU, paving the way for their replacements, mostly Third World (the Philippines, India, and Indonesia) and Eastern European labor on FOC ships using compliant nations (Panama, Liberia, the Bahamas, Malta and Cyprus being the largest FOC sources). These boats now ship more than half of the world's goods. A report from the Canadian Broadcasting Corporation estimated that savings from an FOC registration can be millions of dollars per ship (CBC News online, 6 February 2004).

Recommended Reading

Kaplan, William. *Everything That Floats: Pat Sullivan, Hal Banks, and the Seamen's Unions of Canada.* Toronto: University of Toronto Press, 1987. A detailed history of the CSU and the ISU.

⋈⋈⋈

Between Midnight and the Rooster's Crow

OIL

2005, 66 mins., Canada
Director: Nadja Drost
Cinema-Verité Documentary
Distributor: First Run/Icarus Films

The time between midnight and dawn, when the rooster crows, is when the key decisions for the fate of Ecuador, its economy, and the oil-rich sector in the Amazon jungle are made—in other words, in secret. EnCana, the largest corporation in Canada ($54 billion in 2005), specializes in oil and natural gas. It got the contract to build the Obeduto Crudos Pegados (OCP), the massive pipeline designed to replace Ecuador's nationalized but decrepit pipeline, and to extract crude oil. Eighty percent of the revenue would be EnCana's; Ecuadorean social services would benefit from 10 percent, while debt payment to the World Bank would use up the other 10 percent. In the end even that deal was not good enough for EnCana, which seemed to be concerned that antipipeline protests and perhaps even publicity from a film like this one would make their investment hard to manage. The Chinese, another energy-hungry superpower, bought out Encana's share for one and half billion dollars.

Filmmaker Nadja Drost appears at one point with her hands covered in crude oil sludge. It's her visual reminder of the pollution caused by leaks along the route of the pipe. As she traces the route of the pipeline from its oil fields in the northeastern corner of

Between Midnight and the Rooster's Crow: Ecuadorian boy walking the crude oil pipeline. Courtesy First Run/ Icarus Films.

the country westward to the Pacific Ocean, she notes that the two provinces richest in oil have the worst water, sewer, and electric services, and the highest unemployment. When the pipeline passes through the natural preserve belonging to the indigenous Siona people she discovers, perhaps to her surprise, that they had agreed to the pipeline, but the two motivating factors were a threatened invasion by the military and financial reimbursement.

Drost's talking heads range from EnCana's CEO, Gwyn Morgan, who funds playgrounds and sports teams in Ecuador, to farmers whose crops and bodies bear the scars of toxic sludge and pipes whose gas fires burn twenty-four hours a day. A kinder, gentler Michael Moore, often present in her shots of the pipeline's path, she documents another trouble spot for oil with remarkable tenacity and courage.

Recommended Reading

Perks, Gord. "Celsius 4/11." *Eye Weekly*, 21 April 2005 (online at www.eye.net/eye/issue/ issue_04.21.05/city/enviro.html). Canadian reviewer confesses that compared to the United States "we don't make many Oscar-winning movies, and we don't send our army in to get oil. But after seeing this film, I wonder if that's only because we don't have the same budgets as American filmmakers and oil companies."

⋈⋈⋈

Big Bucks, Big Pharma: Marketing Disease and Pushing Drugs

INTELLECTUAL PROPERTY RIGHTS (DRUGS)

2006, 45 mins., United States
Director: Ronit Ridberg
Agit-Prop Documentary
Distributor: Media Education Foundation

At the simplest level *Big Bucks, Big Pharma* is an extended and precise deconstruction of all those drug ads—for Claritin, Lipitor, Viagra, and so on—that feature beautiful people who can finally mow their lawns, play with their kids, and score better sex. Lipitor, a statin to reduce bad cholesterol (and reduce the incidence of heart disease), for example, is the best-selling drug in the world. But it is one of the almost 80 percent of all "new" drugs released each year by Big Pharma, as the drug companies are known, that are really—as the industry nickname goes—"me too" drugs: they are simply infinitesimal variations on the other three popular statin drugs, Zocar, Vytorin, and Crestor, all of which have fancy ad campaigns of their own.

The film attempts, however, a comprehensive survey of the most egregious means to make the drug industry so profitable and, with the largest phalanx of lobbyists in Washington, D.C., one of the most powerful influences on legislation and the Food and Drug Administration (FDA). Besides "me too" drugs and direct-to-customer marketing (those ads), Big Pharma loves marketing to doctors—free samples to hype, of course, but also gifts, trips, and other perks all in the guise of education. Doctors, we are told, all report that these have no effect on their decision to prescribe certain patented drugs (rather than cheaper generics when available), but they are certain their colleagues are susceptible.

Similarly what the filmmakers and others call "disease mongering" is an effective means of building new markets for normal conditions that can be borne without extensive medication in some cases. But if you have "restless legs syndrome" or adult Attention Deficit Disorder (ADD) or Social Anxiety Disorder (SAD), you probably need an expensive medication. Or not.

Vioxx is of course the drug better not taken, but its advertising budget exceeded that of Diet Pepsi or Bud Light. Clearly Vioxx ads sold more than medical advice. Even though a major journal in 2000 identified the drug as four times more likely to cause a heart attack compared to an older generic drug, Merck did not withdraw Vioxx until 2004. While adverse reactions are often included in the ads, the branding of a drug sells not only a pill but hope and a better lifestyle. Maybe some men who heard the Viagra spokesmen say that erections could last more than four hours believed that was the point and not the warning of an adverse drug reaction.

Featuring a number of experts, including the authors of important books on the subject (Marcia Angell and Katherine Greider), the film is a necessary and revealing companion to the feature film *The Constant Gardener* (q.v.).

Recommended Readings

Angell, Marcia. *The Truth about Drug Companies: How They Deceive Us and What to Do about It.* New York: Random House, 2004. Extensive analysis of the industry by the former editor of the *New England Journal of Medicine*.

Greider, Katherine. *The Big Fix: How the Pharmaceutical Industry Rips Off American Consumers.* New York: PublicAffairs, 2003. Detailed development of the themes of the film.

▶▶▶

Bigger Than Enron

BANKING AND GLOBAL FINANCING
ENRON

2002, 60 mins., United States
Director: Marc Shaffer
Correspondent: Hedrick Smith
TV Documentary
Distributor: PBS

Frontline's documentaries on the Enron scandal and related issues remain essential viewing: *Bigger Than Enron* is one of the most ambitious, as it points to (it seems now) a virtually seamless fabric of accounting, regulatory, and political processes, all of which converged to create one of the largest financial scandals of our time. The related collapse of Arthur Andersen, Enron's auditor and one of the most respected and powerful auditing firms in the world, points to the fatal flaw in Enron's rise and fall: Andersen, like many other firms, became Enron's consultant as well as its auditor; over one hundred of its people worked on the $58 million Enron account, many of them in Enron's Houston headquarters. Since Andersen consulted on one of Enron's most notorious maneuvers to hide debts—its off-the-book or limited partnerships—the auditing firm was not likely to find problems with that arrangement when it submitted its auditing reports.

Off-the-book partnerships—with exciting names like Chewco and Raptor—were elaborate investment schemes that helped Enron always look profitable and subsequently kept their stock price up. Higher stock prices meant that stock options for head executives were worth more, so that building fictitious financial growth on a base of actual accomplishments became the Enron way.

In 1993 the Financial Accounting Standards Board (FASB) recommended that stock options be charged to earnings, that is, become a business expense. Corporate America and especially Silicon Valley exploded in indignation. Dot.com leaders argued it would stifle innovation: Cisco, an Internet routing company, would have its $2.6 billion profit one year cut in half; other high-tech companies would find their profits cut up to 60 percent, according to a Merrill Lynch study Smith quotes. Senator Joseph Lieberman of Connecticut led the charge to keep the stock options off the books. (In the end the FASB only required stock options to be disclosed in tiny footnotes of corporate reports.)

In addition to stock options and seamless auditing-consulting relationships, correspondent Hedrick Smith pursues another of the three most important features of Enron's financial empire building: tort reform. In this instance it was a Republican, Newt Gingrich, whose bill favoring corporate America's desire to stifle shareholder lawsuits against their companies and their auditors, passed Congress easily.

What is "bigger than Enron" were two other high profile scandals that preceded Enron's fall, those of Sunbeam and Waste management. Both also had Arthur Andersen as their auditor-consultant, and both manipulated their bottom line to inflate the value of their stocks. Another harbinger was Andersen's reassignment of Carl Bass, a partner and one of its auditing experts, who had objected to Enron's accounting practices. Smith states that "Enron got so angry at what it called Bass's 'cynicism' that it demanded that he be taken off the account, and Andersen complied." Even some Enron insiders followed him, but that is the subject of another film, *Enron: The Smartest Guys in the Room* (q.v.).

Recommended Reading

Moberg, David, "A Scandal Bigger Than Enron." *In These Times,* 19 February 2002. Although "President Bush pretends that he barely knew 'Kenny Boy' Lay, the major financial backer of his career, many conservatives are pretending that Enron is a scandal of business, not politics." But "at least eight of the most powerful members of the administration, including both Bush and Vice President Dick Cheney, had significant ties to Enron—receiving pay or campaign contributions, investing in the company, or gaining appointment on the basis of Enron's recommendation."

►I►I►I

Blacklist of the Skies

DEREGULATION AND PRIVATIZATION
REAGANOMICS

2006, 98 mins. and 60 mins., United States
Director: Stephanie Saxe
Traditional Documentary
Distributor: Wallach IX Productions (www
.blacklistoftheskies.com)

Although the Professional Air Traffic Controllers Organization (PATCO) strike of 1981 was a defining event for Ronald Reagan's presidency, *Blacklist of the Skies* is the first documentary to review the controversy and assess its effects. Filmmaker Stephanie Saxe, whose father was one of the fired air traffic controllers, offers a detailed, exhaustive, and rancor-free account of the debacle. She interviewed every important figure (especially PATCO's last president, Robert Poli) in the run-up to the strike and uses archival footage for the one figure—Michael Rock, the founder of the union—whom she could not interview personally.

Saxe's access to the men and women who were intimately involved in the union allows the viewer to assess a number of vexing questions associated with the strike. Did the union want and expect the strike to happen, confident that they would win? Did the Reagan leadership of the Federal Aviation Authority (FAA), PATCO's employer, also want the strike because they knew that PATCO could not win? And was PATCO a surrogate for union power, ready to be served up to the Reagan dragon?

We learn that there is a single answer, yes, to all of these questions, but that answer does not make this a simplistic film. The circumstances of working in the federal sector, within a sensitive industry, with strong and idiosyncratic workplace traditions, but without the support of fraternal unions (such as those that represented the airline pilots and the machinists), all complicate the matter.

Saxe leads us, interview by interview, through the history of the union and the preparations for the strike. The early successes in establishing salaries, pensions, and work week schedules are duly noted, as well as the extremely stressful conditions under which the air traffic controllers worked. PATCO may not have learned from its own history, however. Its 1970 strike had been broken with over a hundred members fired—most were later reinstated—with their attorney, celebrity figure F. Lee Bailey, taking much of the blame for the disaster. And more than one viewer will gasp when Saxe explains PATCO's support of Reagan's run for the presidency in 1980, a stance taken by very few unions (the Teamsters come to mind), since the AFL-CIO remained loyal to the Democratic Party.

Although PATCO thought they could win—virtually all their members supported their leadership's handling of contract negotiations and the preparations for the strike—Saxe demonstrates why they were staring at a cloudy screen: Reagan was a grandstander, confident that his threat of firing all of the controllers would find public support. Plus he had 3,500 military air controllers in reserve if he needed them. The pilots and the machinists had found the controllers weak allies in the past, and they made it clear they would not honor their picket lines. Only the Canadian controllers did their bit in not accepting flights from the United States for a short period.

The controllers lost their jobs and Reagan's ratings went up a notch or two. The union's funds were frozen and the union was soon decertified. It isn't easy to take on the lord of rule and regulation, or more precisely, deregulation.

Recommended Readings

Nordlund, Willis J. *Silent Skies: The Air Traffic Controllers' Strike.* New York: Praeger Publisher, 1998. Business school dean (College of West Virginia) offers a detailed and perceptive interpretation of the strike and its context; very helpful on the role of the last PATCO president, Robert Poli.

Shostak, Arthur, and David Skocik. *The Air Controllers' Controversy: Lessons from the PATCO Strike.* New York: Human Sciences Press, 1986. A labor studies professor (Shostak) and a fired controller (Skocik) offer their viewpoints and analysis of the strike.

ᐅᐅᐅ

Blackout

DEREGULATION AND PRIVATIZATION
ENRON

2001, 60 mins., United States
Director: Michael Chandler
Correspondent: Lowell Bergman
TV Documentary
Distributor: Frontline

This sorry tale of the manipulation of California's energy to the point of dangerous blackouts was aired by *Frontline* six months before one of the biggest perps of the crisis, Enron, declared bankruptcy. Lowell Bergman, the *Frontline* correspondent who had been the prime investigator in the tobacco scandal featured in *The Insider* (q.v.), begins his investigation with Energy Alley in Houston, Texas, where companies such as Enron and Dynergy have "pioneered radical ways of buying and selling energy." His first interview is with Jeffrey Skilling, Enron's CEO, who, when pressed by Bergman about the possibility that electricity is "a vital commodity like oxygen" and shouldn't be traded, replies that "in open, competitive, fair markets, prices are lower and customers get better service." Does that make Enron, Bergman asks, "the good guys?" Skilling brags: "We are the good guys. We are on the side of the angels."

Not only did California get terrible service at high prices but eventually, in the summer of 2001, it got no service. At the time of the broadcast, Enron's role in the debacle was not known, so Skilling could say that California's problem was "a ludicrous regulated system," not that it was deregulated. In fact, Bergman argues, "California created a hybrid—part regulated, part unregulated." Utilities like Pacific Gas and Electric (PG & E) "had to buy power at wholesale rates set by the free market, but it would continue to receive payments from retail customers who were paying capped rates."

The California energy crunch was a complicated matter, involving not only (as we learn in *Enron: The Smartest Guys in the Room,* q.v.) some direct manipulation by Enron traders but also drought, hot weather, and a shift of some regulatory powers from the states to the presidential appointees of the Federal Energy Regulatory Commission (FERC). Kenneth Lay's disingenuous dismissal on film—"Every time there's a little shortage or a little bit of a price spike, it's always collusion or conspiracy or something. I mean, it always makes people feel better that way"—was of no help to him when he was convicted of fraud in 2006 and died soon after.

Blackout is one of the best introductions to the complicated ways in which Enron did business. As Bergman says to Skilling: "Electricity was not something that was traded, in a sense, before you guys came along, right? You invented that?" Enron didn't, however, invent trading derivatives—contracts whose value depends on changes in the price of a related or underlying "product" or instrument—but it pioneered using them to (as Bergman says) "trade everything from oil, gas, and electricity to Internet bandwidth and hedges against the weather itself." This remark epitomizes the shift in Enron's history from an energy supply business and to a business that traded energy, related products, and some not so related (bankruptcy insurance, for example).

Blackout does not date because the issues it raises—energy and the powerful figures behind energy policy—remain news. The Supreme Court decision of May 2005, for example, which protected Vice President Dick Cheney's secret meetings to discuss energy policy with Kenneth Lay and other energy corporation executives, becomes an even greater judicial lapse, given the conviction of Lay and Skilling for fraud in 2006, as Bergman lays out the connections among Kenneth Lay, President George Bush II, and Cheney. Like Lay, when asked about CEOs and campaign contributors giving advice on regulating rates, Cheney dismisses the idea of doing business the way he does in fact do

business: "That's the conspiracy theory of public policy. It's irresponsible. It's not true."

Recommended Reading

Clark, Woodrow, and Ted Bradshaw. *Agile Energy Systems: Global Lessons from the California Energy Crisis.* London: Elsevier Science, 2004. Argues that the crises in California (as well as those in the U.S. Northeast, southern Canada, Italy, and England) suggest the failure of deregulated and privatized energy industries.

▶▶▶

Blind Shaft

CHINA
DEREGULATION AND PRIVATIZATION

2003, 92 mins., China/Germany/Hong Kong, in Mandarin with English subtitles
Director: Li Yang
Screenplay: Li Yang, based on Liu Qingbang's novel, *Sacred Wood* (2002)

By combining elements of the classic con film and some muckraking associated with social realist storytelling, Li Yang has created an unusual look at the viciousness of unregulated coal mining in contemporary China and the plight of migrant labor. Two grifters, Song and Tang (played by Li Qiang and Wang Shuangbao), have perfected (they think) a murderous con: they convince a naive fellow migrant worker to pretend to be one of their relatives, murder him below ground after they all take jobs together, and then stage an accident to make the mine owner compensate them for the loss.

So far, so bad. So unscrupulous are the mine owners that they will do anything to hide the lack of safety in their mines. The grifters work hard at their next and—it turns out—final con, setting up a youngster, Yuan (played by Wang Baoqiang) for another dirty job. But he proves lovable and pathetic and poetic justice prevails.

Director Li, a Chinese expatriate whose film is prohibited in China (except perhaps on pirated DVDs), secured valuable location footage until the mine owners realized what he was doing and tried to drive him and his crew away. He was just as successful in filming the street-level life of the provincial cities—the markets, canteens, brothels, and local means of transportation, all of which give an insight into the lives of ordinary people.

He described the situation in production notes for the DVD release: "The safety precautions and facilities in these private coal mines do not meet the basic safety requirements set by the government. The mine owners do not spend money on buying the necessary safety equipment, but rather use huge sums of money to bribe the party cadres and government bureaucrats, in order to obtain the various permits needed to operate the mines. These bureaucrats totally disregard the lives of the miners in these transactions of money and power."

One of the grifters, asked how he can kill, explains his philosophy: "I just eliminate anyone in the path of my fortune." Could this be the philosophy of a new (capitalist) China? One of the hookers, in her own way, sees the changes: when she hears the miners sing "Long Live Socialism," she changes a key lyric to celebrate capitalism as the "sexual climax of socialism." Mao who?

Recommended Reading

Kahn, Joseph. "Filming the Dark Side of Capitalism in China." *New York Times*, 7 May 2003. An "uncompromising look at China's social problems."

⋈⋈⋈

Blue Collar and Buddha

MIGRANT LABOR (UNITED STATES)

1988, 57 mins., United States
Director: Taggart Siegel
Traditional Documentary
Distributor: Filmakers Library

This film delivers on only half its title: we learn in great detail what it means to be a Laotian Buddhist in the small, blue-collar city of Rockford, Illinois, but we certainly never learn what it means to be a blue-collar worker there or even what blue-collar workers think

of the influx of a sizeable number of refugees into a community where diversity had previously meant crop rotation.

This could have been an important film, fleshing out a story that Louis Malle had developed fictionally in his film *Alamo Bay* (see *Working Stiffs*), his dramatization of the clashes between Klan-led native Texan fishermen and refugee Vietnamese who also try to become Texan fishermen. Instead Siegel makes the strange decision of selecting as his representatives of (white) blue-collar Rockford two sets of extremely unpleasant interviewees—a small group of pissed-off Vietnam vets and a slightly larger group of drunks at a bar. At least the former think they have a grievance: they believe that the Laotians are being indiscriminately supported by the Welfare States of America and given the jobs that should have gone to the Vietnam vets. The drunks at the bar don't like the Laotians either, but they are so inarticulate it is mind-boggling that Siegel wasted his film on them. To be fair, there is a very short sequence of real (white) workers interviewed who say, oh yeah, I worked with "them" and "they" are fine.

What we have instead is an extended meditation on the dilemma experienced by transnational and other immigrants: how to worship Buddha and come to terms with an Americanization process that leads so many of the Laotians into Christian churches. (In fact many of these churches sponsored the Laotians in the first place: they would not have been in Rockford, or maybe not even alive, if it weren't for some really nice people.)

The Laotian story is another piece of fallout from the tangled relationships of the United States and Southeast Asian countries. Unlike traditional American immigrant groups, as William Liu, director of the Pacific/Asian American Mental Health Research Center, wisely points out, many Southeast Asians did not plan to leave their countries for economic reasons: they often had anywhere from two hours to two days to run for their lives. (The film actually never discusses when and why they left.) This rupture means that their integration into American culture is likely to be much more strained.

The only assembly line we see in this film is the one many Laotians work in ritually feeding and financially supporting Buddhist monks. And their collars are saffron.

Recommended Reading

Hall, Stuart. "From 'Routes' to 'Roots.' " In *A Place in the World? Places, Cultures and Globalization, ed.* Doreen Massey and Pat Jess, 206–7. New York: Oxford University Press, 1996. Interprets the new immigrant communities using the traditional term "diaspora"—"those who maintain links with their past through preserving their traditions intact" and may or may not be able to return "home."

ᗰᗰᗰ

Blue Vinyl

ANTI-GLOBALIZATION
INTELLECTUAL PROPERTY RIGHTS (PVCs)

2002, 97 mins., United States
Directors: Judith Helfand and Daniel B.
 Gold

Postmodern Documentary
Distributor: Docurama (www.docurama
 .com)

Like many of us, Judith Helfand knows more than her parents and, like many children, seldom wins an argument. In this case, however, when her parents threaten to cover their suburban Long Island home with vinyl or PVC (polyvinyl chloride) siding, Helfand manages to convince them that the dangers of toxic chemical exposure during the manufacture, use, and disposal of PVC products should keep their home from becoming still another—one every three seconds—vinyl-clad home in America. In the end Judith succeeds in getting them to use wood.

Nestled between episodes of the family drama, which play like a happy reality TV show (*Talk to Your Parents?*), Judith and her codirector, Daniel Gold, examine the globalization of PVC. Toting a sheet of blue vinyl siding, Helfand travels to Lake Charles,

Blue Vinyl: Filmmakers Judith Helfand and Daniel Gold on the trail of PVC polluters at the corner of Trust and Corporate. Courtesy Judith Helfand.

Louisiana, the "vinyl capital of America," and Venice, Italy, site of a manslaughter trial of thirty-one vinyl industry executives. (They are eventually acquitted.)

It turns out that Lake Charles may also be the cancer cluster capital of America. Helfand has good reason to be sensitive to such a revelation: early in the film she reveals that she is a victim of her mother's exposure to the toxic drug DES during pregnancy. Despite the crusader credentials this fact affords her, she and her codirector have assembled a deft collection of animated sequences, news footage, and commercials that keeps their very serious quest occasionally silly and usually entertaining. And she gathers some Michael Moore moments, such as when a chemical industry executive reminds us that PVC and table salt are both chlorine compounds. By the end of the film we might conclude that the industry has the intellectual property rights to PVC but not the desire nor the intention of controlling its dangers.

Recommended Reading

Foundas, Scott. "Blue Vinyl." *Variety*, 1 February 2002. Although the reviewer finds the film "distinctly one-sided," he nonetheless concludes that "few viewers of Helfand's pic will likely be re-siding their homes anytime soon."

Stopper, Tim. "Blue Vinyl." World/Independent Film (online at worldfilm.about.com). Reviewer likes the film's "mix of humor and gravity, accessibility and education, conciseness and common sense" and suggests that "the combination of [Helfand's] voice-overs and Marty Ehrlich's original music" makes the film "like a piece of environmental noir."

ᗏᗏᗏ

The Border

MIGRANT LABOR (UNITED STATES)

1982, 107 mins., R, United States
Director: Tony Richardson
Screenplay: Deric Washburn, Walon Green, and David Freeman, from a series of Los Angeles Times articles about illegal Mexican immigrants

The highpoints of Tony Richardson's career spanned both broad, farcical, and satiric gems such as *Tom Jones* (1963) and *The*

The Border: Agent (Jack Nicholson) falls for a border crosser (Elpidia Carrillo)

Loved One (1965) and intense, serious, class-intensive dramas such as *The Entertainer* (1960) and *The Loneliness of the Long Distance Runner* (1962). *The Border* instead is a curious mix of social realism and cop thriller that dramatizes the political issue of policing illegal migration from Mexico. In Richardson's twist on the subject, however, it turns out that a number of border patrol officers are breaking the very laws they are supposed to enforce. The endless attempts by Mexican nationals and "OTMs" ("other than Mexican") at crossing the border, the arrests, the repeated attempts, the new arrests—the cycle seems endless. Charlie (played by Jack Nicholson) succumbs to the easy cash by accepting illegal payoffs, in part to go along with his new pals in his unit and in part to satisfy the never-ending consuming itch of his wife.

Eventually his desire to be a law-abiding officer begins to win out, especially when he begins to fall for Maria (played by Elpidia Carrillo), a young woman who is caught a number of times trying to cross the border. When her baby is stolen by a ring of bad guys that includes Nicholson's fellow officers and supervisor, all hell breaks loose.

Over the credits, Freddy Fender sings "Across the Borderline," which includes these lines: "When you reach the broken promised land / Every dream slips through your hand / You'll lose much more than you ever hoped to find." Fender, whose real name is Baldemar Huerta, is a Tex-Mex singer who has seen the highs (some hit songs) and lows (time in prison): the promised land he sings about and the certainty that something will go wrong permeates virtually every scene in this film.

Recommended Readings

Canby, Vincent. "The Border." *New York Times,* 29 January 1982. Reviewer sees the film as an "angry, brutal melodrama" that is at least "in touch with the ways of lower-middle-class American life."

Taylor, Charles. "The Broken Promised Land." *Salon,* 30 June 1998 (www.salon.com). A long enthusiastic review, using the Fender/Heurta song as a motif: "*The Border* takes dead aim at the senselessness of U.S. immigration policy, the hypocrisy of a country that has long preened as the haven of immigrants while deriving much of its prosperity from cheap, illegal labor and the endless back-and-forth dance between the border patrol and the 'illegals.'"

▸▸▸

Breaking the Bank

ANTI-GLOBALIZATION
BANKING AND GLOBAL FINANCING

2000, 74 mins., United States
Producers: Big Noise Films, Changing
    America, Headwaters Action Video
    Collective, JustAct, Paper Tiger TV,
    Sleeping Giant Productions, VideoActive,
    Whispered Media, and Wholesome
    Goodness
Agit-Prop Documentary
Distributor: Whispered Media

One characteristic of the anti-globalization movement is the cooperation of videographers from various activist and media organizations who pool their footage: this film of the April 2000, protests in Washington, D.C., against the International Monetary Fund and World Bank comes from nine different groups and numerous other participants/videographers.

Besides being a rousing version of the street protests, antic puppet figures, and police attacks, the documentary impeaches the World Bank and the IMF for their reckless policies that exacerbate the poverty and diminishing food supplies of Third World countries.

This documentary is a little more celebrity-centered than other anti-globalization films, using actress Susan Sarandon, filmmaker Michael Moore, and lead singer/guitarist Zack De La Rocha of the band Rage Against the Machine (which disbanded subsequently) as points of inspiration for the rally.

Nonetheless, important issues such as the relationship between militarization, world poverty, and the difficulties of farmers are highlighted by international activists and scientists, such as Vandana Shiva, founder of the Indian group Navdanya, a biodiversity rights group.

Recommended Reading

Shiva, Vandana. *Stolen Harvest: The Hijacking of the Global Food Supply.* Boston: South End Press, 2004. Argues that small-scale farming is superior to agribusiness, especially in the Third World.

⊢⊣⊢⊣⊢⊣

Caribe

OIL

2004, 90 mins., Costa Rica, in Spanish with
English subtitles
Director: Esteban Ramitez
Screenplay: Ana Istaru

On the one hand, biologist Vicente Vallego (played by Jorge Perrugoria) has two beautiful women to fall in love with on beaches near one of the most spectacular of Costa Rican coasts. On the other, he's losing his banana business to the machinations of two global corporations. The banana corporation he has been working with has terminated their contract with him, and an oil company is about to drill offshore and ruin this tropical paradise. And while he is clearly a benevolent boss, many locals see the oil company's arrival as a promise of jobs and care little for potential damage to butterflies and ferns.

Since the close-ups of the remarkable creatures of the Costa Rican jungles and coast are almost as hard to resist as the images of the beautiful cast making love, the film may not make it to the must-see list of Greenpeace activists, despite the attack on the global drive for oil offshore. Vicente himself needs to pay more attention to geopolitics than to Irene (played by Maya Zapata), half-sister to Abigail (played by Cuca Escribano), Vincent's wife.

To a certain extent bananas are old neo-colonial business, while oil is black gold. The switch may seem a little too neat but it is accurate enough. In 2002 the Environmental Law Alliance (www.elaw.org) reprinted a Costa Rican news account (Lauren Wolkoff, "Oil Protests Heating Up," *Tico Times,* 18 January 2002) that foreshadowed the film's non-romantic plot closely: "Ecologists are alarmed by what they perceive as the . . . failure [of Harken Energy of Texas] to address certain minimum requirements in its environmental impact study, which they claim could present grave dangers to the biodiversity of the targeted marine area in the event of a spill or leak."

Recommended Reading

Scheib, Ronnie. "Caribe." *Variety,* 7 June 2005. "Unspoiled tropical beaches and jewel-toned forests" as well as the "imported charms" of the pan-Hispanic cast "make the case against an unscrupulous oil company . . . more eloquently than do the impassioned speeches delivered by script's homegrown activists."

⊢⊣⊢⊣⊢⊣

Chain

WAL-MART

2004, 99 mins., United States/Germany
Director: Jem Cohen
Screenplay: Jem Cohen

Jem Cohen has chosen two remarkably different female characters to navigate the malls and big box stores in this feature film, which often resembles a structuralist documentary. Amanda (played by Mira Billotte) is an American, slacker-like in appearance and language, although by the end of the film she is holding down two low-wage cleaning jobs, one in a big box store and one in a long-stay motel. Tamiko (played by Miho Nikaido) is a Japanese "company" woman, more middle class in appearance, assigned to survey American malls to help her company—which used to manufacture steel—move into the theme park business in America. She is the front person for a project called "The Floating World," a fit metaphor for Tamiko's almost aimless trips into what we think at first are only American malls but we realize (or understand when we view the credits) are malls and big box stores around the world (including eleven different American ones and five from other countries).

Both women are afflicted with different de-

Chain: The endless global mallscape.
Courtesy Antitode International Films.

grees of mall fever and a growing undefined angst. Neither are shoppers—one has no money, the other seems quite casually dressed for a Japanese businesswoman. As Amanda drifts from one bad mall job to the next and Tamiko gathers her impressions of how malls function, Cohen's instinct is to show off the mesmerizing sameness of the mall landscape: we see so many malls, hotel atria, and big box stores—some being built, others being torn down—that when we get a particularly sleek mall glowing in the night sky, we are relieved to be in the presence of something akin to beauty.

The plot of this globalization travelogue is simple: Amanda has managed to cop a mini-DV cam and she films herself in low light mumbling about how she doesn't like to work but she has to do it, while Tamiko moves from hotel to hotel compiling her report. Although they never seem to meet, at the very end we get the impression that Amanda may be working in the hotel complex where Tamiko is staying. At this point Tamiko seems suicidal, as she sees headlines about the slumping Japanese economy and her company seems to be ignoring her e-mailed reports.

A few startling sequences about the disposable and alienating nature of the globalized economy stand out. Amanda admits that she couldn't work at Wal-Mart because she's not much of a "people person," yet when she sees an acquaintance working at an Eckerd drugstore at a mall that is about to be demolished,

she recounts their mall worker solidarity. Amanda had given her free tickets to movies and her friend had given her some stuff from the store. At another, seemingly obscure location, Amanda finds what appears to be a surveillance tape but she—unlike us—does not recognize the "crooked E" logo of the vacant Enron building where the tape was presumably made.

Tamiko for her part tells the story of how her father's company assigned him to stand in a cherry blossom park for almost twenty-four hours so that he could alert his superiors to the exact moment when the blossoms fell—a perfect Japanese cultural moment for them but no doubt a humiliating experience for him.

In the end a bird nests in the lower loop of the B in the Sam's Club sign and a traditional hymn plays. America continues. Cohen made his name as a director of some exciting and well-received musical videos and films (for groups like R.E.M. and Fugazi). Here he has experimented with minimalist mallscapes and a quiet but insistent call for some kind of aesthetic time-out for big box stores.

Recommended Reading

Holden, Stephen. "The Struggle to Find Life in Ordinary Landscapes." *New York Times,* 14 September 2005. The filmmaker "deliberately blurs the lines between fiction, documentary and cinematic essay" but seems uncomfortable that Tamiko asserts that in the United States "big Japanese factories are built where there will be less mixing [of the races] and more racial harmony."

⋈⋈⋈

Chain of Love

TRANSNATIONAL MIGRATION
WOMEN WORKERS AND CHILD LABOR

2001, 50 mins., Holland, in Dutch and
    Tagalog with English subtitles
Director: Marije Meerman
Cinema-Verité Documentary
Distributor: First Run/Icarus Films

Filipino nannies who go abroad in great numbers to work contribute so much to their nation's GNP that the government helps train them, celebrates their comings and goings at the airport, and facilitates their remittances home with bank branches abroad. They are, as one nanny says proudly, "The Mercedes Benz of domestics." They are costly to hire but have a reputation for being clean, efficient, and dependable, unlike, it is implied, migrant laborers from other Third World countries.

The "chain of love" is actually more complex that this title suggests. One of the recipients of this top-notch care, an upper-class Dutch mother of four, who always refers to her nanny as an au pair (which suggests a different relationship), is adamant about the freedom she gains from this hire. We could not live the way we do without it, she insists.

But the real chain of love may come as a surprise to many viewers. A number of the overseas nannies hire Filipino nannies of their own back home! Maternal love is not cheap abroad, but it is in the Philippines. The filmmakers cut back and forth between Melanie, a nanny in Rome, to a cousin who takes care of Melanie's little boy. In the chain of love, it seems, everyone must "pretend" that they are taking care of their own kids.

The film is painful to watch. Like *Do They Catch Children Too?* (q.v.), which focuses on the children of Filipino migrant workers in Israel, the toll of transnational family life is easy to see but hard to assess. The number of interviewees who conclude their interviews by crying nonetheless speaks volumes.

Recommended Readings

Parreñas, Rhacel Salazar. "The Care Crisis in the Philippines: Children and Transnational Families in the New Global Economy." In *Global Women: Nannies, Maids, and Sex Workers in the New Economy*, ed. Barbara Ehrenreich and Arlie Russell Hochschild, 39–54. New York: Henry Holt, 2002. Discusses the effects of the "care deficit" in the Philippines in which perhaps "34 to 54 percent of the Filipino population is sustained by remittances from migrant workers."

———. *Servants of Globalization: Women, Migration and Domestic Work*. Stanford: Stanford University Press, 2001. Parreñas's definitive study—based on numerous interviews—looks at Rome and Los Angeles, "two main destinations for Filipina migration."

⋈⋈⋈

Choropampa

SCARCE RESOURCES (GOLD)

2002, 52 or 75 mins., Peru, in English and
    Spanish with English subtitles
Directors: Ernesto Cabellos and Stephanie
    Boyd
Cinema-Verité Documentary
Distributor: First Run/Icarus Films

Choropampa is a village that happens to sit astride the main trucking route of the Yanacocha goldmine in the Peruvian Andes, the largest goldmine in South America. The mine, whose method of extracting gold is detailed in *The Curse of Inca Gold* (q.v.), is jointly owned by the World Bank, Newmont Mining of Colorado, and a Peruvian partner. When a truck spilled about seventy-five pounds of mercury in the center of the village, the local people almost immediately began to suffer from mercury poisoning and up to two years later many children and adults still had symptoms. It was bad enough that the villagers inhaled poisonous fumes, but a number of them—following ancient ritual—gathered some of what they call *azogue* into little pouches they draped on babies to ward off evil spirits.

The directors alternate corporate videos that explain away the problem with footage of

Choropampa: The mayor of Choropampa speaks out against the Yanacocha goldmine. Courtesy First Run/Icarus Films.

the villagers trying to get the corporation and the government to provide medical aid for their ailments. Alberto Fujimori, Peru's president at the time, tried to reassure the villagers that his government would take care of them. Unfortunately for them, Fujimari soon had to flee because his national security assistant was caught on videotaping selling the supreme court votes that gave Newmont exclusive title to the consortium's access to the gold. (See *The Curse of Inca Gold* for further details on this scandal.) Fujimori fled to Japan to take up the other half of his dual citizenship and left the villagers and their new mayor, Lot Saavedra, the difficult task of winning legal redress or even corporate restitution for their injuries.

When the frustrations of the villagers boil over, the directors are close by to record their blockade of the highway in the middle of the night and also their confrontation with the army. The immediacy of the struggle keeps even the camera crew on the run.

Recommended Reading

Kenney, Charles D. *Fujimori's Coup and the Breakdown of Democracy in Latin America.* South Bend: University of Notre Dame Press, 2004. Reviews the complicated and controversial career of Fujimori.

▸▸▸

Collision Course

DEREGULATION AND PRIVATIZATION
REAGANOMICS

1988, 47 mins., United States
Director: Alex Gibney
Traditional Documentary
Distributor: California Newsreel

Eastern Airlines was the victim of many economic and political forces, including the deregulation of the industry that gave rise to about a hundred nonunion airlines, many of which, such as People's Express, did not remain in business either. Eastern posted enormous losses in 1983, while two major airlines, Braniff and Continental (with Frank Lorenzo at the helm), also declared bankruptcy. Eastern's move to counter the trend was to bring in former astronaut Frank Borman as chairman.

Frank Borman came to the company with a military man's belief in a "strict chain of command." He openly referred to the workers as children and at first reacted to the proposal that management share governance with the workers as equivalent to letting the "monkeys run the zoo." Nonetheless he was able to broker the kind of deal that seemed to be based on sound Reaganomics: the workers would take an 18 to 22 percent wage cut, agree to productivity increases, and change the work rules management found too limiting; the workers would receive a 25 percent stock share, four seats on the board of directors, the right to open the company books, the "right to organize work" by their own "work teams," and pay increases if there was a rise in productivity.

Eastern's plan seemed to work, but the recovery lasted but a year. After a fare war and increased costs for maintaining Eastern's fleet, management demanded a 20 percent wage cut. Enter Lorenzo, one of the models for Gordon Gekko in *Wall Street* (q.v.). Although air passengers do not joke about a "collision course," it accurately describes what happened between the International Association of Machinists and Lorenzo, whose Texas Air acquired Eastern Airlines in 1986. Two more unsuitable partners could hardly have been found: Texas Air (which owned Continental and New York Air) was traditionally anti-union. "We're airline builders, not airline busters," Lorenzo boasted, not too long before selling the airline. After the sale, Borman resigned, but Eastern did not survive.

Although most of the workers and a fair number of their managers at Eastern believed that before Lorenzo arrived they had broken through to a new level of labor-management cooperation that could be a model industry-wide if not for corporations in general, it was not to be. Interviews with these employees lend an air of hopefulness to an otherwise very sober film.

Robert Reich, President Bill Clinton's secretary of labor, provided the film's distributor with this comment: "If up to me, I'd project it on a mountainside and have the audio boom over valley and stream." The flight attendants and the pilots might feel slighted, however, since they seem not to be major players in the drama.

Recommended Reading

Robinson, Jack E. *Freefall: The Needless Destruction of Eastern Air Lines and the Valiant Struggle to Save It.* New York: Harper Business, 1992. Discusses Lorenzo and the unions who squared off against him (the pilots, the flight attendants, and the machinists).

⋈⋈⋈

Commanding Heights: The Battle for the World Economy

OIL

2002, 360 mins., United States
Directors: Greg Barker and William Cran
TV Documentary based on Daniel Yergin and Joseph Stainslaw's *The Commanding Heights* (1998)
Distributor: PBS

Daniel Yergin and his coauthor take the subtitle of their book—"The Battle between Government and the Marketplace That Is Remak-

ing the Modern World"—quite seriously, because the same hocus-pocus that made all of the workers in the oil industry disappear in Yergin's earlier book, *The Prize: The Epic Quest for Oil, Money, and Power*, is operative here as well. Both the film and book about globalization argue that only markets, governments, privatization, and "mixed economies" (strong government role in private enterprise) determine our economic life. Once more workers are invisible, even while downsizing and unemployment are considered inevitable forces.

Commanding Heights nonetheless is a revealing mirror of late-twentieth-century capitalism: in Yergin's view the "commanding heights" are occupied by global corporations whose power rivals that of the rising monopolies of the late nineteenth century, although he is fair enough to point out that these unrestrained monopolies gave rise to government intervention and "regulatory capitalism." Thank God, or at least thank Reagan and Thatcher, however, and the power of the World Bank, because government regulation is now a shadow of its former pelf.

But the series—an extended and quite sophisticated history of economic forces in the last hundred years—is keen to identify the free-market triumph of Reaganomics and Thatcherism as the belated triumph of the ideas of Friedrich von Hayek, whose economic theory that government meddling in the economy was a mistake (and in fact led to totalitarianism) earned him a Nobel Prize in 1974. An opponent of Keynesianism, Hayek and his ideas became Thatcher's ideological underpinning for her campaign to dismantle Britain's regulated and nationalized industries and public services.

The triumph of "free market" capitalism in the 1980s and the dismantling of the Berlin Wall in 1989 ended for what Yergin are two curiously similar economic systems: "totalitarian central planning" in communist countries and protectionist capitalism in the west. Under the leadership of the transnational organizations such as the World Bank, free-market capitalism spread and faltered in a number of economies reviewed by the film: Russia, Poland, India, Bolivia, and Chile. Although the series concludes with a question—

"The Battle Decided?"—there was little doubt about the agenda of one of the key cosponsors of the program—Enron—although its role in the creation of the program has been handled like deposed leaders in the Eastern bloc: it has disappeared.

While not all will agree with its point of view, *Commanding Heights* is a rare exercise in the vindication of one intellectual—Hayek—and gives him credit for changing the course of the world's economic strategy and bringing in the age of globalization.

Recommended Readings

Genzlinger, Neil. "Charting the Mysteries of World Markets." *New York Times*, 3 April 2002. If the film "falls short of explaining how the global economy works or who controls it, it at least gives a sense of what [the WTO] protesters are rebelling against."

"PBS Likes Capitalism More than Commercial Networks Do." *Wall Street Journal*, 28 March 2002. The program is a "paean to private enterprise."

ᐅᐊᐅ

Congo: White King, Red Rubber, Black Death

HISTORY OF GLOBALIZATION
NEOCOLONIALISM
SCARCE RESOURCES (RUBBER AND IVORY)

2003, 84 mins., Belgium/United Kingdom, in English, French, Flemish, and Congolese with English subtitles
Director: Peter Bate
Mixed Traditional and Mock Documentary

Joseph Conrad's *Heart of Darkness* (1902) is probably the most famous exposé of the ivory trade that brutalized the inhabitants of the Congo Free State at the end of the nineteenth century. But ivory was only one of the two resources plundered by the European colonists. The other was rubber, sought for inflatable bicycle tires from the 1880s on. The country was carved out of West Africa and virtually handed to King Leopold II by the Berlin Congress of European nations in 1885. For the next twenty-five years it was literally

his private property, a labor and slave camp for his profit. Whole villages were help captive while their men went into the bush to gather rubber. If they failed to achieve quotas, their hands might be cut off and their families punished or murdered.

Some experts estimate that half the population was killed in this quarter century. Its viciousness inspired some of the first global human rights crusaders and pamphleteers, among whom were African American missionary William Shepherd, who fought against forced labor, and Mark Twain, whose brilliant satire, *King Leopold's Soliloquy* (1905), used the king's own voice to condemn his crimes. The film's title recalls Edward Dene Morel's *Red Rubber: The Story of the Rubber Slave Trade Flourishing on the Congo on the Year of Grace 1906* (1907), which summed up Leopold's rule in this way: "The reek of its abominations mounts to heaven in the fumes of shame. It pollutes the earth. Its speedy disappearance is imperative for Africa, and for the world."

When Leopold was forced to cede his private property over to Belgium sovereignty in 1908 and the Belgians continued to exploit the region's rubber and ivory, even adding copper and diamonds to the list, only the worse excesses of Leopold's era were mitigated. These horrors are developed in the film by switching into a mock documentary mode, dramatizing a trial of Leopold that was never held. Leopold sits in a cage in the dock, like the trial of the Nazi Adolf Eichman in Israel, listening impassively to damning testimony.

Leopold was a member of the European Saxe-Coburg monarchic dynasty: Victoria was Aunt Victoria to him. Part of his unchecked zeal for exploitation and mayhem might have been throne envy since he felt he was considered a minor luminary in the dynasty. Nonetheless the atrocities depicted in Conrad's novel were routine in Leopold's personal African kingdom. And he was guilty of the first great globalization lie: when he gained control of the Congo he told his European peers that "free trade" would be open to them if they allowed him to control these "vacant lands."

Leopold became memorialized in his own

country as the civilizer of the Congo and lies upon lies were told about his leadership. When the Congo was finally liberated from colonial control, only his statues in Belgium remained standing; the Congolese, for their part, sent his statue and that of his principal lackey, explorer William Stanley, to the junkyard. The filmmakers imagine his death in the last moments of the film, uttering the line made immortal by the ivory trader Kurtz in Conrad's novel: "The horror. The horror."

Although the Congo eventually lost its virtually monopoly of rubber by 1930, the forces of neocolonialism and globalism still use the region as a seemingly inexhaustible supply of scarce and valuable resources (*Unreported World*, q.v.). The horror, it seems, is not quite over.

Recommended Readings

Dargis, Manohla. "The Horrors of Belgium's Congo." *New York Times*, 21 October 2005. Agrees that the only sensible term for what Leopold did was "genocide."

Hochschild, Adam. *King Leopold's Ghost.* New York: Houghton Mifflin, 1998. Covers similar ground as the film but adds the story of crusading minister William Shepherd, unfortunately not mentioned in the documentary.

⋈⋈⋈

The Constant Gardener

INTELLECTUAL PROPERTY RIGHTS (DRUGS)

2005, 129 mins., R, United Kingdom/United States
Director: Fernando Meirelles
Screenplay: Jeffrey Caine, from John Le Carre's *The Constant Gardener* (2001)

John Le Carre's novels of cold war intrigue—from the early and quite possibly the best, *The Spy Who Came in from the Cold,* in 1963 through *Tinker, Tailor, Soldier, Spy* in 1974—achieved even greater acclaim when they became, in these two instances, an outstanding film and television series, respectively. Certainly their success owed much to the casting—Richard Burton as the doomed spy and Claire Bloom as his unwitting accomplice in the former and Alec Guinness as the imperturbable and flawed Smiley in the latter.

The Constant Gardener is adapted from Le Carre's thriller about another international target, what he (and others) have called Big Pharma (from PhRMA, the Pharmaceutical Research and Manufacturers of America), the international drug industry. The titular hero is Justin Quayle (played by Ralph Fiennes) who likes to putter in his garden when he's not doing obscure consular tasks for the British government. A young crusader, Tessa (played by Rachel Weisz), heckles him at a lecture but soon leads him out of a domestic Eden (after a precipitate marriage) into the hell of Kenya's campaign against AIDS.

We watch, in horror, as Tessa uncovers, with the aid of a black doctor who some suspect has become her lover, a diabolical plan by a drug company to test their TB drug Dypraxa using AIDS clinics as a cover. This is Le Carre's most explicit drama of globalization, since the motto of the drug company Tessa and the doctor, Arnold Bluhm (played by Hubert Koundé), are investigating is "The World is Our Clinic," a chilling idea that. And remarkably close to what has happened as First World drug companies use Third World patients for clinical tests without the strict protocols required in the United States and Western Europe.

Fernando Meirelles, who directed a very disturbing and violent film about street urchins in a Rio slum (*City of God*), makes a valiant attempt to capture the dense economic base laid down in Le Carre's original novel. In the end he opts for the love story between Justin and Tessa, the apparent scandal of her relationship with Arnold, and the British High Command's collusion with the drug company and locally hired thugs, which culminates in gruesome and exciting events. The latter bring out Le Carre's ability to craft sinister and duplicitous characters.

Meirelles opts for an emotionally satisfying ending—not in Le Carre's novel—which has us believe that the Quayles will be vindicated. The real horror, argues Big Pharma expert Marcia Angell ("The Body Hunters," *New York Review of Books,* 6 October 2005), is that the drug companies wouldn't have to even bother to try to silence their critics.

Le Carre has stated (in *The Nation*) that other globalization topics such as Shell's murderous alliance with the Nigerian oil industry also cried out for examination, but that he became hooked on Big Pharma when he studied the drive for profits and global domination sometimes masquerading as fair trade policy and health campaigns. One of the major goals of Big Pharma, dramatized only lightly in the film, is the curtailment of generic drugs, an especially fatal movement since Third World countries cannot afford the patented drugs of Big Pharma. The WTO has instituted the protocols called TRIPS (Trade Related Intellectual Property Rights), which allow the patenting of organisms (through genetic modification) and stops the use of generic drugs, both of which carry trade sanctions. These results have been extremely satisfying to Big Pharma.

Recommended Readings

Angell, Marcia. *The Truth about Drug Companies: How They Deceive Us and What to Do about It.* New York: Random House, 2004. Extended analysis of Big Pharma's use of Third World clinical trials to avoid FDA scrutiny as well as the practice of acquiring patents for drugs resulting from research sponsored by the government.

Le Carre, John. "In Place of Nations." *The Nation*, 9 April 2001. Extended critique of Big Pharma, one of many targets of "unbridled capitalism" the author considered dramatizing.

Stephens, Joe. "The Body Hunters." *Washington Post*, 17–22 December 2000 (in six parts). Pfizer was sued (unsuccessfully) by parents of children recruited for clinical trials in Nigeria in 1996 of the experimental oral drug Trovan for spinal meningitis instead of a relatively common intravenous drug.

ᐅᐊᐅ

Controlling Interest: The World of the Multinational Corporation

HISTORY OF GLOBALIZATION
NEOCOLONIALISM

1975, 46 mins., United States
Directors: Bruce Schmiechen and Larry Adelman

Traditional Documentary
Distributor: California Newsreel

The title of this controlled but angry political interpretation of multinational corporations speaks to the transition between classic neocolonialism and globalized economic power. The control of Chile was in the hands of an oligarchy consisting of about one hundred companies who held half the industrial wealth, while only two companies made 22 percent of the profits. Multinational oil companies also owned half the coal and uranium deposits. In discussing the economic maneuvers of Ingersoll Rand, a union leader at a company welding plant in Greenfield, Massachusetts, concluded: "Freedom is the freedom for multinationals to make profit in any place in the world."

Although the film was completed after one of the more blatant exercises in American neocolonialism—the military overthrow of the democratically elected government of Chile's Salvador Allende, whose party came to power on the promise of nationalizing the extremely profitable copper mines (among other industries) that made Chile the personal preserve of Anaconda and Kennecott copper companies—the events it chronicles have lost very little of their power to inform and shock.

Controlling Interest is like a lost letter from the militant 1960s, with interviews with Chileans who have been imprisoned and exiled and with one who was tortured for his role in defending Allende's vision of Chile. Similarly, black-and-white footage of unnamed American officers of multinationals show a pasty-faced group of bureaucrats, seemingly interchangeable, who discuss the people of the Third World in stereotypes: locals are good for assembly lines for electronics because of the "native ability . . . to work with their hands," they work for thirty cents an hour, and they don't have any "social distractions" the way we do here. Even the presumably sophisticated George Ball, undersecretary of state for President Jimmy Carter and then a senior partner of the Lehmann Brothers investment firm, does seem very self-conscious: as an example of how a bad thing can turn out okay, he says that after our invasion of the Dominican Republic, things went fine and the people were happy.

Recommended Reading

Aguilera, Pilar, and Ricardo Fredes, eds. *Chile: The Other September 11.* Melbourne: Ocean Press, 2002. Collection of essays from radical points of view memorializing Allende, who was killed on September 11, 1973, and outlining his attempted reforms.

⋈⋈⋈

The Corporation

GLOBAL CAPITAL

2003, 145 mins., Canada
Directors: Mark Achbar and Jennifer
  Abbott
Traditional Documentary, based on Joel
  Bakan's *The Corporation: The Pathological
  Pursuit of Profit and Power* (2004)

One of the turning points in the rise of the modern corporation to political and economic dominance is its assumption of personhood on or about 1886. This was not a religious conversion, but the result of a Supreme Court decision in favor of the Southern Pacific Railroad, which ruled (see Nace) that as "persons" corporations were protected under the Fourteenth Amendment, designed to give freed slaves "equal protection of the laws." As Joel Bakan, author of the film's source book, states: "The corporate person had taken the place, at least in law, of the real people who owned corporations." These "real people," by the way, were the stockholders, but after pioneering "broad popular participation in stock markets," Bakan explains, investors would in practice never exert any control over their corporation.

Historically the great railroad companies of the nineteenth century, led by robber barons, became the templates for the monopolistic corporations whose power persisted through the early twentieth century. As Bakan and the documentary argue, greedy and powerful corporate persons can sometimes be unstable if not pathological. In fact Bakan likes to call— "in a cheeky way" (see Williamson)—the corporation a psychopath because it is governed only by self-interest and is unable to relate to others.

Talking heads, both corporate and establishment types as well as radicals, activists, and critics of corporate excess, appear throughout this documentary, but its case studies, almost all negative with one exception, should make viewers take notice, if not cause alarm. IBM's German subsidiary, for example, had contracts with Nazi agencies for a punch-card system to monitor the disposition of Jewish prisoners.

One of the most involved case studies shows how Monsanto's campaign to introduce Bovine Growth Hormone (BGH), a drug that increases milk production, became a global concern. European countries such as Great Britain refuse to license the hormone. American milk production is up, in part because at least one quarter of American dairy herds use BGH, but the cost is high: additional injections of antibiotics are required to counter cases of infected udders caused by the hormone. And humans face the spread of more antibiotic-resistant bacteria. And when investigative reporters for Fox News had the goods on this bit of corporate knavery, their own media corporation made their lives hell and refused to broadcast their report, which included the damning fact that Monsanto's research for BGH consisted of a ninety-day toxicity trial with thirty rats.

Bad corporation, bad. The one positive case study involves Ray Anderson, CEO of Interface Carpet, who has led his corporation toward a standard of environmental sustainability by imposing strict controls on the use of raw materials and the disposal of pollutants. His company thrived financially nonetheless.

Most, if not all, of the other corporations answer to the narrator's profile: "A corporation is an externalizing machine, in the same way that a shark is a killing machine." If in fact it is psychopathic, how do we treat it? The film doesn't go there (except for Ray Anderson).

Recommended Readings

Nace, Ted. *Gangs of America: The Rise of Corporate Power and the Disabling of America.*

San Francisco: Berrett-Koehler, 2003. Includes a detailed analysis of the definition of the corporation as a person and corporate rights in general.

Scott, A. O. "Giving Corporations the Psychoanalytic Treatment." *New York Times,* 30 June 2004. Overall positive review but adds that "what is missing . . . is any recognition that capitalism survives at least as much on seduction as on coercion" and that while it is a "dense, complicated and thought-provoking film . . . it simplifies its title character."

Williamson, Thad. "Interview with Joel Bakan." *Dollars & Sense,* May/June 2004 (online at www.dollarsandsense.org/archives/2004/0504thecorp.html). Because of the corporate emphasis on short-term profit and the presence of a large labor pool, "there is less incentive on the part of corporations to actually develop relationships with particular communities."

ΗΗΗ

The Crooked E: The Unshredded Truth about Enron

ENRON

2003, 100 mins., United States
Director: Penelope Spheeris
Screenplay: Stephen Mazur, based on Brian
  Cruver's *Anatomy of Greed—The Un-
  shredded Truth from an Enron Insider*
  (2003)

Enron is a great subject for a cheesy movie: you've got Texas, your execs are world-class egomaniacs and crooks running the seventh-largest corporation in America, your chief honcho has been given a nickname by President Bush II, playmates are hired as secretaries and administrative assistants, grinding on tabletops at office parties is routine, and your logo, after which this film is named, kind of looks like a swastika on its side.

In this context, Penelope Spheeris, director of many films, including *Prison Stories: Women on the Inside* (1991) and *Wayne's World* (1992), delivers the goods, combining an exposé of corporate malfeasance with the dramatization of the story of an MBA innocent, Brian Cruver (played by Christian Kane), who gets tempted by easy Enron

money, loses what really matters (his girlfriend) and every penny he earned when Enron crashes, but finally regains his virtue and marries his girlfriend.

Crooked E is based on the memoir/exposé by Brian Cruver, who was hired (by mistake, he is told) at Enron but quickly learns what it takes to be "Enronized" when he is assigned to the bankruptcy division to sell insurance. He adopts the swaggering lifestyle of a financial master of the universe, not seeing that warning signs are everywhere: Arthur Andersen auditors playing video games, company leaders urging everyone to buy Enron stock, and chairman Kenneth Lay's escalating happy talk seasoned with remarks about losses due to "certain structured financial arrangements"—in other words, CEO Jeff Skilling's illegal use of "related party transactions" to disguise the true state of Enron's books.

Cruver has a somewhat mysterious mentor in upper management, Mr. Blue (played by Brian Dennehy) who—when he is not dissing the president of Guatemala on a cell phone—is making speeches about there being "no limits on Enron except the limits you place on yourself" and (eventually when Enron declares bankruptcy) that Enron represents "the globalization of stupidity." He's looking forward to jail, to get some rest.

Spheeris gives Enron world a vibrant and seductive look. Large LED crawl screens in the parking garage tell drivers that "Enron is . . . Ambitious" and Enron TV in the elevators tout the company's virtues and assets. Transitions between scenes are designated with crawl messages that log the day and the roller-coaster ride of Enron's stock price. This is especially appropriate because making its stock price climb was an Enron obsession and its greatest potential fiction.

Just before one of the Playboy playmates on staff tells everyone that they are laid off, Cruver sneaks an inflated contract he negotiated out of his boss's office and destroys it, thereby freeing one of his clients from an ignominious financial defeat. The film can be obvious and hokey, but where else can you learn that a favorite Enron sushi roll consisted of shark?

Since the film was produced by Robert

Greenwald, whose subsequent muckraking documentaries *Outfoxed: Robert Murdoch's War on Journalism* (2004) and *Wal-Mart: The High Cost of Low Price* (q.v.) have caused quite a stir, we can be reasonably sure that the filmmakers tried their best to give us "the unshredded truth about Enron."

Recommended Reading

Fusaro, Peter C., and Ross M. Miller. *What Went Wrong at Enron.* Hoboken: John Wiley, 2002. Comprehensive and readable guide to everyday Enron shenanigans.

⊢⊣⊢⊣⊢⊣

The Curse of Inca Gold

SCARCE RESOURCES (GOLD)

2005, 60 mins., United States
Director: Nelli Black
Correspondents: Lowell Bergman and Jane Perlez
TV Documentary
Distributor: PBS

The melodramatic title refers to the kidnapping of Atahualpa, the last Incan ruler, who told the Spanish under Pizarro that his people would ransom him for gold stacked to the tips of his upreached hand. When the gold arrived, Pizarro promptly murdered him.

The latest betrayal of the descendents of Atahualpa takes the form of strip-mining the hills of Peru for "microscopic" gold. The process used is known as cyanide heaping, in which more than thirty tons of rock are piled on a lined "pond" and cyanide-laced water is drizzled over the heap. The gold combines with the cyanide and is drained into a processing unit. The heap, to my eye, looks incredibly like an Incan pyramid!

The corporate story behind this episode of Incan gold originates in globalized skullduggery. The American company Belmont Gold was in danger of being squeezed out of a consortium of Peruvian and French companies. Its CEO sought out President Alberto Fujimori's right-hand man and national security enforcer, Vladimiro Montesinos, reputed to be

on the CIA payroll, to bend the Peruvian court that would ultimately decide whether the French or American company would gain the gold. Belmont also asked Peter Romero, the U.S. assistant secretary of state for Latin American affairs, to help out on the diplomatic end. The result was virtual control by Belmont.

But an unintended development was that all of Montesinos's deals were captured on videotape and he was forced from office. That was the beginning of the end for President Fujimori as well, but it was not the end of mining-related troubles for the Peruvian people. Farmers living near the Belmont mines became the victims of a toxic spill from a mining truck hauling mercury. This incident is related in detail in the documentary *Choropampa* (q.v.).

Recommended Reading

Bergman, Lowell, and Jane Perlez. "Tangled Strands in Fight over Peru Gold Mine. *New York Times,* 25 October 2005. Companion article to the film by the *Frontline* correspondents; some additional in-depth material.

⊢⊣⊢⊣⊢⊣

Czech Dream

Cesky Sen

GLOBAL CAPITAL

2004, 97 mins., Czech Republic, in Czech with English subtitles
Directors: Vit Klusak and Filip Remunda
Mock Documentary

What do Czechs dream about? Hypermarkets, apparently. The targets of this unusual combination of mock documentary with cinema-verité sequences are multiple. Gullible customers, having experienced the austerity of a communist system that promised to conquer capitalism, fall for an advertising campaign for a fake hypermarket called The Czech Dream. Since Czech shoppers love hypermarkets, they rush to take advantage of the promise of Western-style consumer capitalism.

They are also willing to rush to a hypermarket whose shelves are not only as empty as those in the state-sponsored stores of the previous regime but are in fact not there at all! In an exhibition park outside Prague, the filmmakers spread an enormous fake façade emblazoned with "Cesky Sen" (Czech Dream) and held back the hordes who gathered until the opening bell. As the people rushed across the field toward a store that did not exist, their enthusiasm for a consumer heaven and then their mixture of mystification and anger were captured for the film. Considering the apparent nastiness of the prank, most of the would-be customers accepted their disappointment with remarkable calm, although a few said that fooling people like this was outrageous; another person agreed but added that the "whole country is a scam."

The end of this controversial mock documentary triggers a discussion among the frustrated shoppers of the impending ballot on the entry of the Czech Republic into the European Union, which, it turns out, is another of the filmmakers' targets. A number of the European reviewers of the film noted that the film reflected the moment when the Czech Republic was to join the European Community in the hopes of never facing an empty shelf in a store again. Since the government is spending a small fortune on an ad campaign to get a yes vote on the entry into the EU, the film's supporters on television talk shows argue that the government is itself running another Czech Dream scam.

Film students Vit Klusak and Filip Remunda received a grant to concoct the ad campaign—billboards, advertisements, jingles—for Czech Dream. In fact their primary billboards included lines such as "Do not come" and "Do not spend," slogans that no doubt many consumers regarded as clever reverse psychology. This campaign would have convinced me: great posters, a clever song, promises of giveaways on opening day. But my irony antenna went up as I watched the film, gradually suspecting that not only was the Czech public an object of this scam, but so were we, the viewers: the ad agency and others involved all seem like actors to me, behaving as if they were in a postmodern documentary about the ethics of selling out their expertise.

The film ends with some grumbling among the disappointed shoppers, true, but the original Czech trailer included on the DVD release shows the filmmakers being beaten bloody by some scary-looking customers who—despite the fact that many Czechs interviewed for the film make it clear that hanging out in a hypermarket all day was quite common—were clearly actors. Klusak and Remunda may have based their idea on a fight that happened among customers at an opening of an actual hypermarket: unfortunately, they weren't there that day with their cameras.

Recommended Reading

Bradshaw, Peter. "Czech Dream." *The Guardian,* 24 June 2005. "Those of us who persist in spending our money on something called 'still mineral water' will appreciate this subversive documentary-parable about idiocy and consumerism in the modern age."

ᐅᐊᐅᐊᐅᐊ

Dance with Farm Workers

CHINA
MIGRANT LABOR (OTHER THAN
  THE UNITED STATES)

2001, 90 mins., China, in Mandarin with
  English subtitles
Director: Wu Wenguang
Cinema-Verité Documentary

Viewers, guided by the title perhaps, expect a film about Chinese folk dancers. The dancers on this stage, however, are construction laborers who have migrated to Beijing from Sichuan in search of employment. They are part of the army of migrant workers who are transforming the urban Chinese cityscape. Ironically, the hall they are rehearsing in is a former textile factory that will become an amusement center, the kind of project that would hire them as day laborers.

The thirty workers are recruited in part because they like the pay: thirty yen a day (a little less than four U.S. dollars). Eventually they enter into the spirit of what could only be called a postmodern industrial/labor happening, staged by dance professionals from the Beijing Living Dance Studio. The dance protocols involve workers' movements—climbing ladders, rolling barrels, walking on catwalks—which have a certain charm when abstracted into a repetitious movement choreographed for all thirty workers.

At the Berlin International Film Festival in 2002 director Wu Wenguang noted the workers' first interest had been their pay: "It was only some time later that they discovered that they, the lowest of the low, would be standing center stage." And although he wanted his "film to be very close to the reality and the people of the society of China today," the film of the rehearsal had to be "mediated through my own personal views" (program notes). The result is the kind of dance not usually seen in the Chinese countryside but in a First World avant-garde studio.

A Darker Side of Fair: The "fairer" standard of beauty. Courtesy Documentary Educational Resources.

Recommended Reading

Leary, Charles. "Performing the Documentary, or Making It to the Other Bank." *Senses of Cinema,* July 2003 (online at www.sensesofcinema.com). Calls Wu's work "performative writing," that is, "the documentary form and the dance/performance form are inseparable, part of the same creative impulse."

⋈⋈⋈
A Darker Side of Fair

INTELLECTUAL PROPERTY RIGHTS
  (CHEMICALS)

2004, 25 mins., India, in English
Director: Deepak Leslie
Traditional Documentary
Distributor: Documentary Educational
  Resources

What do Indian beauty queens, models in Madras, and Bollywood stars have in common? Fair skin color, despite a deep mythological tradition in India that seems to favor dark and sometimes blue and earth-colored heroines and goddesses.

Multinational corporations such as Unilever,

Clinique, and L'Oreal have created lightening creams with names such as Fair, Fairever, Fair and Lovely, and Lovely Fairness, as if the thesaurus is stuck in *F*. These creams, mostly ammonia products that bleach the skin with some risk, have carved out an enormous market share in India and neighboring countries, for whom a light or Caucasian complexion is touted as a ticket to romantic and even economic success.

Director Deepak Leslie reviews other traditional forms of Indian literature and culture that favor fair skin, suggesting the influence of the colonizing powers, especially in the imperial British era. Contemporary advertisements, perhaps not surprisingly, tout fair skin most outrageously, even showing the failure of some dark-skinned women to get a man or get ahead. The film also explores the influence of this code on arranged marriages, a staple of Indian culture.

Recommended Reading

Joshi, Ruchir. "Neither Fair nor Lovely." *Hindustan Times,* 25 March 2006. Columnist laments that many Indians "are very racist towards others but even more so towards ourselves."

►I◄►I◄►I◄
Darwin's Nightmare

GLOBAL CATASTROPHES
SCARCE RESOURCES (FISH)

2004, 107 mins., France/Austria/Belgium, in
    English, Russian, and Swahili with English
    subtitles
Director: Hubert Sauper
Cinema-Verité Documentary

One nightmare in this film involves the Nile perch, a vicious predator fish—often six feet long, three hundred-plus pounds—which, when introduced into Lake Victoria in Tanzania in the 1960s, devoured all the native fishes. Despite its ugliness, its large fillets were desirable for food. Russian and other importers flew enormous cargo planes into the region to pick up tons of fillets to sell on the international market; secretly the planes, especially the Russian ones, flew in with weapons and ammunitions for sale to the numerous warring peoples and nations in the region.

The second nightmare, in the opinion of director Hubert Sauper, is globalization, or, more precisely, the victory of capitalism: it has seduced or destroyed its enemies. He wrote that he "could make the same kind of movie in Sierra Leone, only the fish would be diamonds, in Honduras, bananas, and in Libya, Nigeria, or Angola, crude oil" (2004 London Film Festival program notes), in brief, the scarce resources the powers of globalization compete for.

Sauper's camera has captured a living nightmare precisely: local fishermen lose their jobs to bigger companies, while women and children buy the rotting carcasses of the perch after they are filleted. African and World Bank officials make deals, while Russian pilots hook up with Tanzania prostitutes as their planes are serviced. The civil wars in the region claim numerous casualties: it is, Sauper asserts, as if you had 9/11 every day in the Eastern Congo alone.

Few films have been able to capture both the failures and absurdities of the transition from neocolonialism to globalization. To supply fish fillets to Europe and other destinations, a local economy is destroyed, a country is put at risk through civil war, and a former First World country joins the select company of arms dealers who place profit above statecraft. If Darwin ever wakes up from his nightmare he will find at least two factors yoked to natural selection he paid insufficient (perhaps understandably) attention to: greed and politics.

Recommended Reading

Scott, A. O. "Feeding Europe, Starving at Home." *New York Times*, 3 August 2005. The reviewer calls the film a "harrowing, indispensable documentary" and "a work of art." Sauper has turned "fugitive, mundane facts . . . into the stuff of tragedy."

►I◄►I◄►I◄
A Day without a Mexican

MIGRANT LABOR (UNITED STATES)

2004, 100 mins., R, United
    States/Mexico/Spain, in English and
    Spanish with English subtitles
Director: Sergio Arau
Screenplay: Sergio Arau, Yareli Arizmendi,
    and Sergio Guerrero

This crossborder coproduction was a box-office hit in Mexico. Although it is a one-joke film, it is a funny joke: imagine a day in California when the entire Mexican and Mexican American population literally disappears in a flash, as if they were first choice in the Rapture, one disgruntled fundamentalist whines. Flash titles explain what we see before our eyes: since 90 percent of all farm workers are Mexican, fresh vegetables and fruit are no longer available. Since almost all the domestic workers and yard workers have disappeared as well, none of those tasks at private homes get done either. More surprisingly, perhaps, 20 percent of all school teachers are gone too.

The director uses a mock doc style, with lots of phony newscasts about rich people trying to trim their own lawns and even newscasters as principal characters, including Lila

Rodriguez (played by Yareli Arizmendi, a Cuban Mexican American) who, although she is typecast by her employer as a Latino voice on the air, does not disappear. Eventually, in an adoption joke, we learn why.

Director Sergio Arau expanded a short film (included on the DVD issue) to make this feature film: either one makes the point well, although the feature adds some ethnic jokes designed to offend, albeit comically. If anyone hadn't realized that Mexicans and Mexican Americans are in California to stay, not just to pick crops and leave, this film is for them. Nonetheless, it is one of the first feature-length global comedies with a message. That message was reinforced on May Day 2006, when millions of immigrant workers took a holiday to protest anti-immigration laws: many commentators referred to it as a "day without immigrants."

Recommended Reading

Taylor, Ella. *L.A. Weekly,* 14 May 2004. Film swings from a "heavy-footed satire about white California's assumptions that all Latinos are Mexicans and ignoramuses" to a "misbegotten tragic social realism centered around a small group of white and Latino characters who must deal with the fallout."

ᗛᗛᗛ
Deadliest Catch

SCARCE RESOURCES (FISH)

2005–6, two seasons of 10 and 9 episodes, respectively, 60 mins. each
Producers: Thom Beers and David McKillop
TV Documentary Series

Why do 253 fishing boats converge on Dutch Harbor in Alaska to hear an announcement from the Alaskan Fish and Wildlife Authority about the length of the Alaskan king crab harvest season, four to twelve days max, during frigid November? The answer is the almost 16 million pounds of crab up for grabs. At just under $5 a pound, the haul is worth about $75 million. The risks are formidable: a virtually 100 percent injury rate, twenty-hour shifts, wet decks, and freezing temperatures.

The early episodes in the first season of this Discovery Channel series are exciting if you love crabs or crab pots. By episode six, finally and sadly, we also get some sensational television: a boat goes missing, another ship loses someone overboard, and the fatality count is six in just one short season in the Bering Sea, supporting the series' title. At the end of the first series, one crab season has ended and another begins: a risky job, one of the most dangerous in the global competition for the scarce resources of the sea.

We don't have to love crab, however, to be mesmerized by the hard and dangerous work these small crews carry out. (Maybe it helps.) The crews are mostly American but with enough international participation—it is one of the Samoans who goes overboard—to remind us that this is a globalized industry. The work is repetitive—pile up giant metal crab pots, bait them, dump them overboard, retrieve them, do it again—but the conditions vary enough to keep our attention. Gale force winds are not unusual in these waters, not to mention freezing temperatures and high rolling seas. Although you see it often enough that flinching may not seem inevitable, when two-hundred-pound crab pots careen down the gangplank at a fair clip, dragging a line that just misses ensnaring a worker's leg every time, it's hard not to react.

Despite the fierce competition the captains and crews all pull together when a may day call goes out. One minute they are hoping to outmaneuver a competing boat for what seems a likely spot, but the next minute they stop work and search the sea for missing comrades. With POV shots and a cinema-verité style, the filmmakers keep us on the edge of our gunnel most of the time. Alaskan king crab is in the middle range of most environmentalists' list of acceptable fish not threatened by overfishing in the global market, but this ranking depends on which quota system is used: in the first season the entire fleet had a quota and may the best fishermen succeed, but in the second season the quota is by ship alone, making the task less competitive between ships but no less dangerous.

Recommended Reading

Gates, Anita. "With King Crabs, a Seaman's Life is Not a Happy One." *New York Times*, 26 April 2005. The reviewer worries that the Discovery Channel really wanted a disaster to happen so they could film it; one finally happens after the review appeared.

ᚺᚺᚺ

Death in the Garden

La mort en ce jardin
The Diamond Hunters

HISTORY OF GLOBALIZATION

1956, 104 mins., Mexico/France, in Spanish with English subtitles
Director: Luis Buñuel
Screenplay: Luis Alcoriza, Gabriel Arout, Luis Buñuel, José-André Lacour, and Raymond Quenean

Luis Buñuel's reputation as a director in the last forty years is based on his glossy, absurd, sexually provocative films such as *Belle de Jour* (1967) or *The Discrete Charm of the Bourgeoisie* (1972). These films depict a displaced upper middle class whose irrational pretensions to wealth and glamour were often punctured by film's end. They were usually big-budget productions with international stars (e.g., Catherine Deneuve).

Buñuel's other films are black-and-white, low-budget explorations of the underclasses and working classes as they confront and sometimes defeat the absurdities of the global capitalist system. With the exception of the early (1933) *Land without Bread* (in *Working Stiffs*), a semidocumentary exploration in the Spanish hinterland, all of Buñuel's films in the 1950s were made in Mexico.

The plot of *Death in the Garden* is pure Buñuelian absurdity: a frontier diamond field, virtually a playground for anarchists, exists in an unnamed Latin American fascist dictatorship. Prospectors, hustlers, prostitutes, soldiers of fortune, policemen, and priests all coexist in this region. Because it has no name,

the country could be anywhere in Latin America. And because it is "too free," one character says, it is unstable and open to government interference. It becomes a crossroad of neocolonial forces because of its scarce resources, a pattern that will persist through the era of globalization.

Enter Shark (played by Georges Marchal), a soldier of fortune who leads the diamond workers in a rebellion against the state; he himself blows up the local police station. Obviously the central government will not put up with this, and his group of rebels and misfits, swirling with love affairs and potential jealousies, decamp for the jungle. At first, Shark's ragtag band, which includes a prostitute, a miner, a trader, and a pacifist priest, looks like they may have lucked into a Garden of Eden, so attractive are the surroundings away from the city. Soon the difficulties of survival tear them apart.

In a Buñuelian universe, anarchy on a political level often gives way to anarchy on a personal level. What begins as political drama ends up with personal misfortune: unlike *Illusion Travels by Streetcar* (in *Working Stiffs*), anarchy and love cannot stay on the tracks.

Recommended Readings

Buñuel, Luis. *Objects of Desire: Conversations with Luis Buñuel*. Ed. and trans. Paul Lenti. New York: Marsilio Publishers, 1992. Good detailed interviews.

Durgnat, Raymond. *Luis Buñuel*. Berkeley: University of California Press, 1968. A very helpful survey of Buñuel's career.

ᚺᚺᚺ

A Decent Factory

CHANGES IN THE WORKPLACE: WORLDWIDE

2004, 79 mins., United Kingdom/Finland/France, in English, Finnish, and Chinese with English subtitles
Director: Thomas Balmes
Cinema-Verité Documentary
Distributor: First Run/Icarus Films

Since the standard of a "decent factory" in the business world is usually predicated on the views of such experts as Milton Friedman, Nobel Prize winner in economics—"The one and only social responsibility of business is to make profits"—it will come as a shock to some that Nokia, the Finnish communications corporation, has an ethics compliance executive (Hanna Kaskinen) and appears interested in what she has to say.

Thomas Balmes begins his quest for a decent factory (after quoting Friedman) with a visit to a resort, an all-male retreat where important business is discussed. The top managers of Nokia appear, mostly naked, in this first sequence and earnestly set the stage (in discussions) for their desire to document the company's requirement of fair labor practices at its Chinese supplier, where their phones are manufactured.

Neither Nokia's Hanna Kaskinen or Louise Jamison, a British consultant, both of whom occupy center stage for most of the extended Chinese sequences in the film, were invited (apparently) to the party. The filmmakers may be making a low-key Scandinavian observation here. Or maybe not.

In any case Kaskinen, the relatively rare female Nokia exec, seems much more concerned that one of the managers of their Chinese supplier, a European with a British accent, makes bad jokes most of the time. Meanwhile another manager, who is Chinese, describes himself as "middle" management but seems to be in charge: when the ethics team spots teacups near some chemical cleaning supplies, he orders an immediate movement of the supplies to . . . the kitchen!

By the end of the film we know that Nokia knows. What they do with what they know is not so clear. The facts remain that China willfully exploits its workers even by some of its wishy-washy laws. Where else but in a communist country could workers have such a hard time getting a minimal wage and decent hours?

Recommended Reading

Dargis, Manola. "When Preaching Globalized Ethics is Just Corporate P. R." *New York Times*, 29 June 2005. The film is "a cursory, irritatingly facile look at the human cost of globalization," especially weak in its "underwhelming revelations" about the Chinese labor situation.

▶◀▶◀

The Diamond Life

NEOCOLONIALISM
SCARCE RESOURCES (DIAMONDS)

2000, 7 mins., United States
Directors: Stephen Marshall and Josh Shore
Online Agit-Prop Documentary
Distributor: Guerilla News Network (www.guerrillanews.com)

It is perhaps fortunate that not every image in this "News Video," as the Guerrilla News Network calls its online films, is crystal clear, because the graphic images of dismembered Freetown, Sierra Leone, adults and children are hard enough to watch as it is. They are the victims of attacks in 1999 by a rebel force, the Revolutionary United Front (RUF), led by a dismissed army corporal, Foday Sankoh, who sold what the filmmakers call "conflict diamonds" to bankroll their operations.

The Guerilla News Network presents traditional agit-prop subjects in online videos laid over a soundtrack by prominent and cool musicians: Peter Gabriel provided both the funding (from his activist group, Witness, which funds video equipment for populations undergoing human rights attacks) and the music for this history of the civil war in Sierra Leone. The film is also a critique of such diamond merchants as De Beers of South Africa, who currently buys two-thirds of the world's diamond supply, including diamonds—the film argues—from RUF.

The filmmakers argue that rebel groups like the RUF can exist only because of globalization: stop the payments for scarce resources and the violence against civilians should decrease. Many of the images of young people whose hands have been cut off are hard to look at, but they recall the earlier era of colonialism in Africa when King Leopold's private Congo Free State used the same methods to force workers to retrieve rubber (see

Congo). Under neocolonial control De Beers and South Africa built immense wealth because of state-sanctioned control of vast gold and diamond resources and the black workers who toiled to retrieve them.

Guerrilla News Network believes it has a formula for attracting young people to political issues. Too often, the filmmakers explain, documentaries ignore the powerful methods of mainstream media and advertising that have successfully gained the attention of consumers everywhere. Why not, they argue, steal some of their power but with a different message? In a related book, *True Lies*, Stephen Marshall and Anthony Lappe argue that "there can be no serious hope to reform the national media unless the progressives can learn to compete against it, or at least learn from its appropriation of pop-cultural aesthetics." Otherwise, they conclude, cultural life will continue being a "spectacle . . . orchestrated by billionaire globalists with former high-level political strategists running the show."

Recommended Readings

Holt, Cody. "Information Warriors." Video Systems, 1 January 2003 (on line at preview .videosystems.com/coverstory/video_information_warriors/index.html). Extensive discussion of the film and the Guerrilla News Network.

Marshall, Stephen, and Anthony Pappe. *True Lies*. New York: Plume Books, 2004. Extensive critique of the mainstream media and its neglect of important stories; also targets some progressive organizations for their laxness and lack of media savvy.

ᑭᑭᑭ

Diamonds and Rust

CONTAINERIZED SHIPPING
SCARCE RESOURCES (DIAMONDS)

2001, 73 mins., Namibia/Israel, in English, Hebrew, and Spanish with English subtitles
Director: Adi Barash and Ruth Shatz
Cinema-Verité Documentary
Distributor: First Run/Icarus Films

The *Spirit of Namibia* is a diamond mining trawler: it vacuums the sea floor off the coast of southwest Africa, pumps diamond ore to a screening deck, where its crew extracts the diamonds. If that were not a remarkable feat in itself, the fact that it happens at all is even more remarkable, as it depends on a Namibian crew, Cuban officers, an Israeli security officer, all supervised by the white South Africans managing this De Beers diamond company operation.

The filmmakers spent ninety days on this rusting vessel, which functions more like an offshore platform than a ship. Nonetheless it totes up millions of dollars worth of diamonds, while a crew member earns less than $40 a week. While De Beers leads the global market for diamonds, its global crew sails virtually to nowhere.

This virtually derelict ship will eventually make its way to the ship dismemberment workshops on the beaches of India and Pakistan (see *Workingman's Death*). We think of container ships or massive oil tankers as the sleek engines of the globalized economy: the filmmakers remind us that too many other ships remain in service, at a risk to humans and the environment both.

Recommended Reading

Kehr, Dave. "Haitian Capitalism and a Hunt for Diamonds in the Sea." *New York Times*, 8 May 2002. A film "that chugs along as listlessly as the ship itself, discovering moments of value in a sea of ennui."

ᑭᑭᑭ

Dirt

MIGRANT LABOR (UNITED STATES)

2003, 91 mins., United States
Director: Nancy Savoca
Screenplay: Nancy Savoca and Richard Guay

Nancy Savoca has had success directing comic films about working-class Italian American women (*True Love*, 1989, and *Household Saints*, 1993) and codirecting (and cowriting) the intensely serious HBO miniseries on abortion, *If These Walls Could Talk* (1996). In *Dirt* she dramatizes the life and hard times of undocumented domestic workers in contemporary Manhattan. Dolores (played by Julietta Ortiz) is a Salvadoran maid to wealthy Upper East Side families, supporting herself, her husband, and her son, and scrimping to save enough money to build a house back home.

When she loses one of her jobs working for a well-off Latino family—the lady of the house is a politician who has denounced illegal immigrants and cannot take a chance on Dolores anymore—the advice she gets from another immigrant is accurate enough but hardly helpful: "You don't smile enough." Savoca's decision to focus closely on Dolores makes this an intimate and sympathetic look at how undocumented workers are less than a paycheck away from losing their foothold in America. Her life in the bowels of a big apartment building finds her bonding with the elevator operator, another domestic worker, and the doorman, immigrants all. She focuses much of her anger not on the difficult customers she must flatter but on a Latina neighbor who is into Santeria and may have ratted out her husband's fellow immigrant workers at a restaurant.

When Dolores's husband dies in a construction accident (having switched jobs because the restaurant wouldn't hire undocumented labor any more), all that she has worked for seems to come apart. It costs $12,000 to take his body back to El Salvador. Her son, who has honed his computer skills hacking into his school's secure system, fights going back: it is no longer his country, he complains.

Savoca's depiction of Dolores as a victim of globalized labor is also evident when Dolores returns home to El Salvador. It turns out that she is now perceived as different by her family—she's lost weight, she's "more independent," she smokes—and she decides that she needs to go "home," which turns out to be New York. Her last speech sums up why she can survive: "I have work because there is always dirt, and even if it is not there, people want someone to take care of it. I take care of it."

Recommended Reading

Scheib, Ronnie. "Dirt." *Variety*, 6 December 2004. Actress Julieta Ortiz "lights up" this "audience-grabber as tightly condensed and emotionally resonant as its title," representing "an entire underclass of illegal immigrants scrambling for survival."

▶▶▶

Dirty Pretty Things

MIGRANT LABOR (OTHER THAN THE UNITED STATES)
SEX WORK/TRAFFICKING
TAXI DRIVERS

2003, 97 mins., R, United Kingdom, in English and Somali with English subtitles
Director: Stephen Frears
Screenplay: Steve Knight

Stephen Frears uses two of the most common immigrant urban workplaces—a hotel and a taxi service—to limit the viewer's attention so inexorably that it seems only immigrants live in London. He has created one of the first thrillers to confront realistically one of the darkest sides of the metropolis—the trafficking of human organs.

Okwe, a Nigerian doctor (played by Chiwetel Ejiofor) has two jobs: minicab driver during the day and hotel porter at night. The hotel's immigrant staff, trooping in night after night as if punching a time card at a factory, includes Senay (played by Audrey Tantou), a Turkish woman who has fled an arranged marriage and who rents a couch in her apartment to Okwe. Always in the background of the gradually revealed horrors of this film is the inevitable attraction between Senay and Okwe, although the latter has a family back home. Add to this attractive pair a hooker, Juliette (played by Sophie Okonedo, who costarred in *The Hotel Rwanda* [2004] and has the best comic lines in the film), and the hotel night manager, Sneaky (played by Sergi Lopez), whose illicit trade in human organs provides the scary premise of the thriller, and you have a film as captivating as it is disturbing.

The plot begins and ends with a bang. Okwe is sent to a room whose toilet is plugged. He understands what has done it: a human heart. Okwe's obsession with this heart leads him and Senay along some violent paths until in the end his skill as a doctor becomes part of a poetic justice that many viewers will find difficult to watch.

Frears has captured the life and loves of Indian and Pakistani immigrants to London who are beginning to join the middle class in *Sammy and Rosie Get Laid* (1987) and *My Beautiful Launderette* (1985), as well as Irish working-class life in *Liam* (2000), but with *Dirty Pretty Things* he creates a city in which the underclass survives because it can outwit a virtually invisible enemy.

Recommended Reading

Ebert, Roger. "Dirty Pretty Things." *Chicago Sun-Times*, 1 August 2003. "It is a story of desperation, of people who cannot live where they are born and cannot find a safe haven elsewhere."

▸◂▸◂▸◂

Diverted to Delhi

OUTSOURCING AND OFFSHORING

2002, 55 mins., Australia
Director: Greg Stitt
Distributor: Filmakers Library

Since unemployment among college graduates in India is quite high—some estimates put it at 30 percent—many of them take special courses that will train them to work in India's massive call center industry, the ultimate digital industry of globalization. Director Gregg Stitt follows four students who take such a cross-cultural training course at North Star College in Delhi, attempting to improve their English skills, learn about other cultures (especially America, England, and Australia), and practice being customer-friendly.

Stitt also follows another group at the EXL call center, this one enrolled in an in-house training course for employees whose English skills are already strong. The goals here are higher—facility at colloquial English, knowledge of American sports and geography—in short, ways to make themselves pass as just another American operator at the end of the helpline.

This billion-dollar industry in India is the direct result of outsourcing by almost half of the American Fortune 500 companies. Even smaller companies opt for outsourcing, but recent reports (see Stone) indicate that in a digital center such as Bangalore wages have risen, making the economic deal for American companies not quite as sweet. Some major companies, Stone reports, are finding that the language skills and expertise of the call center operators did not meet the quality they ex-

Diverted to Delhi: Indian call center students study English, Elvis, and Einstein. Courtesy Filmakers Library.

pected and they withdrew their contracts and created American call centers again.

It is a tribute to the filmmaker's empathetic involvement with the four North Star College students that we root for them as they try to master colloquial English. They must not only sound right but also be conversant with slang and the familiar activities of their target countries. They have to say "not a problem" with gusto and conviction as if they grew up in New York or Chicago. Needless to say not all Indian speakers can wrap themselves around these phrases. Of the four aspirants Stitt follows the only two of them (both attractive women) to get hired by a call center; the two men at the time of filmmaking were still unemployed. To my eye and ear there seems to be some gender selection at work, since I would have guessed the employment result (based on their skills) quite differently. But the film is a fascinating journey with these students nonetheless.

Recommended Reading

Stone, Brad. "Should I Stay or Should I Go?" *Newsweek*, 19 April 2004. The magazine's Silicon Valley correspondent weighs the pros and cons for American corporations of the Indian call center tidal wave.

▶◀▶◀▶◀

Divine Carcasse

NEOCOLONIALISM

1998, 59 mins., Belgium/Benin, in French,
    Fon, and Yoruba with English subtitles
Director: Dominique Loreau
Ethnographic Fiction

Using the hybrid form of ethnographic fiction pioneered by Jean Rouch (see *The Jaquar Quartet*), the director puns on the "body" of a 1955 Peugeot imported into the Benin port city of Cotonou by Simon, a European philosophy teacher. The film opens with an immense cargo ship disgorging not only this special car but many others, the colony's highly desired commodities of the mother country. Although other Benin locals eye the Peugeot, they are told that it is for a European only.

This European car generates illusions: Simon's friends say that it should help him pick up girls. But a man who is preparing a lecture on Plato's Myth of the Cave—in which objects may appear real but are actually shadows of a higher reality (the things themselves)—will probably not be a date magnet. When his car doesn't perform well and, suspicious of an object he discovers under the hood that may be a fetish, he gives the car to Joseph, his cook, who thinks he can raise his family's fortunes by turning it into a taxi. That plan falls through when, during an *egungun* ritual or trance, Joseph's ancestors tell him about a family curse that must be released. To the scrap heap the Peugeot goes, soon to be turned into an actual fetish by an artist, a metalworker who transforms strips of metal into a formidable spirit force.

The car has finally become divine. So accomplished is the metalworker that we see in documentary-like sequences the scraps of metal becoming another being, Agbo, the ram god, commissioned by the village elders of Ouassou. The new "body" of the car travels by boat again to its new home, standing sentinel at the village perimeter like the good master of the night it is supposed to be.

Secondhand neocolonialism becomes first-class colonized semideity: the perennial struggle in Africa films between modernizing forces and cultural traditions is resolved in a curious way. As a car the Peugeot works fitfully; as a divinity it works superbly. As a former colony Benin must turn shadows of things into realities.

Recommended Reading

Gorman, Suan. "From (French) Automobile to (Beninois) Agbo: Mythology, Modernity, and Divine Carcasse." EnterText (Brunel University), Winter 2004–5 (online at people.brunel.ac .uk/acsrrrm/entertext/4_2/gorman.pdf). Discusses the film as a vehicle for changing mythologies, how "European mythology changes when confronted with an unfamiliar landscape."

▷▷▷
Dockers

CONTAINERIZED SHIPPING

1999, 100 mins., United Kingdom
Director: Bill Anderson
Screenplay: Jimmy McGovern and Irvine
   Welsh

One of the longest—and to most of the dockers involved—frustrating strikes in recent British history began in 1996 when five dockworkers at Mersey Docks and Harbour Company (Liverpool) were fired for walking off their jobs when they refused to work overtime without pay. When about five hundred coworkers agreed not to cross their picket line, they were fired too. The two-year standoff generated significant antagonisms between the men and their union, the Transport and General Worker's Union (TGWU), as well as between Tony Blair's New Labour Party and the traditionally pro–Labour Party union families. New Labour expected the TGWU to defuse the militancy, following the typical pattern formed during the Thatcher years—force the union into a strike they cannot win, offer a bribe or two (redundancy pay), and when that is refused, attack the workers with nationalized police units (see *The Battle of Orgreave*).

Two years into the strike, Liverpudlian writer Jimmy McGovern (later known for his screenplays for *Liam,* 2000, and *Sunday,* 2002), was invited to participate in a writers' workshop set up by the dockers and their wives to compile a history of their struggle. He had written some pro-docker essays for newspapers, including one in which he stated that the head of the TGWU "blamed the dockers' defeat on [Thatcherite] anti–trade union laws which New Labour is pledged to retain." Instead McGovern argued that "the dockers lost because their union leadership blew it," and besides that the leadership supported Blair and what his new party stood for ("When You're a Liverpool Docker, It Never Rains But It Pours," *Observer,* 1 February 1998).

The writers' workshop turned its focus to drafting the script for this film. The central story of the strike remained intact, but a composite family of characters was created to provide the drama with a family focus. Docker Tommy Walton and his wife Jean Walton (played by Ken Stott and Crissy Rock) have a son who is also a docker. Tommy's best friend, Macca Macaulay (played by Ricky Tomlinson) decides to scab. A momentum for their victory seems to build: the women organize an active support group; Liverpool soccer star Robbie Fowler, after scoring a goal in a big televised game, lifts his shirt to reveal a T-shirt supporting the dockers; and initially the union and New Labour listen.

Needless to say, the dockers don't win in this film as they did not win in real life, and to this day the debate about the strike continues. A number of critics have argued that the Liverpool strike proves that New Labour is old Thatcher in new Blair bottles. Certainly the triumph of globalization on the British docks is a combination of containerization and Thatcher's assault on the militant unions on the docks (see Hunter).

Recommended Readings

Bohanna, John Henry. "Dockers." *Labour Net,* 26 July 1999 (online at www.labournet.net/docks2/9907/film.htm). Extensive positive discussion of the film.

Hunter, Bill. *They Knew Why They Fought: Unofficial Struggles and Leadership on the Docks, 1945–1989.* London: Index Books, 1994. A critique from the left of the history of dockworkers' struggles before the Liverpool strike.

▷▷▷
Dot Con

DIGITALIZATION
ENRON

2002, United States
Producers: Martin Smith and Saran Silver
TV Documentary
Distributor: PBS

A dot.com is not always a "dot con" but this *Frontline* documentary traces the great

Internet bubble of the 1990s, trying to make sense of the financial rise of dot.com companies that were not profitable at the time of their initial public offering (IPO) of stock and had in fact never been profitable. The 4,700 companies that registered with American stock exchanges between 1990 and 1995 were expected to be profitable; the turning point, *Frontline* and others have argued, was 1995 when Netscape went public when it was not yet earning any profits. During the bubble, when it was assumed that the Internet was changing business forever, companies would pursue venture capital—or themselves be pursued by venture capitalists—and their stock prices would rise. It was as simple as that.

Or not. The IPO really involved two different kinds of stock sales. Before the IPO, a complicated financial show takes place, beginning with a "bake off" (investment bankers make their pitch to do the IPO), followed by a "road show" (the selected bank visits mutual fund managers and big hedge fund investors) to lock in some allocated stock. Ordinary investors get to buy only during the "aftermarket," when the stock is actually listed. The abuse of the system comes with the initial allocated stocks: once the price begins to rise, sometimes as much as 400 percent even on the very first day, the managers "flip" the stocks and sell them for major profits.

In his interview on film, Michael Barach, the former CEO of MotherNature.com (online sales of vitamins and other heath and fitness supplements), calls the IPO system "legalized bribery." "It's favor-building," he adds, since an investment banker may still have some of his lower price allocated stock to distribute, let us say, for $13 a share when the price on the ticker has already reached $42: "You get a call. . . . And you can sell it and flip it right then and there." Ordinary investors, not always insiders, can come in only during the aftermarket, when the price is $42 a share, or even higher.

Frontline also dissects the tendency of stock analysts to be "cheerleaders" and not critical enough. In the worst cases, a stock analyst (Scott Ehrens for Bear Stearns, for example) kept making positive recommendations to buy a software stock (Digital River, an online sales consultant company) to keep "the stock pumped up." What the analyst did not reveal was that his company was one of the firms that had led the IPO and so had a vested interest in rising stock prices. Sam Burstyn, an attorney involved in investigating IPO problems, concluded: "The fact that an investment banker is underwriting a public offering does not mean that it's a sound investment . . . but that the IPO is merely an exit strategy for the insiders." One of the major promoters of IPOs—Credit Suisse First Boston—settled with the Securities Exchange Commission (SEC) for a $100 million without admitting any wrongdoing, but many other cases are still going forward.

The Internet bubble of the 1990s now joins some of the great financial bubbles of the past—the seventeenth-century Dutch Tulipmania or the eighteenth-century South Sea Bubble—as indicators of global financial instability. And although *Frontline* does not develop Enron's involvement with virtual trading and stock pumping, that company is a large part—if not one of the largest—of the bubble-making apparatus (see Lowenstein).

Recommended Readings

Cassidy, John. *Dot Con: The Greatest Story Ever Sold.* New York: HarperCollins, 2002. Offers a similar analysis of the stock market culture of the 1990s when it hit the much touted information superhighway, not to mention the rise of day trading and IPOs.

Lowenstein, Roger. *Origins of the Crash: The Great Bubble and Its Undoing*. New York: Penguin, 2004. Add executive overcompensation and compliant auditors to *Frontline*'s mix of factors and the result is this crystal-clear analysis of the bubble, especially in relation to Enron.

Do They Catch Children Too?

MIGRANT LABOR (OTHER THAN THE UNITED STATES)

2003, 49 mins., Israel, in English, Hebrew, and Tagalog with English subtitles
Director: Hedva Galili-Smolinsk
Cinema-Verité Documentary
Distributor: Ruth Diskin Films

Two children running through their neighborhood streets, playing games, and speaking Hebrew to each other and those they encounter is routine in an Israeli city. Except the children in this film are Filipinos born in Israel and cousins—Ryan is the son of Carlito, and Nato the son of Carlito's sister Luz—whose parents came on work visas, which, in Carlito's case, turned out to be fraudulent. Many of the cousins' games reflect the fact that Carlito is in jail awaiting deportation: the boys play policemen arresting people or prisoners escaping from a jail. It's Ryan who asks if he'll be deported as well: "Do they catch children too?"

This documentary is a child's eye view of what must seem like an irrational world. The children are remarkably well adapted to Israeli life and are virtually trilingual (Hebrew, English, and Tagalog). The attendant at a phone shop immigrants use to call home sums up their parents' dilemma: if you go home to visit family and friends, you cannot come back, so you stay to do our work.

The filmmakers touch on the lives of some other immigrants—one from Ecuador, another from Ghana—focusing on the disruption of their children's lives. All of the children seem understandably obsessed with missing their parents, planes flying overhead, jails, and deportation. In their view, all of these are too closely related for comfort. Ryan, for one, is very concerned about how dark he appears: he knows he doesn't look Israeli enough, that is, white.

We visit a school where many of these children are enrolled: except for what seems to be the uneasiness in the air about certain students and/or their families gone missing, it could be a multicultural classroom in many lands. And perhaps that is, in the end, the main thing to take away from this film, but Ryan, who at one point we observe chanting his lessons in Hebrew, goes back to the Philippines to join his father.

Resource

Ellman, Michael, and Smain Laacher. *Migrant Workers In Israel.* Online at fidh.org/mag moyen/rapport/2003/il1806a.pdf. A report from the International Federation for Human Rights and the Euro-Mediterranean Human Rights Network that is harshly critical of Israel's handling of guest workers.

⊢⊢⊢

Edge of Darkness

GLOBAL CATASTROPHES
THATCHERISM

1985, TV series, 6 episodes of 55 mins. each,
    United Kingdom
Director: Troy Kennedy Martin
Screenplay: Troy Kennedy Martin

Although this popular British television series of the 1980s is primarily a political thriller, it shares some characteristics of postapocalyptic films in which unsafe nuclear installations and radiation sickness ramp up the viewers' anxiety considerably. *Edge of Darkness is* also a profound political attack on the Thatcherite state and its (marginally) criminal paramilitary and dangerous secret state apparatus of internal repression and control. To this surefire mix of skullduggery and statecraft the film reflects the fact that Britain has for years operated a semisecret plutonium processing plant at Sellafield, Cumbria, on the coast of the Irish Sea, making money by extracting plutonium from the world's nuclear waste. Although the film does not explicitly explain the leading British role in this global market, novelist Marilynne Robinson's *Mother Country* has, and the implications for disasters on a global scale are real.

What the director has done is tuck a Sellafield-like radioactive plant in a mineshaft and added a subplot of an investigation of the contested election of a union mining leader, reminding viewers of the disastrous 1984–85 miners' strike (just recently concluded) and the notorious mineworkers' leader Arthur Scargill. He includes footage of clashes between strikers and the police on a television news program, as well as a public speech by Thatcher in which she explains how nuclear power leads to world peace.

The plot itself is heartbreaking: Ronald

Edge of Darkness: CIA agent Darius Jedburgh (Joe Don Baker) joins the search for the secret plutonium processing plant.

Craven (played by Bob Peck), a Yorkshire policeman, learns of the shooting death of his only daughter. She has been a university activist against nuclear power, part of a semisecret group called Gaia, but Craven really never understood what her activism entailed. She accompanies him as a ghostly presence throughout the film, occasionally giving him advice, but ultimately making Craven more desperate, daring, and inconsolable. Craven begins to gather evidence of a secret plutonium-processing plant that leaked and polluted a nearby reservoir. When Gaia daringly investigated the mineshaft that houses the facility, shadowy figures in the government order their execution.

The film is a very intricate, dense, politically charged roller coaster. It ranks with *Boys in the Blackstuff* (see *Working Stiffs*) and *Our Friends in the North* (q.v.) as a contender for one of the most critically ac-

claimed British television series in the last twenty-five years.

Recommended Readings

Broad, William J. "U.S. Has Plans to Again Make Own Plutonium." *New York Times*, 27 June 2005. With leftovers from Russia in short supply, the call is out to make Plutonium 238, "hundreds of times more radioactive than the kind of plutonium used in nuclear arms" so that "inhaling even a speck poses a serious risk of lung cancer."

Lavender, Andrew. "Edge of Darkness," in *British Television Drama of the 1980s*, ed. George W. Brandt (Cambridge: Cambridge University Press, 1993), 102–18. Careful discussion of the themes and political implications of the series.

Robinson, Marilynne. *Mother Country*. New York: Farrar, Straus & Giroux, 1989. A novelist's outraged attack on British policy that created and maintained the Sellafield plutonium processing plant in Sellafield in the Lake District.

⋈⋈⋈
Edit

LABOR HISTORY

2003, 94 mins., South Korea/United States, in
    Korean with English subtitles
Director: Changjae Lee
Postmodern Documentary

We are used to self-referential filmmakers who are political and funny—Michael Moore in the United States, for instance, or Mark Thomas in England. But Changjae Lee is a very serious self-referential filmmaker indeed. His autobiographical film about his decision to censor his own news film about college-educated activists who take blue-collar jobs has some impressive and witty flourishes (including at least one shot in which he, a second filmed image of himself, and his shadow all coexist), but he takes himself and his subject very seriously.

And he should: the two Koreas remain an artifact of the preglobalized cold war, with South Korea getting much press as the democratic alternative to the harsh communist North. Lee took a job with a South Korean television station and filmed three college grads—two who worked for the national train system and a third who was the head of the metalworkers' union. All three projected a fair and balanced attitude toward their jobs.

To get his film on the air Lee had to re-edit the film, tone down the positive vibes, and insert some interviews with college grads who quit their blue-collar world for executive pay and perks. Now he has re-edited the original film once more, reinstating the earlier deletions and adding footage about himself throughout this self-critical and somewhat self-accusatory period of his life.

And, despite the self-referential flourishes, we get inside some of the tumult of the South Korean labor movement, especially in the 1980s when a repressive government routinely attacked student and labor demonstrations.

Recommended Reading

Scheib, Ronnie. "Edit." *Variety*, 31 March 2005. An "existentialist curio should prove a potent, if esoteric lure for the small but swelling ranks of experimental docu aficionados."

⋈⋈⋈
E-Dreams

CHANGES IN THE WORKPLACE: NORTH
    AMERICA
DIGITALIZATION

2001, 94 mins., United States
Director: Wonsuk Chin
Cinema-Verité Documentary

Combining Internet ordering with urban bicycle delivery in the heyday of startup and IPO frenzy led to entrepreneur Joe Park's Kozmo.com, a company that guaranteed delivery of drinks, snacks, and videos to its web customers within the hour. Growing from ten employees to four thousand in just three years (1998–2001) and in eleven cities at its peak, Kozmo.com attracted millions in venture capital and even some exclusive deals with companies such as Starbucks. Although Park had experience in investment banking, he didn't—as he will eventually admit—know anything about running a company.

Some of the illusions of Park's fellow execs are amusing now. Stephen Carl, the content editor, offers his perspective: "A long time ago it was about the Great American Novel. Then all of a sudden it became the Great American Screenplay. It's now the Great American Business Plan." However shaky this may be as cultural history, Carl certainly has a point. That Park and his buddies named the company after their favorite drink—a cosmopolitan—may be less relevant, although one Korean investor asks what the company's name means. Park makes the mistake of telling him that it means "nothing."

But as we know from other dot.coms, many of the twenty-somethings didn't know too much either. What they knew—or thought they knew—was that if they could just get the company going long enough they could cash out their stock after a big IPO. When Internet stocks collapsed in April 2000, Kozmo.com went down as well. The much-anticipated IPO never happened and even though—in Park's words—"our customers consider us rock stars," ignoring profitability for too long meant that the company could not survive a downturn in stock value.

What did Kozmo.com lack? At one point one of the kozmonauts asks another young startup guy if he had any "grown-ups" working with him. Probably a lack of understanding basic labor issues contributed to its demise as well. We see some scenes of the chaos that results when no paychecks greet the men and women who deliver the goods: at one point a supervisor hands over his own money to two delivery guys ($100 each) to tide them over until the checks come in. At another point, in Park's attempt to reassert control over his faltering company, he notes that the specter of unionism looms and worries that in the San Francisco Bay Area Asian Americans were more likely than not to go union.

Joe's parents ran a successful dry cleaning business in Philadelphia. Modest, no doubt, but they are still in business. Globalization means, among other things, a digital network linking customers, company, and manufacturer. Whether it also needs bicycles is doubtful.

Recommended Reading

Scott. A. O. "Chronicling a Bubble Called Kozmo.com." *New York Times,* 11 January 2002. Review emphasizes Park's role: "He is too young to be tragic, too lucky to be heroic; his story is like a Dreiser novel redone as an Archie comic, or a pilot for the WB network."

▶▶▶

Enron: The Smartest Guys in the Room

ENRON
OIL

2005, 109 mins., R, United States
Director: Alex Gibney
Traditional Documentary, based on

Bethany McLean and Peter Elkind's *The Smartest Guys in the Room: The Amazing Rise and Scandalous Fall of Enron* (2003)

Alex Gibney's extended adaptation of the best-selling exposé of Enron is the clearest cinematic introduction to the Enron scandal: it combines a history of the company and a virtual psychobiography of its leading figures. The film reviews the key moments in Enron's rise and fall—its movement from an energy transmission company to a virtual trading company, its cult of personalities—Kenneth Lay, chairman of the board and friend of the Bush family, Jeffrey Skilling, president and CEO, and Andy Fastow, chief financial officer—and its giddy celebration and profit-taking during the California energy crisis of 2000 (see *Blackout*). Most of their controversial financial maneuvers—such as mark to market accounting, which claims future deals as immediate profits and off-the-books partnerships that hid company debt—are explained here, but the film develops at great length the way the company's energy traders, with the blessing of the figures at the top, were able to maneuver through some tight loopholes in the law and at other times simply bypass the law when it came to trading energy, facilitating California's disaster.

Gibney includes not only the relatively well-known early Valhalla, New York, scandal in 1987 when the company covered up the outright fraud of two traders who eventually went to jail, but also the outrageous Silver Peak, Nevada, incident when trader Tim Beldan diverted upward of 2,900 megawatts of energy bound for California through a 15 megawatt "spigot" in Silver City. The move earned Enron upward of $7 million because, under the rules, congestion in the delivery resulted in increased payments to the trader. Of course other California energy maneuvers earned Enron millions, such as moving energy out of California and then selling it back at higher prices or urging generating plants to shut down for unnecessary maintenance until the price rose.

The filmmakers came upon a treasure trove

of audiotapes with Enron traders exchanging cheat stories and gloating about stealing money from California's grandmothers. At one point a fire under a transmission line is reported—Gibney obligingly cuts to a similar fire—and one of the traders, realizing that this will decrease supply and drive up the prices even more, says, "Burn, baby, burn!"

Gibney uses Bethany McLean and Peter Elkind, the source book's authors, as his authoritative interviewees and also points to the *Fortune* magazine article written by McLean, "Is Enron Overpriced?" which marked the beginning of the end for the crooked E. Footage from the Simpsons' cartoon in which the Enron stock is on a roller-coaster ride that heads straight to the poorhouse for investors, as well as Enron's own commercials and video parodies (including one in which Skilling invents a scheme called Hypothetical Future Value, the essence of mark to market accounting), round out this informative analysis of the culture of greed and power. The soundtrack closes with Tom Waits's riveting song, "God's Away on Business": "Who are the ones that we kept in charge? / Killers, thieves, and lawyers."

Recommended Readings

Gibney, Alex. "The Straight Dope on the Crooked E." *International Documentary*, June 2005, 8–10. Director's statement about the film, with comments on the score.

McLean, Bethany. "Is Enron Overpriced? *Fortune*, 5 March 2001. The author asked the question—"How exactly does Enron make its money?"—that Enron's accountants and leaders did not want asked.

◄◄◄

EPIC 2014

DIGITALIZATION

2004, 8 mins., United States
Directors: Matt Thompson and Robin
   Sloan
Online Mock Documentary (www.robinsloan
   .com/epic)

This flash video is a conceptual trip in the form of future history: it assumes, with some accuracy, that our globalized communications system was created by American inventions and entrepreneurship. We begin in 2014 as the fictional Museum of Media History is reviewing the last thirty years of the convergence of journalism and the Internet.

Amazon.com (and its "automated personalized recommendations" system of customer contacts) and Google (echoing Amazon.Com, "it treats links as recommendations") merge in 2006 to form Googlezon. Google had already launched its Google Grid, "a universal platform that provides a functionally limitless amount of storage space and bandwidth to store and share media of all kinds," incorporating the functions of a number of classic (and actual) Internet, media, and communications services Google either purchased—TiVo and Blogger—or had already launched on its own—Gmail and GoogleNews. The resultant media network is powerful indeed.

Mighty Microsoft attempts to contest Googlezon's media hegemony by creating Newsbotster, "a social news network and participatory journalism platform," based on its ownership of Friendster, but when Googlezon unleashes EPIC (Evolving Personalized Information Construct), the battle of the Internet giants is over. Not only does Microsoft cry uncle but the mighty emperor of print media, *The New York Times,* after a defeat in the Supreme Court contesting Google's use of its "facts" from its online edition, gives up the Internet in favor of a limited (and, it is supposed, retrograde) "print newsletter for the elite and the elderly."

Although the video, like a PowerPoint presentation, is light on visual variety, it suggests the vague supercorporation dominance characteristic of dystopian science fiction. Every person's own EPIC provides what old-fashioned news people would call a subjective sample of the news but one that is certainly closer to even our contemporary scene. With EPIC, we would be living in the ultimate version of Wikipedia—the "sprawling chaotic mediascape is filtered, ordered, and delivered" with everyone contributing a part of the input: "blog entries, cellphone cam images, video reports," and of course text messages of all kinds merge with investigative reports. The whole package is customized to each recipient "using his choices, his consumption habits, his interests, his social network . . . to shape the product."

The directors issued a sequel (really just an extension) of *EPIC 2014* titled *EPIC 2015* (2005, both available at epic.makingithappen .co.uk), which added other Internet and media developments—podcasting, GPS, and Google Maps—to allow EPIC to follow a user and his personal or other contacts through a handheld screen. One could watch the EPIC films and assume most of this synergy is already in place.

Recommended Readings

Geller, Masha. "The Demise of the Fourth Estate." *iMedia Connection*, 7 February 2005 (online at www.imediaconnection.com). Discusses "how Google and Amazon could destroy the news media."

Lamb, Gregory M. "Is 'Googlezon' in Our Future?" *Christian Science Monitor*, 19 December 2005. Quotes futurist Paul Saffo approvingly: What *EPIC 2014* demonstrates is the "fundamental transition" underway "from mass media to personal media."

Nisenholz, Martin. Speech at the Interactive Media Conference and Trade Show, San Diego, 8 May 2003 (online at www.internet-press.net/ news/newsevents11.htm). The inspiration or impetus of the film—a speech by the CEO of *New York Times* Digital Edition—which probes numerous changes affecting journalistic practice.

ᐅᐊᐅᐊ

Extreme Oil

OIL

2004, 3 episodes of 60 mins. each
Producer and Writer: William Cran
Executive Producer: Stephen Segaller
TV Documentary Series

As the world gulps seventy-seven million barrels of oil daily, the search for new sources of energy becomes intense, dangerous, and sometimes (it may be argued) criminal. This PBS television series reinforces the concept of oil as *one*, if not the *key*, indicator of globalization. In the first episode, "Pipeline," the filmmakers follow the 1,100-mile Baku-Tbilisi-Ceyhan pipeline from the Caspian Sea to the Mediterranean Sea, including a stop in Azerbaijan, where the filmmakers were arrested. The second episode, "The Oil Curse," documents the struggles of two oil-producing countries, Ecuador and Angola, to reap some benefits from the oil companies' extraction of millions of gallons of oil from their countries. The final episode, "The Wilderness," brings the viewer to the contentious oil-producing grounds of Canada and Alaska, especially the latter's Arctic National Wildlife Refuge. In all of the episodes, the producers attempt a balance that sometimes the subject resists and sometimes subverts. If drilling in Alaska ruins the caribou habitat, for example, can the situation ever be reversed and the safety of the animals assured? In Alberta, possibly a model for the Alaskan enterprise, even the oil producers refer to their product there as "the world's worst oil."

Producer Willian Cran, who made two other television documentaries about the history and politics of oil, *The Prize* (1992) and *Commanding Heights* (q.v.), has stated (on the PBS website for the series) that the brief for *Extreme Oil* was to film outside the obvious locations in the Middle East. Each region would suggest a different theme—environment in Alaska, geopolitics in the Baku pipeline region, and "the curse of oil" in the Third World. Ironically, he suggests, "there's a strong case to be made that oil makes poor countries poorer."

This series is an excellent introduction to the major dilemmas about oil faced by the leading guzzlers. Whether such a thirst can ever be slaked may not be answered so easily.

Recommended Reading

Martell, Ned. "Wilderness to War Zones: In Relentless Pursuit of Oil." *New York Times,* 13 September 2004. Worries that the film is sometimes "simplistic" but acknowledges its perception of the use and search for oil as a global addiction.

Farmingville

MIGRANT LABOR (UNITED STATES)

2004, 78 mins., United States
Directors: Catherine Tambini and Carlos
   Sandoval
Cinema-Verité Documentary

Farmingville, a mostly suburban community of fifteen thousand residents, sits in virtually the geographical center of Long Island. With easy access to major interstates, it also features a number of commercial greenhouses and building supply stores. In the late 1990s it experienced a spurt in the number of Hispanic workers living in town and seeking jobs as day laborers with contractors and other employers. Picking up some drywall and Mexican workers became routine.

But not acceptable to a number of the local residents, especially when the number of Spanish-speaking residents hit 10 percent of the existing population. Activists on both sides soon squared off in what would become one of the flashpoints in the handling of globalized migratory labor. "Illegal aliens are the invaders" read one sign of a local group organized under the name of Sachem Quality of Life (Sachem being the local Indian name of a Farmingville high school); "They treat us all like dogs all the time," complained one of the Hispanic workers. In confrontations played out across the United States—see Austin, Texas, in *Los Trabjadores*—it was only a matter of time before things would get out of hand.

The local Sachem Quality of Life leadership soon brought in national anti-immigrant leaders to bolster their case. In most instances these national figures had already established themselves on the far right side of the scale of debate—the Federation for American Immigration Reform (FAIR), for example. Propaganda images of Mexicans crowded together in hovels and men menacing women on street corners joined a real increase in traffic from both contractors' and workers' vehicles in fueling the xenophobic debate. When a young mother, a pedestrian, was stuck and killed by a Mexican worker who skipped bail and disappeared, the situation deteriorated rapidly.

Two neo-Nazi youths were arrested for attempting to murder two Mexican workers they had kidnapped, and although they eventually received twenty-five-year sentences, until the court case wound its way through the courts, no compromises seemed possible. Groups of immigrant rights advocates and Long Islanders' United against the Hate pushed for a job-hiring site, while anti-immigrant groups fought to push the workers out by organizing further demonstrations against the hiring site.

By 2003, when the filmmakers began to gather all their material for a final edit, no hiring site had been authorized and a group of local high school youths had been arrested for firebombing a house where day laborers lived.

Recommended Readings

Arseneau, Adam. "Farmingville." *DVD Verdict*, 23 November 2004 (online at www.dvdverdict.com). Argues that it is "the story of small-town America suddenly dropped headfirst into a class and race war, absolutely confused as to how it got there in the first place, struggling to restore a sense of normalcy to its streets."

Stevens, Dana. "When the Pursuit of a Living Wage Leads to Violence." *New York Times*, 29 October 2004. Positive review: an "unusually sensitive and sophisticated piece of investigative journalism (to gain their subjects' trust, Ms. Tambini and Mr. Sandoval lived and worked in Farmingville for nine months during the filming)."

Fear and Trembling

Stupeur et tremblements

CHANGES IN THE WORKPLACE: WORLDWIDE

2003, 107 mins., France and Japan, in
   French and Japanese with English
   subtitles
Director: Alain Corneau
Screenplay: Alain Corneau, from Amélie
   Nothomb's novel, *Fear and Trembling*
   (1999)

The stereotypical Japanese salary man or woman is a model of conformity, obedience, group-thinking, and repressed emotions. Although it may seem counterintuitive to cheerleaders of American capitalism who value (they say) boldness and individual striving, Japanese corporations have clearly been successful, innovative, and even rewarding places to work, either despite or because of these stereotypical qualities.

As if to put the stereotype to the test, this unusual comedy adapts an autobiographical novel written from the point of view of a Japanese-speaking Belgian woman who takes a job as a translator for the Yumimoto Corporation, a huge export/import multinational corporation, based in Tokyo: Amélie (played by Sylvia Testud) thinks she has her dream job because she has always wanted to become "a true Japanese woman." She is assigned to Fubuki (played by Kaori Tsuji), one of the few women in her unit, a woman of poise and exquisite beauty, which the camera, in obedience to Amelie's voice-over, dwells on lovingly. The ancient advice—approach the Japanese emperor only with "fear and trembling"—seems to be transferred to Amélie's many male (imperial) supervisors, but with Fubuki she detects, she believes, a sisterly bond. When she manages to advise a male coworker about a campaign related to Belgium and he makes a successful presentation, she has the illusion that she can make it in this male-dominated world.

Alas, through turns of plot both funny and horrifying, most involving her being treated rudely and given demeaning tasks at every turn, Amélie begins to realize that she has violated one of the bedrock rules of the Japanese corporate workplace: by displaying initiative and causing her immediate supervisor, Fubuki, to lose face, her career is in jeopardy. Even though she penetrates some of the mysteries of this company in its global outreach, her best career trait ends up being stoicism.

Recommended Reading

Scott, A. O. "Help Wanted: Young, Naïve Masochist." *New York Times,* 19 November 2004. The director's "mildly perverse sensibility

turns the conflict of cultures into a psychodrama that is at once lighthearted and intense."

▶◀▶◀▶◀

Fishing in the Sea of Greed

SCARCE RESOURCES (FISH)

1998, 45 mins., India, English and Hindi with
    English subtitles
Director: Anand Patwardhan
Cinema-Verité Documentary
Distributor: First Run/Icarus Films

The competition between a factory (fishing) ship and a typical Indian, coastal, four-person boat is off the scale: one ship can catch and process fish a thousand times faster than the Indian ship but with corresponding harm to the ocean and its supply of fish. Even compensatory schemes devised by the World Bank to develop coastal aquaculture by building saline shrimp ponds often backfire: any breach in the low earthen walls results in the salination of ground water, deterioration in drinking water, and the ruin of nearby fields.

Anand Patwardhan dwells on the problems but attempts to offer a film about organizing against the trends that potentially affect hundreds of small communities of fish harvesters and fish workers. Even the villagers who could afford to launch small fishing trawlers could not compete with the "foreign ships," as the villagers labeled them. Instead, led by the National Fishworkers' Forum and inspired by the nonviolent tactics of Gandhi, the villagers of the Kanyakumari region at the southern tip of the Indian subcontinent turned to a variety of strategies to protect their livelihood.

The film follows the gradually escalating tactics of the National Fishworkers' Forum and its supporters. A hunger strike by one of their leaders and the burning of a mock wooden factory ship (imitating Gandhi's burning of foreign cloth during his campaign for national self-reliance) build support for a massive harbor blockade in Bombay, when factory ships and other container vessels were turned away by demonstrators on boats of all sizes.

The film ends on an optimistic note, as India hosts the first annual World Fisheries Day, sponsored by the World Forum of Fish-workers and Fish Harvesters. The hard work of enforcing a government law on coastal zone protection—up to five hundred meters from the coastline—to keep sand mining, mangrove estuary destruction, and aquaculture pollution under control remains on the agenda.

Recommended Reading

Hoskot, Ranjit. "Netting the Conscience." *The Hindu Magazine* (online at www.hinduon net.com/folio/fo0104/01040320.htm). Surveys the filmmaker's career and his close contact with the fishing villages he filmed.

▶◀▶◀▶◀

Fish Is Our Life

SCARCE RESOURCES (FISH)

1994, 28 mins., United States
Director: Peregrin Beckman
Cinema-Verité Documentary
Distributor: Documentary Educational
    Resources

Visitors to Tsukiji Market, Tokyo's largest wholesale fish market, see such a plenitude of fish that the warnings of scarcity in the oceans must seem like tall tales. Peregrine Beckman films these fish lovingly, as he explores a handful of the 1,100 family-owned businesses that participate in the seven auction houses at the market. Husbands and wives work together, often specializing in a single species or related fish.

The subtitle of the most comprehensive book on Tokyo's fish markets, Theodore Berstor's *Tsukiji*, is "The Fish Market at the Center of the World." Although the phrase may seem like hyperbole, in terms of the globalization of fishing (that is, overfishing), it is an apt metaphor for the Japanese culture of fish consumption. Tsukiji Market, the largest seafood market in the world, handles almost 90 percent of the volume of fish sold in Tokyo and 20 percent in all of Japan.

This film will be a revelation even if the viewer has seen other fish markets: the sheer volume of operation and size of the incoming fish are remarkable, as are the labor-intensive, small operations that process the fish for the auction sales. The film does not comment on overfishing, however, reserving its narration for the briskly professional workers and owners of the fish business.

Recommended Reading

Bestor, Theodore. *Tsukiji: The Fish Market at the Center of the World.* Berkeley and Los Angeles: University of California Press, 2005. Detailed ethnographic account of the market.

Fish is Our Life: Cutting fish at Tsukiji Market, the "Fish Market at the Center of the World." Courtesy Documentary Educational Resources.

Le Franc

BANKING AND GLOBAL FINANCING
NEOCOLONIALISM

1994, 45 mins., Senegal, in Wolof with
  English subtitles
Director: Djibril Diop Mambéty
Screenplay: Djibril Diop Mambéty

The star of this artful blend of traditional African storytelling and symbolic economic discourse about both ends of the spectrum of wealth—street markets and international currency markets—is Marigo (played by Dieye Ma Dieye) who plays a *congoma*, a home-made blend of guitar, drum, and harmonica, on the streets of Dakar, Senegal. His landlady

Le Franc: Marigo (Dieye Ma Dieye) carries his winning ticket stuck to a door. Courtesy California Newsreel.

(played by Aminta Fall) has confiscated his instrument, and so he is doubly compromised—can't pay her, can't earn any money without his instrument. As luck would have it, he spots a thousand-franc note dropped by a lottery customer at the market stall belonging to Langouste (played by Demba Ba), a colorfully dressed dwarf. Langouste forces Marigo to use the note to buy a sure winner, ticket 555.

The lottery is called Devaluation, a radio announcer proclaims, a protest against France's "international swindle of supply and demand" when it devalued the West African franc by 50 percent in 1994. He goes on to predict a great competition for prizes because Kus, the Dwarf God of Fortune, is embossed on every ticket.

Of course Marigo wins, but his effort to get his ticket redeemed provokes his comic odyssey across the crowded city streets, city dumps, and what looks like a destroyed mosque. To protect his ticket, he had pasted it with a powerful glue to his door, underneath the poster of his hero, Yaadikoone, a Senegalese Robin Hood. The lottery board will redeem his ticket only if they can read the control number on the reverse side, and so it's off to the oceanside to free the ticket from his door. He teeters from street to street, from bus stop to market, carrying his door.

Mambéty uses flashbacks and flashforwards in intriguing ways throughout this short film. At one point Langouste points at a man who cracked under the strain of winning the lottery and we see that he looks like (virtually *is*) Marigo carrying a door! Another time Marigo is crossing a desolate stretch of the city, and he turns suddenly to confront a double of himself playing his congoma. Is this the Marigo of the future? Or the past?

Both of Mambéty's two short films in this volume, *Le Franc* and *The Little Girl Who Sold the Sun,* feature street people, "people [who] will never have bank accounts; for them, each day presents questions of survival" (see Givanni). Mambéty's skill in placing these people in a global perspective is remarkable.

Recommended Reading

Givanni, June. "African Conversations." *Sight & Sound,* September 1995, 30–31. Interview with the filmmaker about his career.

ᗅᗅᗅ
From Mao to Money

CHINA
GLOBAL CAPITAL

2001, 28 mins., Denmark, in Danish with
   English subtitles
Director: Frank Esmann
Cinema-Verité Documentary
Distributor: Filmakers Library

Although this short but revealing entry into the debate on China's future asks whether China is heading for market communism or communist capitalism, by film's end there really is no other response than the one given in the last lines of narration: "The journey from Mao to money is nearly over." A two-class system seems firmly in place, sometimes referred to in the film as the rich and the poor but in fact is the reflection of what Mao always predicted ("top party people taking the capitalist road") and what Deng Xiaoping's oft-quoted aphorism ("It doesn't matter whether a cat is black or white as long as it catches mice") memorialized.

And while Mao is a ghostly presence in the film—Zong Sehn, the leading rich capitalist and motorcycle factory owner featured, was once a Red Guard, part of Mao's army of youth to protect his legacy—it is Deng who is quoted approvingly. Zong Sehn lives in a house that could be a nouveau riche American McMansion, while his workers—part of the one hundred million estimated rural folk who migrate to the cities for jobs—are in crowded dormitories.

There are few times—at least in the films in this book—that the WTO is welcomed enthusiastically, but Zong is ecstatic about China's acceptance into that club. It will mean, he says, that China now has to play by the international rules for capitalists. By the way, he confides, corruption is inevitable in our rapidly expanding economy, especially this first stage: the civil servants make demands on the new capitalists, but we pay them to do things for us.

This "socialism with a Chinese face" means McDonald's on main street and skyscrapers on the horizon. It also means construction workers sending almost all of their pay back home, like migrant workers worldwide.

Recommended Reading

Sull, Donal N., and Yong Wang. *Made in China: What Western Managers Can Learn from Trailblazing Chinese Entrepreneurs.* Boston: Harvard Business School Press, 2005. Numerous accounts of Chinese managers and venture capitalists conquering new capitalist territory.

ᗅᗅᗅ
From the Other Side

De l'autre côté

MIGRANT LABOR (UNITED STATES)

2002, 98 mins., France, in English, French,
   and Spanish with English subtitles
Director: Chantal Akerman
Postmodern Documentary
Distributor: First Run/Icarus Films

Illegal Mexican immigrants would not normally come to mind when thinking of subjects for Belgian minimalist filmmaker Chantal Akerman, known for her *Jeanne Dielman, 23 Commerce Quay, 1080 Brussels* (1975), a difficult but compelling microscopic view of a single mother, part-time prostitute, and obsessive-compulsive. Akermann has now used her trademark long takes on the U.S.-Mexican border, as her camera visits both the beauty and the horror in the stories of illegal immigrants "from the other side."

Akerman alternates interviews with cranky Americans, distraught Mexican families, and surprisingly sympathetic officials, all of whom recognize the dangers inherent in the American policy of superpolicing the easiest entry routes for illegals, thereby forcing them to use the dangerous desert routes. The dangers of heat and water deprivation are obvious enough, but there is also a vigilante spirit among Americans who object to people sneaking across their ranches in the middle of the night.

Appropriately ambiguous in its point of view, the film drives us back and forth across the border, with the towns of Agua Prieta in Mexico's Sonora province, and Douglas, Arizona, and its nearby ranches. In interviews on the Mexican side of the border, family members tell of lost ones, sometimes abandoned by their smugglers, the "coyotes." The Americans are not subtle racists, making it clear that they will shoot trespassers if necessary, although occasionally a sympathetic voice is heard, such as a sheriff in Arizona who criticizes the "calculated consequence" of the "bad strategy" that forces the illegals into the desert route.

Some of the most eerie and compelling long takes are actually special effects photography taken from patrolling border police helicopters, using spotlights and infrared photography to track the illegals making their way across the desert at night.

Although Akerman's sympathy clearly lies with the Mexicans who are driven by poverty to seek a dangerous solution to their problems, her decision to take sides in her film was not always enough: "I want something to be expressed in all of its complexity, something that must therefore be a resonance of what is already there, usually hidden, but definitely there, in others, in the spectator" (interview on First Run/Icarus Films at www.frif.org).

Recommended Readings

"Border Policy Must Change to Halt Deaths." *Arizona Republic*, 19 June 2002. In an editorial the newspaper scoffs at "the entire country," which "is in tacit agreement with immigration hypocrisy" that immigrants are not really wanted for jobs to keep "costs down for business and consumers."

Kehr, Dave. "Inching Toward America, So Near but So Far." *New York Times,* 20 February 2003. A positive review: this is "a spare, painterly and scrupulously unsentimental look at the plight of illegal Mexican immigrants."

Madigan, David. "Police Investigate Killings of Illegal Immigrants in Desert." *New York Times*, 23 October 2002. Reports from Arizona on a possible "vigilante terror campaign to stop the flow of immigrants from Mexico."

Rooney, David. "From the Other Side." *Variety,* 6 June 2002. Her "unhurried approach" gives the film a "poignancy and bleak poetry that more informative, fact-based reporting might have lacked."

◄►◄►

The Future of Food

INTELLECTUAL PROPERTY RIGHTS (GMOs)

2005, 88 mins., United States
Director: Deborah Koons Garcia
Agit-Prop Documentary

The future of food? In a word, bad. Monsanto, the leading pesticide company, has purchased every major seed company they could find and have trolled the federal seed archives all with only one goal: to patent seeds and reverse the centuries-old (and worldwide) tradition of farmers using their own seed to grow the food we eat.

Deborah Koons Garcia's documentary explains in chilling detail what it means to patent—for the first time in history—the essence of life. Holding such a patent gives Monsanto and other corporations the right to genetically modify the food we eat. Furthermore, when these genetically modified organisms (GMOs) spread, usually by accident, into unmodified fields, farmers have been held liable for damages for using a company's seeds without permission.

Such corporate knavery has been upheld by the Canadian Supreme Court when Monsanto discovered some of their Roundup Ready plants in an unauthorized field. Such plants have a genetic marker that makes them resistant to Monsanto's favorite pesticide, Roundup, and hence the company's patented plant survives the attack while other plants do not. The farmer who lost the case argued that the seed simply blew into his field. If the relatively progressive Canadian Supreme Court is supporting (however narrowly with a 5 to 4 vote) Monsanto's outrageous maneuver, what chance would American farmers have if they took their similar cases to a higher court?

Garcia concludes this convincing film with a brief report on Monsanto's "suicide seed" that will terminate its own plant self after one growth cycle. Isn't there a dystopian novel yet about this?! We should not forget, Garcia reminds us, of alternative greenmarkets and antibiotech activists who are leading the fight for pure food. It's a small comfort.

Recommended Reading

"Film Clips." *San Francisco Chronicle,* 30 September 2005. The filmmaker "has taken a complex subject and made it digestible for anyone who cares about what they put into their stomachs."

▸▸▸
Ghost in the Shell

EARTH AS COLONY

1995, 82 mins., Japan/United Kingdom, in Japanese with English subtitles
Director: Oshii Mamoru
Animation screenplay: Kazunori Itu, based on Shirow Masamune's manga (adult comic book), *Ghost in the Shell* (1989–90)

The opening title of this Japanese anime indicates that globalization has become interplanetary: "In the near future, corporate networks reach out to the stars, electrons and light flow throughout the universe. The advance of computerization, however, has not yet wiped out nations and ethnic groups." For cyborgs—a kind of misunderstood ethnic group in this film—what's left of their humanity or identity is called the "ghost" in their mostly artificial bodies or "shells."

Anime, or Japanimation as it is sometimes called, doesn't respect genre boundaries: *Ghost in the Shell* is simultaneously science fiction, film noir, and a political thriller, all furnished with a cyberpunk dude and a babe, a close relation to the mise-en-scène of *Blade Runner* (1982). But this is no ordinary babe: she is Major Kusanagi, a voluptuous cyborg

in Section 9, a security police detail, who is partnered with Batô, still another cyborg (but with a little more human in him), a hunk with a seen-it-all attitude. We are in the year 2029, and (mostly) humans and (mostly) cyborgs have reached a kind of grudging equality, if not mutual regard. Kusanagi and Batô are called on to investigate an American "ghost hacker" called the Puppet Master, who is guilty of a number of crimes against the global order: "stock manipulation, illegal information gathering, political engineering, and several acts of terrorism." Sound familiar?

In fact like most science fiction the drama is really a commentary on contemporary misdeeds, in this case the corporate drive for global power, except that this Puppet Master can be much more sneaky. As he seems to have no permanent human body he is now a self-conscious program in search of a new shell or human form. He knows about the security group, Section 9, but it turns out he was originally created as Project 2501 of the Ministry of Foreign Affairs (or Section 6), who often distract our heroes with the pursuit of globe-trotting sleazoids. Rivals within any government are also not future news, but these groups mimic our own global conflicts (and sometimes accommodations) between multinationals and security forces (see *Syriana*).

When the Major finally gets her software into the Puppet Master's temporary shell, she finds out that he wants to merge with her. Finally, after seeing all these beautiful bodies, we think, some sex! Or at the very least a Frankenstein and his mate moment? But no, the Puppet Master is more platonic: we are "mirror images of one another's psyche," he tells the major. The slightly kinky ending is unexpected and I leave it to the viewer to discover, but Oshii launched a sequel, *Ghost in the Shell: Innocence* (2004), and then franchised the concept to another director, Kenji Kamiyama, who did a television series called *The Ghost in the Shell: Stand Alone Complex* (2002–5), both of which move toward some potentially R-rated subjects but never quite get there.

In Oshii's sequel, for example, Batô investigates a new line of sex robots, the *gynoids*, who have turned on their masters: they are the product of a multinational corporation that, having at first moved into the special economic zone for them called the Northern Frontier, has decided to continue their illegal implantation of "ghosts" (identities stolen from young girls) into the gynoids from an offshore floating industrial ship beyond the reach of the government.

The television series moves into a post–World War III society, with an uneasy peace between the former antagonists, the American Empire, and the unnamed Japanese government. One plot line links a number of episodes in which non-Japanese Asians immigrate illegally into Japan after World War III, workers at first acceptable to rebuild a war-torn country.

Like *Metropolis* (2001), another anime classic, this film recognizes that sanitation workers will still have a job to do in the future. What gets top billing, nonetheless, are the forces of globalization at the top of the corporate world still competing for economic dominance.

Recommended Reading

Ebert, Roger. "Ghost in the Shell." *Chicago Sun-Times,* 12 April 1996. Although the film "is too complex and murky to reach a large audience," he "enjoyed its visuals, its evocative soundtrack (including a suite for percussion and heavy breathing), and its ideas."

◄►◄►◄►

The Girl in the Café

ANTI-GLOBALIZATION

2005, 94 mins., United Kingdom/United
    States
Director: David Yates
Screenplay: Richard Curtis

Whenever the G-8 or WTO meets, the police keep the inevitable anti-globalization protestors far away from the leaders on high. Imagine that one of the protestors—an attractive, young woman, of course—has managed to share a hotel room with a male staff member of the British delegation to a G-8 summit. She gets to mingle with prime ministers and chancellors of the exchequer. What would she do?

She would lecture on the need to stop compromising and to confront seriously "extreme poverty" because somewhere a child dies every three seconds. Or at least this is what the somewhat mysterious Gina (played by Kelly Macdonald) does at a London café one day when she chats up Lawrence (played by Bill Nighy), an assistant to the British chancellor of the exchequer. Gina, a naive, shy ex-con falls into a relationship with the equally shy bureaucrat, who lives for work, lives for paper actually, he says, reports and documents. He has so many tics that we are surprised Gina finds him attractive, but his dry wit and encyclopedic knowledge of the miseries of the world's poor wins her over. They make a less glamorous couple than Bill Murray and Scarlett Johansen in a similar May-December romance (*Lost in Translation,* 2003), but there is at least a burning issue in their drifting relationship that ignites her passion and eventually his as well.

Aside from the unlikely pairing of Gina and Lawrence, the subject of the world's poor has rarely been presented in such a romantic way. Although the film was made for the purpose of educating the public about the role of the G-8, it has a surprising soft spot for the British delegation who do, in the end, the right thing, influenced by Gina's determined attempts to make them understand what dying children really means.

Lawrence knows the horrors of extreme poverty statistically, but Gina wonders why he never includes a picture of a dying child in his reports; he admits that such a report would indeed be transformed.

Recommended Reading

Lowry, Brian. "The Girl in the Café." *Variety,* 19 June 2005. Reviewer likes this "understated and moving" film, noting that its "improbable romance proves a thought-provoking, modestly scaled affair that somewhat awkwardly affixes an overt political message onto its more marketable core."

▶▶▶

The Global Assembly Line

HISTORY OF GLOBALIZATION

1986, 58 mins., United States
Director: Lorraine Gray
Traditional Documentary
Distributor: New Day Films

This film is one of the earliest and still relevant examinations of globalization, using Mexico and the Philippines as the exemplars in the Global South that have become home for numerous factories formerly based in the United States. It is especially clear about what it calls the feminization of offshoring, as it documents the managerial preference for teenagers and unmarried women, who are considered more pliable and more nimble with their fingers.

The historical context of the maquiladoras (border factories) in Mexico, perhaps less well known than the factories themselves, provides the viewer with another lesson in the politics of migratory labor: when the *bracero* program of controlled labor was ended in 1965, many of the returning workers, mostly men, were expected to take the jobs of the newly developed maquiladora program. Gradually the percentage of women in the program climbed to 90 percent, where it stayed for years.

The Philippines, particularly Manila, was also an early host country for offshore assembly plants, making not only textiles but electronic parts such as semiconductors. Dictator Ferdinand Marcos and his wife, Imelda, extolled the virtues of putting young women to work in these factories: "Only beautiful products can come from happy people," the gnomic Imelda intones. Unfortunately, as the film documents, the "happy people" had to contend with noxious fumes and eye-straining work.

The film documents early signs of unrest in the system, as there was even the equivalent of a maquilaldora general strike in Reynosa in 1983. When a reporter for Reynosa's American sister city, McAllen, Texas, tried to report on the Reynosa strike he was arrested allegedly and tortured. This outcome was closer to what was already the norm in places such as the Philippines under the Marcos regime.

Recommended Reading

Goodman, Walter. "New Directors/New Films . . . *Assembly Line.*" *New York Times,* 18 April 1986. Notes prophetically that "the record laid out powerfully here is of heightened protests and tougher crackdowns. No one expresses much hope for reconciliation or accommodation. It is difficult to disagree with Bishop Desmond Tutu, who is interviewed at length, that the future looks bleak for anything but more of the same, and worse."

▶▶▶

The Globalisation Tapes

ANTI-GLOBALIZATION
NEOCOLONIALISM
WOMEN WORKERS AND CHILD LABOR

2002, 71 mins., United Kingdom
Producers: Joshua Openheimer and Christine Cynn
Agit-Prop Documentary
Distributor: Vision Machine Film Project (www.visionmachine.org)

This film originated as an unusual collaboration of the Indonesian Independent Workers' Union of Sumatra Plantation Workers (Perbbuni); the International Union of Food, Agricultural, Hotel, Restaurant, Catering, Tobacco, and Allied Workers' Association (IUF); and the London-based Vision Machine Film Project. For the most part, the professionals turned the filmmaking over to the plantation workers themselves. They traveled to various work sites and villages to listen to their fellow workers detail harsh working conditions and also to offer their analysis of the principal causes for much of this distress.

The thesis of the film is simple enough but devastating in its implications: through waves of repressive colonization (Dutch empire), neocolonization (the American-led overthrow of the nationalist leader Sukarno by Suharto, memorialized in the feature film, *The Year of*

Living Dangerously, 1982), and globalization (the World Bank and the International Monetary Fund), workers on the ground and their leadership have been brutalized and impoverished.

What makes this a successful film, however, is that local filmmakers and workers remain, for the most part, front and center. Their efforts are supported with some hip postmodern editing of captions, montages, and provocations, such as this rhetorical exchange: "Why is 'globalisation' an English word? Because the Javanese didn't colonize the whole world." The interview with a worker who gathers the fruit pods for palm oil details his daily wages ($1.14/day). But to earn even that, he has to have his son work, without pay of course: "I can't make my quota if I work alone." He cuts and pulls down from the trees giant pods weighing about eight pounds each, and he must gather seventy of them each day. Another extended interview features the women who spray Gramozone (which consists of parquat, an Agent Orange ingredient), in a circle around each tree. The women wear no goggles or masks and suffer the obvious consequences of dealing with such poison.

The film also provides a capsule history of Indonesia and how it has come to be essentially a vassal of the World Bank and the IMF. The trade unionists hope to organize not only Indonesian workers but also their counterparts in other developing nations. Otherwise, one of them says, the companies will just relocate to another former colony in the Third World.

A number of unusually and compelling sequences punctuate this ideal companion to John Pilger's *The New Rulers of the World* (q.v.), another documentary analysis of the World Bank and the IMF in Indonesia. A soccer match played by elephants and an interview with a leader of one of Suharto's death squads remind us of the strange old days, while the soundtrack at the end includes the songs "We Shall Overcome" and "Solidarity Forever," suggesting some "new" old ways.

Recommended Readings

La Botz, Dan. *Made in Indonesia: Indonesian Workers since Suharto.* Boston: South End Press, 2001. An essential study of the role Indonesian workers played in the 1998 overthrow of President Suharto and their ongoing struggle with globalization and issues of human rights.

Pilger, John. *The New Rulers of the World.* London: Verso, 2002. Essays on Indonesia and other countries victimized by transnational organizations.

▶◀▶◀

Global Village or Global Pillage?

ANTI-GLOBALIZATION

1999, 27 mins., United States
Director: Jeremy Brecher
Traditional Documentary, based on Jeremy Brecher and Tim Costello, *Global Village or Global Pillage* (1998)

Instead of limiting the film to explanations of how globalization works or how it exploits, the director has assembled a team of anti-globalization analysts and experts to chart grassroots organizing at both the local and international levels. The film uses traditional documentary interviews and footage as well as animation (by labor cartoonist Mike Konopacki) and song, with a voice-over narration by actor/activist Ed Asner.

The film explains how organizations, supported by environmental groups and organized labor, have reversed some of the negative aspects of the seemingly inevitable expansion of capitalist investment, especially in countries in the Global South. And it is these countries where globalization hits hardest: "Third World countries are being forced to race to the bottom," concludes Dennis Brutus, anti-apartheid activist and poet. "They have to compete with each other, outbid each other, in offering cheaper labor than their competitors and also offering more stringent legislation to control labor. So you get both repression and increased poverty."

One of the animated sequences shows satirist Jonathan Swift's Gulliver as a global corporation pinned down by Lilliputian activists and workers of the world. Calling this the "Lilliput strategy," the filmmakers suggest that anti-globalization campaigns in 1999 helped cancel about one fifth of the immense debt the Global South has accrued in transactions with transnational organizations such as the World Bank and the IMF.

Less encouraging is the testimony given by Janet Pratt, whose job not only disappeared when her Westinghouse factory "went south," but who was recruited by her company to go to Juarez to train Mexican workers to do her job.

Recommended Reading

Brecher, Jeremy, Tim Costello, and Brendan Smith. *Globalization from Below*. Boston: South End Press, 2000. More of a how-to guide than Brecher and Costello's *Global Village or Global Pillage?* both books nonetheless lay out the broad social movement that offers alternatives to traditional top-down (it's unstoppable) advocates of globalization.

ᐳᐸᐳᐸᐳᐸ
Grupo Alavio Films

CHANGES IN THE WORKPLACE: WORLDWIDE

The Face of Dignity, 2002, 58 mins.
Zanon: Building Resistance, 2003, 18 mins.
For a Six-Hour Workday, 2004, 20 mins.
The BAUEN Workers' Cooperative, 2004, 20 mins.
La Forsta Belongs to the Workers, 2005, 52 mins.
Thermal Spa Cacique Pismanta Cooperative, 2005, 50 mins.
Agit-Prop Documentaries
Producers and Distributors: Grupo Alavio (www.alavio.org)

The Grupo Alavio videographers take their inspiration from the Argentine *crotos* (hobos or bindle stiffs, to use the Industrial Workers of the World equivalent) who traveled the open road looking for work in the early twentieth century. They were anarchists, concealing their pamphlets in their bags or *avio*, a term denoting provisions or equipment (probably what we would call today a kit bag). Members of Grupo Alavio travel to various sites of struggle in Argentina, especially those involving the "recuperated" or occupied fac-

tories. Their style is cinema verité and their goal agit-prop, since the videos are intended to be shown not only to the workers and families involved in the struggle but to serve as the means of instructing others how the factory takeovers worked.

Four of the six films involve factories or work sites abandoned by their owners for various reasons. In some cases the owners felt their profit margins were not sufficient to continue production, although in at least one instance—La Foresta, a beef slaughterhouse—the film implies that some Argentine capitalists have discovered an alternative means of making money: take government subsidies for their businesses, but don't use the subsidy on site.

In other instances the owners would let the factory run down and expect to recoup any losses by selling off the equipment, the approach used by the owners of Zanon, the biggest ceramic tile factory in Argentina and perhaps all of Latin America. The owners did not pay the indigenous Mapuch people for their clay or the workers their back pay, two new ways of committing fraud.

Factory takeovers are an attempt by Argentine workers to exert control in the face of their country's defaulting on World Bank and IMF loans. With Argentina in recession and jobs disappearing, the workers in these factories—as well as the unemployed featured in two of the films—organized to take economic and political action to safeguard, or demand, jobs.

All of the films develop in a similar way: we are taken by the filmmakers inside the organization of workers or the unemployed, meet some of their leaders and attend some of their assemblies, and witness presentations before government agencies or demonstrations attempting to gain legitimacy for an occupied factory. In *La Foresta Belongs to the Workers* at first the workers' organization is turned down by the judge overseeing the factory's case, but then a successful presentation at a county board gives them the right to use the equipment in place. They still need, the workers note, the real estate too. Their slogan—"Occupy/Resist/Produce"—only gets them so far. Many of the people worked twenty to thirty years for La Foresta's previous owners, and their rallying cry reflects their frustration: "La Foresta belongs to the workers. . . . If you don't like it you can go to hell!"

The Face of Dignity focuses on the equally aggressive tactics of an activists' council of the unemployed in Solano, a Buenos Aires suburb. They debate whether to "cut the road" and establish a barricade of burning tires because, in part, they have been excluded from the global economy. See *The Take* (q.v.) for a wider, politically broader interpretation of these struggles.

Recommended Reading

Trigona, Marie. "Anarchist Film during the Spanish Civil War." *Revolution Video* (online at www.revolutionvideo.org). One of the activists in the Grupo Alavio discusses historical agit-prop films to establish a continuity of filmmaking with the Grupo Alavio today.

ᐅᐅᐅ
Gutted

CONTAINERIZED SHIPPING
SCARCE RESOURCES (FISH)

2004–5, 60 mins., United Kingdom/United
    States
Director: David Peat
TV Documentary
Distributor: PBS

There may be more than one way to save the cod from overfishing and eventual extinction in European waters, but this BBC Scotland documentary, "re-versioned" (see Heffernan) for PBS in the United States, documents the rather startling approach of the European Union (EU): regardless of the condition or age of the cod fisher's boat, scuttle and gut it. End of boat, salvation of fish. Or is it that simple?

Of course it isn't. Fish all over the world are being caught unto oblivion, if not legally (in season, within territorial limits, quotas recognized) then illegally (no hatches battened). Globalization has provided the factory

ships, and the First World (mostly but not exclusively) has provided the appetites. The list of endangered fish species grows alarmingly every year. This film want us to create a list of endangered fishermen.

We follow the misfortunes of the formerly successful Scots family of Sandy West, whose beautiful, relatively new boat, the Steadfast—purchased for more than $2 million—is hauled ashore and destroyed. In stories such as these the family is caught in the maws of Brussels, capital of the EU, not capitalism. The Steadfast was one of 235 boats destroyed in five years. West reports that his son went off to work on an offshore oil rig, another feature of the globalized economy off the Scottish coast.

The West family was only one of the folks in Fraserburgh affected: the entire village fleet was decommissioned. The film also features one activist group of wives, the Cod Crusaders, who traveled far and wide to take their message to the public. Director David Peat also couldn't resist filming another boat, this time a $35 million factory trawler, hard at work gathering tons of herring for the Japanese and Russian markets. That type of fish made a comeback, but at whose expense?

The BBC changed the original UK broadcast date from early to late June 2004. It seems that the European Union was holding elections in mid-June and thought the film was not a good PR piece for the transnational body. They were right.

Recommended Reading

Heffernan, Virginia. "Preservation Takes Priority, and the Fisherman Struggles." *New York Times*, 23 August 2005. The reviewer is very cranky about the "re-versioning" or re-packaging of the film for American audience, suspecting that along with subtitled Scots accents, Scots militancy is being suborned.

ᐅᐅᐅ
H-2 Worker

MIGRANT LABOR (UNITED STATES)

1989, 70 mins., United States
Director: Stephanie Black

Mixed Traditional and Agit-Prop Documentary

Belle Glade, Florida, is where Edward R. Murrow's *Harvest of Shame* (in *Working Stiffs*), the classic documentary about migrant workers, filmed its opening scene in 1960. In the 1980s as many as 10,000 Jamaican and other Caribbean workers lived there as virtual serfs on sugarcane plantations six months of the year. Federally subsidized American companies use the H-2 designation for agricultural workers when there are (supposedly) no American workers available to do the job and the work is seasonal or temporary. Of course by definition all migrant workers cope with those conditions, but the work on the sugarcane plantations requires, in the words of company reps, special skills.

The special skills that Jamaican workers provide were learned on the sugarcane plantations at home before those plantations collapsed because of unfavorable trade regulations. The men fly in to Florida, are bussed to their dorms resembling a minimum security prison, and bussed back and forth to hard, dirty, and sometimes risky work in the fields. For this they receive minimum wage, but the director cuts to their pay stubs, which shows that they pay 10 percent of their gross for "travel" and 33 percent for their room and board.

A number of talking heads justify this extraordinary program. Some of the men at one point vote with their feet and try a work stoppage until they received their due. Which turns out to be a swift trip back to Jamaica. The men left behind make the best of things, exchanging (by voice-over) surprisingly cheery letters with loved ones and dancing to their own beat.

The director and her crew had to film a number of sequences secretly. Bravo for their nerve.

Recommended Readings

Kliot, Jason. "H-2 Worker." *Cineaste* 18, no. 1. "Through a subtle mixture of adroit editing, vital subject matter, and, quite simply, determination, *H-2 Worker* rises above its genre."

Schaefer, Stephen. "Bring the Cane Fields' Pain to Cannes." *USA Today*, 14 May 1990. An account of the film's production.

Wilkinson, Alec. *Big Sugar: Seasons in the Cane Fields of Florida*. New York: Knopf, 1989. A history of the scene, including the story of the 1942 indictment of U.S. Sugar Corporation for enslaving their black workers.

▶▶▶

The Hidden Face of Globalization

ANTI-GLOBALIZATION
WAL-MART
WOMEN WORKERS AND CHILD LABOR

2003, 30 mins., United States
Producer: Crowing Rooster Arts
Agit-Prop Documentary
Distributor: National Labor Committee
(NLC)

The never-ending wrong the National Labor Committee raises in its ongoing campaigns against labor abuses in the globalized markets is usually this: multinational corporations want their intellectual property rights (their logo or the brand) protected by law, but they reject laws protecting workers on the grounds that they harm free trade. In fact most transnational organizations such as the World Bank agree with them: environmental and labor laws are often prohibited under trade agreements with WTO members.

The "hidden face" is of course that of women and children. In this film the NLC demonstrates the gross violations of wages and hours that young women and children must endure to make the garments in a Disney sweatshop in Bangladesh. Despite Disney's own code of conduct, conditions remained deplorable at least through 2003. The NLC has consistently taken the stand that these factories should not close—Disney should not "cut and run"—but that conditions and wages should be improved.

The NLC follows the young women from home to work and back again. Interviews bring their real faces out in the open. But after they began complaining, Disney took its orders away from the Shah Makhdum factory,

The Hidden Face of Globalization: Women walk to work in Bangladesh. Courtesy National Labor Committee.

where many of them had worked for eight years and where output went mainly (70 percent) to Disney. In effect both workers and sweatshop were simultaneously punished.

Recommended Reading

National Labor Committee. *Wal-Mart's Shirts of Misery.* New York: National Labor Committee, 1999. Pamphlet with data supporting the NLC's argument in the film about Bangladeshi sweatshops.

⋈⋈⋈

High and Low

Heaven and Hell

CHANGES IN THE WORKPLACE: WORLDWIDE HISTORY OF GLOBALIZATION

1963, 142 mins., Japan, in Japanese with
   English subtitles
Director: Akira Kurosawa

Screenplay: Eijiro Hisaita, from Ed McBain's novel, *King's Ransom* (1959)

Akira Kurosawa's reputation as a world-class director is based first of all on his samurai films in general and two films in particular that many rate in the top echelon of film classics: *Rashomon* (1950) and *The Seven Samurai* (1954), both historical dramas of medieval Japan and fascinating studies of human behavior using the conventions (and pretensions) of the warrior genre. Perhaps less well-known are his social realist films, including *High and Low.* On the surface this is a kidnapping film but one that transcends its police procedural genre because of its economic and cultural weight.

Through clever financial maneuvering, Kingo Gondo (played by Toshiro Mifune), an executive in a big shoe company, is poised to seize control of the entire company. He has set

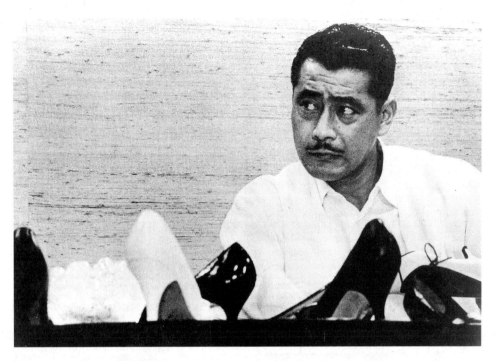

High and Low: A shoe executive (Toshiro Mifune) confronts a choice between morality and profits.

aside a significant sum of money to accomplish this, but just as he is to launch his takeover bid, his son is kidnapped and the ransom requested is of course his takeover money. He and his hitherto devoted wife face a complex dilemma when they learn that the child kidnapped is actually his son's playmate, their chauffeur's son, because of a mistaken identification. Now the moral dilemma is sharp: is he willing to use his money for another person's son?

It is an exquisite rendition of a relentless Japanese theme: private morality versus public loyalties, the resolution of which, according to a number of commentators, has led to Japanese industrial success (see Attanasio). The fact that he hesitates at all convinces his wife to pack her bags and one of his previously loyal business subordinates to betray him.

Although the film seems so rooted in Japanese culture, one might be surprised to discover that it is actually a fairly close adaptation of Ed McBain's *King's Ransom,* from his 87th Precinct mystery series. Kurosawa does transform the novel's American CEO, who is quite contemptible in his unwillingness to give up on his takeover aims, into an obviously conflicted individual who eventually agrees to the do the right thing, and he adds the urban geographical divisions that highlight the economic divide of the principal characters captured in some fascinating camera angles. Thus the kidnapper in the working-class, crowded tenements in the city spies with a telescope on the hilltop estate of the shoe executive. Both film and novel retain the corporate dance that executives and their underlings engage in: what seems on the surface to be so characteristically Japanese in

Kurosawa's vision turns out to be part of the American corporate scene, at least filtered through Ed McBain's somewhat hardboiled approach to all human relationships.

In the 1950s Japan's economic growth was phenomenal—almost 10 percent a year. Kurosawa's film reacts to that growth with an ethical deathtrap. Impossible to predict is Japan's next step onto the global stage, but Kurosawa (as Yoshimoto points out) set his film in Yokohama, Japan's leading port city for over a hundred years and one of the Japanese cities then most intertwined with foreign business and culture. Kurosawa also continued to challenge his audiences with films about both high (*Ran*, 1985, an aging warlord turns his kingdom over to his sons) and low (*Dodeskaden*, 1970, set in a shantytown).

Recommended Readings

Attanasio, Paul. "High and Low." *Washington Post*, 7 November 1986. Highlights the "general dilemma of modern Japanese life—the conflict between humane values and the rigid loyalties that have made for its commercial success."

Yoshimoto, Mitsuhiro. *Kurosawa: Film Studies and Japanese Cinema*. Durham: Duke University Press, 2000. Detailed analysis of the film, with emphasis on the psychological (the CEO and kidnapper share certain traits) and the locations ("the spatial organization of the city partly accounts" for the kidnapper's act).

ㅏㅓㅓ

How Yukong Moved the Mountains

Comment Yukong deplaça les montagnes

CHINA
LABOR HISTORY

1976, 660 mins., France, in French and
    Chinese with English subtitles
About Petroleum, 81 mins.
The Pharmacy, 74 mins.
A Woman, a Family, 101 mins.
The Generator Factory, 120 mins.
The Fishing Village, 95 mins.
A Barracks, 54 mins.
Story of the Ball, 11 mins.
Professor Tsien, 12 mins.

A Performance at Peking Opera, 30 mins.
Training at the Peking Circus, 14 mins.
Craftsmen, 13 mins.
Impressions of a City, 55 mins.
Directors: Joris Ivens and Marceline
    Loridan
Cinema-Verité Documentary

The title of Joris Ivens and Marceline Loridan's twelve-part series of films about the China of the Cultural Revolution of the 1970s comes from a peasant fable, one Chairman Mao enjoyed telling: Yukong set out to move by hand two mountains blocking the path to his house, believing that it would take his sons' sons and their future generations of sons to succeed in moving the mountain. His neighbors mocked his resolve, but heaven intervened and did it for him. Mao concluded: "Our heaven is none other than the masses of the Chinese people." In the 1970s, the overwhelming majority of Chinese people were peasants. (In recent years, however, the migration of peasants to the new factory cities has changed and complicated this traditional dynamic: see *Railroad of Hope*.)

It is curious, then, that Ivens and Loridan—despite the ambitious length of the project—focused on Chinese workers, not peasants, but they could not do it all. What they did do—oil fields, a pharmacy, a generator factory, a fishing village, to name just a handful of their subjects—was a remarkable exploration of the average Chinese worker, his or her family, and workmates and how they participated in the political and cultural life of their collectives, whether they be factory or army or other worksite based.

What is of special interest to us years later is the films' emphasis on participatory decision-making and the self-critical work style. Both are Maoist virtues that have virtually disappeared in the new China of hierarchical control of the factories, which are, in any case, no longer universally under state management. Especially revealing then, in retrospect, is *About Petroleum*, the first film, because it represented for Ivens and Loridan an attempt at China's self-sufficiency in energy. Again this was a Maoist virtue long abandoned as China expanded its industries and sought to buy oil abroad and even, in one famous moment in 2005, tried to buy an American oil company.

For Thomas Waugh (see below), the cinematography of Ivens and Loridan reflected their acceptance of the Chinese emphasis on decentralized decision-making and "minimized their own subjectivity." Using both close-ups and long takes (and cinema verité, in general), the couple was able to film the "perpetual self questioning and self awareness which impels [the Cultural Revolution] forward at its roots." Waugh also argues that two of the twelve films (*A Woman, A Family*, focusing on a woman welder and union official, and *The Fishing Village*, about a collective of women who fish) are explicitly feminist and that one of the most politically important films (*The Generator Factory*) demonstrates a unique Cultural Revolution communications form, the *dazibao* or wall poster.

Rarely seen and undistributed, like so many of Ivens's films, *How Yukong Moved the Mountains* remains a testament to a major phase of Chinese labor and cultural history. As we see these films today, especially *The Generator Factory*, the China of today seems both close (disregard for environmental issues and no helmets or safety glasses for the workers) and far (worker-centered discussions on how to run the factory).

Recommended Reading

Waugh, Thomas. "Filming the Cultural Revolution." *Jump Cut*, nos. 12–13 (1976): 3–6 (also online at www.ejumpcut.org). Detailed and extended analysis of the film and the directors' experience in China.

◄►◄►◄►

The Human Cost behind Bargain Shopping

WAL-MART

2005, 60 mins., United States
Producer: Dateline NBC
Correspondents: Chris Hansen and Richard Greenberg
TV Documentary

What distinguishes this *Dateline NBC* program on sweatshop conditions in the Bangladeshi factories that make products for the U.S. market is the use of a hidden camera. (The show actually has a hidden camera division.) *Dateline* presents their investigation into the "human cost behind bargain shopping" in three parts. The first shows a person masquerading as an American clothing buyer visiting and questioning a Bangladeshi factory manager whose company supplies Wal-Mart, Sears, and Kohls. The clothing buyer is Charles Kernaghan, the National Labor Committee activist whose career has been spent exposing sweatshop conditions around the world (see *The Hidden Face of Globalization* and *Mickey Mouse Goes to Haiti*).

In the second part a *Dateline* crew goes back to the factory with a hidden camera and also films candid interviews with employees off site. In the last part Masuma, one of the sewing machine operators interviewed previously, is brought by the National Labor Committee to the United State where she visits a Wal-Mart in Connecticut.

Two versions of the truth emerge. The factory manager lies about pay and hours, saying that his company adheres to the national law that mandates a maximum sixty-hour week and the minimum wage—just under twenty cents an hour. We learn from the hidden camera and candid interviews that the workers are kept sometimes as many as twelve to fifteen hours a day and not paid the minimum wage.

What *Dateline* uncovers—and other TV documentaries such as *Is Wal-Mart Good for America?* (q.v.) confirm—is that many foreign factories are being trained by Wal-Mart's penny-hoarding regimen. When one Bangladeshi exec tried to get Wal-Mart to pay him one cent more per garment, Wal-Mart pressured him for a two-cent cut. (Wal-Mart's written rebuttal to the program, available on *Dateline NBC*'s website, denies this allegation.)

When Masuma visits Wal-Mart in Connecticut she spots exactly the same kind of jogging pants she was sewing stripes on back home. The price of one pair is the equivalent of one week's pay for her. If she were paid twenty-five cents more an hour, she says, she would finally be able to provide an adequate diet for her family.

Recommended Reading

Rivoli, Pietra. *The Travels of a T-shirt in the Global Economy: An Economist Examines the Markets, Power, and Politics of World Trade.* New York: Wiley, 2005. A daring idea: follow a T-shirt from purchase to its origins (Texas cotton but Chinese weaving) and ultimately its recycling.

▶◀▶

Human Error

Below the Belt

CHANGES IN THE WORKPLACE: NORTH
    AMERICA
GLOBAL CATASTROPHES

2005, 95 mins., United States
Director: Robert M. Young
Screenplay: Richard Dresser from his own
    play, *Below the Belt* (1997)

By combining a computer-generated landscape with special effects, a lurid Technicolor palette, and what only could be described as an industrial compound in a Third World country, Robert M. Young has moved from the progressive social realism of his earlier films—*Nothing But a Man* (in *Working Stiffs*) and *Alambrista* (q.v.)—to a hyperrealism that is as much theater of the absurd as it is a postapocalyptic or even an alternative (fantastic) universe.

Originally designed to be filmed at abandoned factories (such as oil and sugar refineries) in Puerto Rico, Young instead created an industrial plant that appears to be engineered for a chemical process. All we see are vats with bright green waste and pipes spewing toxic smoke. Behind the factory runs a river so polluted that the factory waste flowing into it makes no change in its appearance. It catches fire at one point, like the legendary Cuyahoga River Fire in Cleveland in 1969 whose oil-fed flames were five stories high. But it's just business as usual at this plant, which is transformed during a surrealistic dream sequence into an assembly line cranking out what looks like squashed metal TVs, each of which is embedded with a single human head.

We meet the new hire, Dobbitt (played by Robert Knott), trying to make sense of his new position as "checker" with a coworker, Hanrahan (played by Xander Berkeley,) as they suffer under the petty micromanaging of their boss, Merkin (played by Tom Bower). The more the men talk, the less they work; most of the time they exchange stories and not-so-veiled barbs. They are the white managers of a mostly black workforce, many of whom look like they have stepped one time too many in a pool of poisonous liquid and at least one of whom falls into a vat of deadly-looking gook. To the very end we never know what they really manufacture, and that is certainly Young's point about industrial outposts run by multinationals in the age of globalization: "They're making something they laugh about," Young told an interviewer for *Millimeter Magazine* (1 January 2004, online at digitalcontentproducer.com), "but you never know what it is. You know it's bad for the world."

Recommended Reading

Martel, Ned. "Unresolvable Disputes on the Assembly Line." *New York Times,* 16 September 2005. In this "avant-garde commentary on corporate detachment and office politics, grown men act immeasurably childish when enslaved to a factory."

▶◀▶

Human Trafficking

SEX WORK/TRAFFICKING

2005, TV miniseries, 2 segments of 120 mins.
    each, United States
Director: Christian Duguay
Screenplay: Agatha Dominik and Carol
    Doyle

Can films about sleazy topics avoid being sleazy? Lifetime, the cable channel that calls itself "Television for Women," takes a stab at a "no" answer. A film about sex slavery has a salacious story line by definition, but using the conventions of a crime thriller helps the viewer focus on the more disgusting side of globalization.

During the course of the film we see three Soviet and Soviet-bloc women, ages sixteen to twenty-one, two twelve-year-olds hidden in Manila, one American girl literally snatched from her parents' side while touring Manila, and one relatively mature twenty-one-year-old, all headed for the sex slave operation controlled by a master criminal, Sergei Karpovich (played by Robert Carlyle). The fact that three of the women end up in America and a fourth one is an American enables Kate Morozov (played by Mira Sorvino), a New York City detective who joins the Immigration and Customs Enforcement, a division of Homeland Security, to lay siege to the crime network after she sees the body of still another teenage girl who has committed suicide rather than submit to sex.

The film is part of Lifetime's campaign, Stop Violence Against Women, which features major stars in key roles: in addition to Sorvino and Carlyle, the miniseries features Donald Sutherland as Kate's boss. Given the subject, the filmmakers have to cope with fairly graphic realism. Teenage girls have their clothes ripped off, their beautiful bodies exposed, amid too many shots of leering potbellied men undoing their belts.

Still, the film assures that no one can use the term "sex work" for what these girls do, since they have been kidnapped or tricked into serving as sexual slaves, brutalized, and forced to work in brothels and porn studios, many of which seem to be located in New Jersey.

The global reach of sex trafficking is reinforced by the four major story lines, which crisscross until the exciting resolution. Karparov oversees an empire whose flunkies seduce a waitress in Prague, trick a hopeful model in Kiev, kidnap an American twelve-year-old in Manila, and buy another twelve-year-old from her parents in northern Luzon, and transport all of these girls to the United States illegally.

Recommended Reading

Stanley, Alessandra. "Selling Sex, That Renewable Resource." *New York Times*, 24 October 2005. The miniseries may offer "less moral complexity" than some accounts of the industry, "but it does an effective job of dramatizing a scourge that is too often packaged for prurience."

⋈⋈⋈

Hyenas

Hyenes

NEOCOLONIALISM

1992, 113 mins., Senegal, in Wolof with English subtitles
Director: Djibril Diop Mambéty
Screenplay: Djibril Diop Mambéty, from Friedrich Dürrenmatt's play, *The Visit* (1956)

In filming his adaptation of Friedrich Dürrenmatt's *The Visit*—or more precisely, Dürrenmatt's play as filtered through the 1964 film adaptation directed by Bernhard Wicki and starring Ingrid Bergman—Djibril Diop Mambéty kept the original story but gave it a Senegalese flavor. Billed as a representative of the World Bank, an incredibly rich woman, Linguere Ramatou (played by Ami Diakhate), returns to Colobane, the town of her birth—and, we eventually learn, her shame. In revenge for vicious treatment by her former lover Dramaan Drameh (played by Mansour Diouf), who had paid two other men to say they had slept with her, she promises the village elders to bankroll her economically depressed hometown if they will only do just one little thing for her: kill Drameh. Of course they refuse, with high moral statements about the sanctity of life; of course they gradually give in as they are seduced by the consumer goods "the visitor" can produce for them.

Both Drameh and Ramatou, Mambéty implies, are marginalized people: in the end, they are of Colobane but not acceptable to Colobane, for very different reasons. The townspeople, dressed in rice bags, literally devour Drameh like the hyenas they repre-

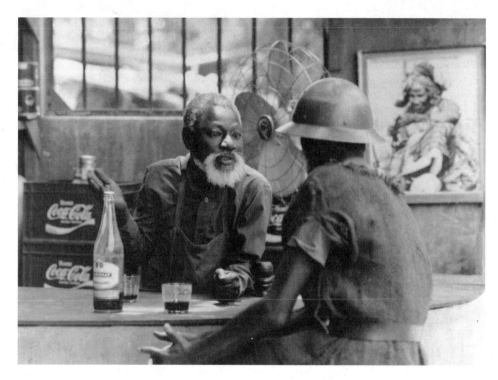

Hyenas: Sengalese merchant Dramaan Drameh (Mansour Diouf) defends his past behavior. Courtesy California Newsreel.

sent. After he vanishes, the town itself disappears under the blade of the bulldozer: what will rise in its place (Senegalese audiences would know) is "the real-life Colobane, a notorious thieves' market on the edge of Dakar" and, it turns out, the childhood home of the director (see Ukadike).

Even within the renaissance of African filmmaking at the end of the twentieth century, Mambéty was unusual, adapting a modern German play to African conditions. But more than that: acknowledging his culture's neocolonial background, he borrowed elephants from the Masai of Kenya and hyenas from Uganda, and to make it global, he borrowed Ramatou's bodyguard from Japan and imitated scenes from the annual Carnival of Humanity of the French Communist Party in France. Why? "My task was to identify the enemy of humankind: money, the International Monetary Fund, and the World Bank. I think my target is clear."

Recommended Readings

Pfaff, Francoise. *Twenty-Five Black African Filmmakers.* New York: Greenwood Press, 1988. An overview of Mambéty's career.

Stack, Peter. "African Parable of Greed." *San Francisco Chronicle*, 14 June 1995. Stresses Mambéty's vision of "the destruction of traditional values in Africa" by "European and American capitalism" in a remarkably beautiful and "funny, barbed parable."

Ukadike, N. Frank. "The Hyena's Last Laugh." *Transition* 78 (1999): 136–53. Interview with Mambéty and extensive discussions of his career and this film.

◄►◄►◄►

I Heart Huckabees

WAL-MART

2004, 106 mins., R, United States,
Director: David O. Russell
Screenplay: David O. Russell and Jeff Baena

Leaving aside one absurdity—that after saying "I Love New York" for a generation people are suddenly supposed to say "I Heart New York"—David O. Russell's strange satire has as many targets as Wal-Mart has aisles. On the surface Albert Markovski (played by Jason Schwartzman) is a failed liberal environmentalist: he has managed to save literally only one large rock from the site of a new branch of Huckabees, a big box chain whose headquarters—but none of the actual stores—fills the screen on occasion. Albert's environmental allies are tricked by Huckabees' lie that its new store will fulfill their goal of "open spaces." Huckabees' CEO, Brad Stand (played by Jude Law), and Dawn (played by Naomi Watts), his curvaceous girlfriend and Huckabees' ad icon, have modeled their motto on Wal-Mart's: "One store, one world."

But, like some of the business comedies of the 1950s, such *Desk Set* or *The Solid Gold Cadillac* (see *Working Stiffs* for both), the filmmakers are almost more interested in the romances and comic intersections of the characters than the corporate pursuit of cash and/or efficiency at any price.

The price, of course, is one's soul. Both corporate Brad and environmentalist Markovski hire the same two Existential Detectives, Bernard and Vivian (played by Dustin Hoffman and Lily Tomlin), to keep tabs on them and help explain their life choices. This pair of clowns are really Freudian therapists who forego intrusive questioning for outright voyeurism. Their greatest rival is another Existentialist Detective, Catherine (played by Isabelle Huppert), who soon convinces Albert, using her sexy French ways, that her blend of comic rough sex and masochism is better for him than anything else.

In the meantime Dawn, the heartthrob of Huckabees, thinks the company's ads should feature her dressed like an Amish milkmaid rather than in the halter top and short shorts she used to favor. In a manner somewhat similar to *Three Kings* (1999), Russell's earlier and brilliant film about the first Iraqi war (although with none of that film's consistent narrative verve), *I Heart Huckabees* shoots first and looks for a target later. Unlike big box real life, there are no workers in this film, no anti-union

campaigns, and even no actual Huckabees' store: it's all, Russell suggests, an elaborate illusion we pay for with our anxieties.

Recommended Reading

Dargis, Manohla. "On a Stroll in Angstville with Dots Disconnected." *New York Times*, 1 October 2004. Overall a very positive review, it is especially interested in firefighter Tommy (played by Mark Wahlberg), who sees through much of the world's illusions and feels its pain—"child labor, melting icecaps, the works."

▸◂▸◂

I Like to Work

Mi piace lavorare—mobbing

CHANGES IN THE WORKPLACE: EUROPE

2004, 89 mins., Italy, in Italian with English subtitles
Director: Francesca Comencini
Screenplay: Francesca Comencini

Whatever its origins in Italian popular vernacular, "mobbing" is the term used by Italians for the process by which a company applies psychological pressure and job humiliation to force an employee to resign. Bound often by union contract and strong national labor laws, Italian employers cannot fire a worker so easily. Instead they resort to petty job reassignments and snubbing to make a worker feel so unwanted they leave. (See *Fear and Trembling*, which suggests that Japanese business culture also uses such methods as routine modus operandi.)

Although the phenomenon is obviously widespread, the contemporary usage owes much to Heinz Leymann, a German-born Swedish researcher who popularized the concept of psychological bullying based on his studies of animal psychology in the 1980s and who subsequently opened a clinic for treatment of its victims (see his website at www .leymann.se).

Anna (played by Nicoletta Braschi) seems to be the unlikely target of an office vendetta. Her company has been sold to a multinational corporation and her supervisors are under pressure to shake things up. They began to reassign her from her usual post to more and more trivial tasks. She hangs on, however, despite the psychological toll and the disruption of her family life that the bullying causes; as a single parent she cannot give up her job. This is an extremely sympathetic portrait of a woman who at first has absolutely no idea that she has somehow been targeted. Indeed the film suggests that a fair amount of the bullying is in fact irrational and unconscious behavior on the part of her puffed-up supervisors.

Recommended Reading

Gravois, John. "Mob Rule." *Chronicle of Higher Education*, 14 April 2006, A10. Review of Leymann's research and a discussion of the phenomenon, citing studies that indicate "mobbing occurs most in institutions where workers have high job security."

▶◀▶◀

Inch'Allah dimanche

Thank God It's Sunday

MIGRANT LABOR (OTHER THAN
   THE UNITED STATES)
NEOCOLONIALISM

2001, 98 mins., France and Algeria, in French
   and Arabic with English subtitles
Director: Yamina Benguigui
Screenplay: Yamina Benguigui

French law and French culture governed the North African immigrants who came to France after World War II from the former colonies: the men were to be invisible in the public arena and they would return home when their services were no longer needed. But the work did not end. By 1974, Algerian women and children were finally allowed to join their husbands, although they were not necessarily welcomed. The memory of France's loss in the Algerian War of Independence (1954–62) lingered among many native French citizens.

Director Yamina Benguigui was born in France of Algerian immigrants, political activists who fought for Algerian independence. She tells the story of Zouina (played by Fejria Deliba), who in 1974 has come to an unnamed French provincial town with her three children and her husband's bossy mother, Aicha (played by Rabia Modadem), to join her husband. Ahmed (played by Zinedine Soualem) expects his wife to live Algerian style under the thumb of his mother. In part because she has no traditional Algerian peers and in part because she senses opportunities she would never have back home, Zouina follows a daring assimilationist path, sneaking out on Sundays and following the lead of a new friend, a French woman who works at the local makeup factory.

Zouina is doubly isolated, however, as an immigrant woman who struggles in one culture that she resists and in another she does not understand. Since any sign that these colonized citizens of France were integrated into their new society were rare—although the film has a few hopeful moments—the film cannot totally resolve Zouina's dilemma. Eventually her descendents will become a new kind of French resident, but until that time—and with its own tragedies evident in the riots in France in 2005—Zouina will not go back and may not be permitted to go forward.

Benguigui has noted in an interview that ironically women who remained behind often entered the public arena more resolutely in the new postcolonial Algerian society. But Benguigui's career has placed her in a struggle with French culture, fighting "to be able to work on subjects like this, subjects and realities that France isn't necessarily willing to acknowledge."

Recommended Reading

Alexander, Livia. "French-Algerian: A Story of Immigrants and Identity." *Satya Magazine* (online at www.satyamag.com/may02/index .htm), May 2002. Helpful interview with the director.

▶◀▶◀

The Inheritance

CHANGES IN THE WORKPLACE: EUROPE
GLOBAL CAPITAL

2003, 115 mins., Denmark, in Danish with
   English subtitles

Director: Per Fly
Screenplay: Per Fly and Kim Leona

When the patriarch of a Danish family commits suicide, he sets in motion a Shakespearian drama of succession for the leadership of the steel company he has mismanaged for a number of years. Ulrik, his son-in-law (played by Lars Brygmann), had been promised the top post even though he does not seem to be a leader. His son, Christoffer (played by Ulrich Thomsen), was always his father's first choice, but after a turn at the helm he decamped to Stockholm to run a restaurant and marry a beautiful actress. The Lady Macbeth of the piece, his mother, Annelise (played by Ghita Nørby) demands that Christoffer return as he is the only one with the talent to save the company.

Per Fly's film reflects our era of global corporate mergers. It becomes apparent that the Danish bankers will support Christoffer only if he downsizes his work force and consents to merge with a French competitor. To pull off this merger he must fire his brother-in-law and a number of others close to his family, including a foreman who babysat him. To remain competitive he must destroy all family ties and repress all emotion. His mother's temperament becomes his: when told by the bank to downsize 170 of his 900 employees Christoffer's reaction is to reduce the figure to 130. His mother tells him to fire 200 instead: that way a clear message of his control will be sent.

The film achieves an unusual and careful blend of family and corporate affairs: in the collapse of the families of the national bourgeoisie, Per Fly suggests, we see the collapse of the national corporation. Or vice versa.

The Inheritance is the upper-class segment of a trilogy: the first, *The Bench* (2000), was about working-class alcoholics; the third, *Manslaughter* (2005), featured middle-class individuals from the 1960s who run amuck.

Recommended Reading

Holden, Stephen. "An Executive's Hard Choices and the Toll They Take." *New York Times*, 9 July 2004. The film "is much too canny to be a glib anti-corporate screed" because "each excruciating decision Christoffer makes is critical to the company's well-being."

⋈⋈⋈

The Insider

INTELLECTUAL PROPERTY RIGHTS (TOBACCO)

1999, 155 mins., R, United States
Director: Michael Mann
Screenplay: Eric Roth and Michael Mann, from Marie Brenner's essay, "The Man Who Knew Too Much," *Vanity Fair*, May 1996

Director Michael Mann has been known for his stylish television shows (*Miami Vice*, 1984–89) and filmmaking (*Heat*, 1995, and *Collateral*, 2004) about conflicted cops and

The Insider: The whistleblower (Russell Crowe) conferring with the reporter (Al Pacino).

interesting bad guys. With *The Insider* he has created what could only be called an anticapitalist thriller: he adapts the suspense and violence characteristic of his usual crime-centered genres to the drama of a tobacco industry whistle-blower who feels that his life is threatened.

One of the greatest frauds of the modern era was perpetrated by the giant tobacco companies. The CEOs of these companies—whom the film and others refer to as the Seven Dwarves—testified under oath that all their research indicated that nicotine was nonaddictive. In fact they knew, as Jeffrey Wigand (played by Russell Crowe), who was the head of R & D for Brown & Williamson knew, that the industry not only understood the strength of the addiction but also developed specific chemical additives to heighten it.

The corporation knows that Wigand is not trustworthy with their secret, and they make him sign a confidentiality agreement. His need for health insurance for his family makes his compliance likely. Eventually he is tempted by crusading journalist Lowell Bergman, who wants him to do an interview with Mike Wallace (played by Christopher Plummer) for *60 Minutes* so badly he promises him the moon. But the show does not air: the threat of a lawsuit brings even the producers of *60 Minutes* to its knees. Wigand is now caught between the truth and a vindictive company.

Mann uses many genre elements of filmmaking—the sudden appearance of unknown figures in the night, eerie landscapes bathed in light, unexpected calls, and threatening messages—to convey the assault on Wigand, as it gradually becomes known that the billions in tobacco profits may be jeopardy. What Wigand knows is explosive and threatening. The business of a global company has rarely seemed so scary, in real life or on the screen.

Recommended Reading

Maslin, Janet. " 'The Insider': Mournful Echoes of a Whistle Blower." *New York Times*, 5 November 1999. Extols the complexity and style of the film: "Once Hollywood had a favorite folk tale: that the lone truth teller battling political or corporate evil would triumph" but in this tale

"almost every character is compromised by business considerations."

⋈⋈⋈

The Island

EARTH AS COLONY
INTELLECTUAL PROPERTY RIGHTS (GMOs)
SEX WORK/TRAFFICKING

2005, 136 mins., PG-13, United States
Director: Michael Bay
Screenplay: Caspian Tredwell-Owen, Alex Kurtzman, and Roberto Orci

While it may be a cliché that science fiction literature and film are more criticisms of contemporary society than speculations about a future world—think H. G. Wells's satire of Victorian social Darwinism in *The Time Machine* (1895)—*The Island* tries hard to make the future seem just an extension of, well, now. Ben & Jerry's ice cream is still for sale in 2019, and other corporate heavies such as Mack truck, Michelob Light, and Cadillac all get to pose for their (branded) close up. The villain of the film is also a corporation, the kind of future organization typical of such films as *Blade Runner* (1982): whoever controls the science controls the globe.

The science in *The Island* is cloning human beings. In this instance the clones are insurance products for individuals who for $5 million get to have a clone ready for spare parts (kidney, heart, etc.) when the need arises. To keep business humming the corporation makes the clones docile (maximum mental age is 15), isolates them in a sealed enclosure because—they believe—they are survivors from a contaminated and now lifeless world, and gives them the pseudo hope that they can win a lottery and be transported to the Island, the last safe natural habitat on earth.

One clone, Lincoln Six Echo (played by Ewan McGregor) begins to exhibit an unexpected curiosity about his limited world: Why do we wear white? Why is Tuesday always tofu night? He is attracted to Jordan Two Delta (played by Scarlet Johansson) who—remember, they are emotionally and mentally teenagers—tries to teach Lincoln how to scam the equivalent of a high school cafeteria worker but eventually is much more successful as his pupil learning how to French kiss him.

Although the science in the film is not entirely crystal clear, the insurance product was originally going to be an undifferentiated organism of body parts, but that idea didn't work out. A failure of stem cell research perhaps? A critique of same? Hard to say, because the politics of the film are also murky: Roger Ebert and other critics are bothered by the seeming independence of the megacorporation from any government scrutiny, but that is a feature that comes with the genre.

The look of the film and the exposition of the plot provide an intriguing first hour or so, but then the film descends into what may be a record for the number of car chases. The teenage clones get lots of exercise running from the corporate hit men, as they break out into the real world, which turns out, of course, not to be contaminated at all, unless you count the congestion they encounter on the Los Angeles freeways. Director Michael Bay does go in a few directions others have avoided: the birth of a baby to one of the clones, for example, and the subsequent euthanizing of the mother as the baby is handed over to human parents is a sequence that will generate a shudder or two.

Bay channels films such as *Coma* (1978) for the harvesting of human spare parts, *Logan's Run* (1976) for the biosphere and limited life span of the clones, and *Blade Runner* for the corporate manipulation and creation of humanoids. Like *Blade Runner*, the film suggests that curiosity makes us human, but Bay uses another old standby of the tradition: the hero develops a conscience and a desire to rescue fellow clones and kick some corporate butt. We have a satisfying collapse of the clones' biosphere, and in an ending exactly the same as *Logan's Run* we witness the clones streaming to freedom. How their policyholders are going to react is maybe part of a sequel.

With almost no exceptions, postapocalyptic science fiction posits a powerful global corporation that loses out to the little people. Even though the globe itself is at risk, usually a small band of humans (or their equivalent) get to light out for the territories and freedom. *The Island* plays some variants on this familiar scenario and even manages to hang a CEO in the end.

Recommended Reading

Ebert, Roger. "This Island is No Paradise." *Chicago Sun-Times*, 22 July 2005. Compares the film unfavorably to Kazuo Ishiguro's novel *Never Let Me Go* (2005) because the film doesn't sufficiently pursue an important part of the novel's message—that "the real world raises many of its citizens as spare parts; they are used as migratory workers, minimum-wage retail slaves, even suicide bombers."

ⵗⵗⵗ

Is Wal-Mart Good for America?

CHINA
WAL-MART

2004, 60 mins., United States
Director: Rick Young
Correspondent: Hedrick Smith
TV Documentary
Distributor: PBS

In just one program, *Frontline* develops a remarkable perspective on two of the most important players in globalization—China and Wal-Mart. In fact viewers may easily come to the opinion that Wal-Mart is some kind of equal international partner of China, so thoroughly have the fortunes of both been intertwined. The numbers are amazing: of the $36 billion imported to America from China in 2003, Wal-Mart accounts for almost half or even more of that figure, with a low estimate of $15 billion and a high estimate of $30. (One would think these figures would be a matter of record, but it has not always been in Wal-Mart's interest to publicize its close ties with China after decades of promoting the mantra "Buy American.")

Correspondent Hedrick Smith takes us on a tour of three aspects of Wal-Mart's global effect. We visit Terminal Island, where the twin container ship ports of Long Beach and Los Angeles processed 28 million tons of Chinese goods in 2004, up from 2 million tons in 1990. Wal-Mart, the number one customer, welcomes entire ships with six to eight thousand containers each. The cranes, operated by unionized longshoremen (a significantly reduced work crew compared to precontainer days), cost $6.5 million each and were also made in China.

The next two ports of call are landlocked: Circleville, Ohio, where an RCA plant, Thomson Consumer Electronics, employed a thousand workers from a local population of only thirteen thousand. When Wal-Mart demanded, as it always does, the lowest possible cost of goods for its stores, Thomson outsourced its manufacturing to China. (And Wal-Mart built a supercenter in the field next to the vacant Thomson plant.)

The final visit is to an Australian businessman who opened Hayco, a business in a town north of Shenzhen, China, that supplies electric toothbrushes and home-cleaning products to big American companies like 3M, Procter and Gamble and Wal-Mart. He relies on the low wages of Chinese workers, most of them migrants from rural areas, to keep his costs so low that Wal-Mart will agree to buy his goods. But it is Wal-Mart who calls the shots: "Wal-Mart has reversed a hundred-year history that had the retailer dependent on the manufacturer," argues Nelson Lichtenstein in the film; now the "retailer is the center, the power" of the supply chain.

As an introduction to the essence of Wal-Mart, *Frontline*'s compact presentation is hard to beat. Many other documentaries emphasize Wal-Mart's impact on American markets and workers, but *Frontline* makes the connections global.

Recommended Reading

Bonacich, Edna, and Khaleelah Hardie. "Wal-Mart and the Logistics Revolution." In *Wal-Mart: The Face of Twenty-First Century Capitalism*, ed. Nelson Lichtenstein. New York: New Press, 2006, 163–87. How Wal-Mart and China move their goods around the world.

▷◁▷◁▷◁
It's All True

HISTORY OF GLOBALIZATION
LABOR HISTORY

1942 (1993), 86 mins., B & W and color, G, United States
Directors: Richard Wilson, Myron Meisel, and Bill Krohn, using film sequences directed by Orson Welles
Mixed Traditional Documentary and Ethnographic Fiction

Even those viewers familiar with Orson Welles's masterpiece *Citizen Kane* (1941) or the cloudy left-leaning politics of his early career may find enough irony in *It's All True* to last until still another lost masterpiece of Welles is uncorked. The young Welles was sent, improbably enough, to Brazil as part of the American government's plan to solidify our relationships with South American dictatorships who might be susceptible to Nazi wiles or perhaps their gold.

Welles planned a three-part Latino tour of a film: a child's story in Mexico (*My Friend Bonito*), carnival in Rio (*The Story of Samba*), and a homage to an amazing sea journey of four fishermen along Brazil's eastern coast (*Four Men on a Raft,* formerly known as *Jangadeiros*). Enough footage from this incomplete project survives to give us a sense that this would have been an unusual film in keeping with a number of projects (Sergei Eisenstein's *Que Viva Mexico* and John Steinbeck's *The Forgotten Village,* for example, both in *Working Stiffs*) that examined the poor and Indian workers in Latino countries in the 1930s and 1940s.

Brazil in the 1940s was run by the dictator Getúlio Vargas, who ruled with some Nazi sympathizers close to the throne. Welles himself was a semi-lefty. Thus when he came upon the samba schools, he realized that they represented an extraordinary presence, representing an implicit challenge to the status quo with their racial diversity and hill-shanty poverty. What he didn't realize, perhaps, was that such sentiments would not be popular with Brazilian cryptofascists or RKO for that matter.

Robert Stam argues that Welles's film "constituted a radical departure from Hollywood modes of production and norms of cultural representation." The celebration of heroic fishermen and the mixed race and black Brazilians mark this film as an unusually sympathetic interpretation of a culture too often regarded as only exotic.

Welles's project was further compromised by the drowning death of one of the *jangadeiros* during filming. Such a tragedy emphasizes the dangers faced by the raftsmen, of course, but Welles wanted to capture the spirit and survival skills of mestizo workers. Stam concludes that *It's All True* is an ode "to Africanized-indigenized mestizo commmunties" and a refutation of the "myth of the lazy native." Only some of that ode survives.

Recommended Readings

Ebert, Roger. "It's All True." *Chicago Sun-Times,* 27 October 1993. "In its more heroic moments it looks like something by Sergei Eisenstein."

Higham, Charles. *The Films of Orson Welles.* Berkeley: University of California Press, 1970. Includes a chapter on *It's All True*, with detailed analysis of the film's surviving footage, stills, and a history of the production.

Stam, Robert. *Tropical Multiculturalism.* Durham: Duke University Press, 1997. Stam's "comparative history of race in Brazilian cinema and culture" includes an excellent chapter on the production and Brazilian context of the film.

⋈⋈⋈

The Jaguar Quartet

MIGRANT LABOR (OTHER THAN THE UNITED STATES)
NEOCOLONIALISM

Jaguar, 1954–67, 91 mins.
Petit a Petit, 1969, 90 mins.
Cocorico! Monsieur Poulet, 1974, 90 mins.
Madame L'Eau, 1992, 90 mins.
France and Niger, in French with English subtitles or voice-overs
Director: Jean Rouch
Ethnographic Fictions

Distributor: Documentary Education Resources

Jean Rouch's unusual cinematic exploration of the former French colonies of the southwest Ivory Coast—the Gold Coast (now Ghana), Togo, Dahomey (now Benin), and Niger—evolved from both necessity (synchronizing sound and speaker was not possible then) and intention (following nonprofessional actors in their quest for jobs and economic security). His is an invaluable record of short-term or annual migratory labor in Africa beginning in an era when such topics were virtually ignored or considered only a subject for anthropologists.

Rouch filmed extensively in the field, using individuals who would "play" themselves in typical situations they faced trying to make a living. In postproduction Rouch used voice-over narration in which they remember what happened, make jokes, and sometimes reflect upon a given action, a continuation of what Rouch believed was a dialogue between his participants and himself, an "audio-visual feedback" (see Bickerton).

Although Rouch did not use the term "quartet," these four feature-length films use the same three nonprofessional actors from Niger who, in the first film, *Jaguar,* migrate east through Dahomey (through the home of the naked Somba people whom the men mock for their savage ways) to cities in the Gold Coast. Lam, the herdsman, takes a job as a cattle herder for a butcher in Kumasi, while in Accra Illo, the fisherman, becomes a dockworker and Damoure, formerly unemployed, becomes a foreman at a lumberyard. The three friends regroup in Kumasi, and with the aid of a fourth friend, Duma (who has tried gold mining), they set up a market stall, Petit a Petit, to sell everything under the sun. Despite the success of the stall, the homesick men head back and show off their wealth and "western" manners, become "jaguars," slick and confident men with money, sunglasses, playing the role of "wild boys," as cool as can be ("I only speak English," says Damoure, but "let's show the poor people" what we brought back home).

The other films in the quartet are all variations on this initial journey and the economic realities of French colonialism. In *Petit a Petit* (*Little by Little*) their stall has prospered and the men decide they need to travel to Paris to learn how the French live in tall apartment buildings: when they return home to Niger their construction scheme to build a similar building fails and they assemble in a straw hut to think in African terms. In *Cocorico! Monsieur Poulet* (*The Crowing of the Rooster*) the men form a company to take chickens into the bush for resale; their pathetic Citroen leads them into supernatural episodes as they live as "marginal" workers, in Rouch's voice-over, trying to outmaneuver "the economic absurdity of the system."

Madame L'Eau (*Madam Water*) tackles the African problem of drought. The men try to find an alternative to expensive electric pumps that carry the water of the gradually receding Niger River to their fields. They travel to Holland to find experts who will consult (for no fee) on how to transport water. After rejecting technologically advanced steel windmills they hit upon a simple plan: a wooden windmill that local carpenters can construct. A month after bringing back a kit and a helpful engineer, it works successfully on the Niger, even irrigating a field of tulips.

Although Rouch had already begun *Jaguar*, *Moi, un noir* (*I, a Negro,* 1959) was the first film he released using his characteristic approach. In that film he cast a different set of three men to travel from Niger to Abidjan in the Ivory Coast as casual laborers. It was his intention, he said, to "mix fiction with reality" since "fiction is the only way to penetrate reality." A more controversial film, *Les maitres fous* (*The Crazy Masters*), was banned after its release in a number of African countries because it depicted members of the Hauka, an anti-French sect, mocking colonial officials. Rouch's innovative filmmaking, as Bickerton argues, came at "the moment of decolonization in West Africa," when "Rouch was not only uniquely open to the transition but, through his camera, an active participant in the process."

One of the remarkable happenstances of *Jaguar* is the inclusion of scenes of the assassinated nationalist leader Kwame Nkrumah campaigning. This footage turned out to be unique, as the leaders of the CIA-sponsored military coup d'etat that deposed Nkrumah in 1966 systematically destroyed any visual records of him. This political erasure was unfortunately part of neocolonial realpolitik when colonies gained political independence and national elites colluded with the former colonial powers.

Recommended Readings

Bickerton, Emilie. "The Camera Possessed: Jean Rouch, Ethnographic Cineaste, 1917–2004." *New Left Review* 27 (May–June 2004): 49–63. Argues for Rouch's special role in adapting Robert Flaherty's participatory filmmaking (in which Flaherty encouraged Nanook of the 1921 film *Nanook of the North* to comment on the rushes of the film and then included those comments in the final cut) to an "anti-colonial ethnography."

Rouch, Jean. *Cine-Ethnography.* Minneapolis: University of Minnesota Press, 2003. The definitive edition of Rouch's writings; also extensive interviews and discussions with the filmmaker, on all of his projects including *The Jaguar Quartet.*

Stoller, Paul. *The Cinematic Griot: The Ethnography of Jean Rouch.* Chicago: University of Chicago Press, 1992. Detailed discussion of Rouch's method and many of his ethnofictions.

▶▶▶

Knock Off

ANTI-GLOBALIZATION

2004, 45 mins., Germany/United States,
  English with some German subtitles
Directors: Anette Baldauf and Katharina
  Weingartner
Cinema-Verité Documentary
Distributor: First Run/Icarus Films

"F is for Fake," proclaims the title of one of Orson Welles' lesser-known films. And of the many consumer capitals of fake New York City is one of the biggest, especially a strip extending from Canal Street in Chinatown and nearby Soho, up Broadway the length of Manhattan, with stops at both Times Square and Harlem thrown in the mix. The *Knock Off* filmmakers see the trade in fakes as rebellion

Knock Off: Avoiding the logo police in New York City. Courtesy First Run/Icarus Films.

against corporate branding: the film's subtitle is "Revenge on the Logo." They film anticorporate activist Hyun Lee's gleeful speech: "The only way we can survive is to outsmart the system: piracy and doing things off the books, that's part of how we survive."

Most shoppers who buy knock-offs of luxury consumer goods will probably applaud the speech of one of the shoppers interviewed: "You find it on Canal Street and feel like you're fooling the world. I got this! And no one knows it's a fake."

The German filmmakers love the New York City streets and it shows: they linger over shots of Prada's flagship store in Soho, conceived as a performance space for shoppers, a Times Square rally with Rev. Billy of the Church of Stop Shopping, and a raid on a salesman's stall on Canal Street during which a policeman cheerfully explains how they will grind the confiscated watches to pieces.

At one point the film comes to a brief philosophical turning point, when the subject of Gucci handbags and their knock-offs are discussed: what if Gucci is outsourcing the production of these bags to the same factory in China where the knock-offs are being made? Although the film does not pursue this puzzle of globalization it gives the shoppers we see in the film a moment's thought before they go ahead and buy—which?

Recommended Reading

Land, Joshua. "Screed is Good." *Village Voice,* 4 January 2004. Suggests that the film "never quite manages to account for the mysterious appeal of designer labels, but it does embrace the relevant if unoriginal idea that the knockoff is often even better than the real thing."

▶◀▶◀▶◀

Life and Debt

EXPORT PROCESSING ZONES
TRANSNATIONAL ORGANIZATIONS

2001, 86 mins., United States
Director: Stephanie Black
Traditional Documentary

"How can the machete compete with the machine?" a Jamaican farmer asks in distress when two staple industries of the Jamaican economy—milk for internal consumption, bananas for export—decline because of the Jamaican government's agreement with the WTO and the World Bank to abandon local subsidies. With trade barriers no longer in place, cheap imported milk powder undercut domestic milk production, and the Jamaican banana industry—a modest 5 percent of the world's market compared to Chiquita's and Dole's combined share of 95 percent—was hauled before the WTO because it had a tariff-free exclusive contract with the United Kingdom. When the WTO ruled in favor of the United States, acting mainly in the interests of Chiquita, Jamaica's locally owned plantations were no longer viable. Soon banana workers' wages plunged to $1 per day, and the model imposed on the country's plantations was that of the Chiquita plantations of Honduras, where workers were routinely brutalized and in many cases killed by their own military.

Two stories alternate in *Life and Debt*: in one, American tourists come to Jamaica to play, drink, swim, and sightsee; in the other, Jamaica as an independent economic entity dies. The two stories are related, of course, but the mechanism of the relationship has been obscured by glossy photographs of beaches and bikinis. This "island in the sun" (to use its 1950s nickname, as well as the title of a Hollywood melodrama, included in *Working Stiffs*) lost its economic self-sufficiency because the main forces in globalization—the WTO and World Bank—made it an offer it could not refuse.

What did Jamaica gain by accepting loans from the World Bank? The right to have the Kingston Free Zone, an Export Processing Zone where identical gray garment factories assemble materials carted a short distance from containerized boats and reloaded when the garments are finished. In short, another global sweatshop, where workers earn $30 every two weeks. In one remarkable sequence, we see Asian workers—imported from where?!—being bussed in when Jamaican workers refuse to work.

The filmmakers highlight a secret report from the World Bank, which stated that Jamaica has "achieved neither growth nor poverty reduction." This is an exemplary documentary about the mechanisms of globalization. Its voice-over narration comes from Jamaica Kincaid's *A Small Place*, written about Antigua not Jamaica, which suggests that this is a regional story as well.

Recommended Readings

Holden, Stephen. "One Love, One Heart, or a Sweatshop Economy? *New York Times*, 15 June 2001. "The movie offers the clearest analysis of globalization and its negative effects that I've ever seen on a movie or television screen."

Kincaid, Jamaica. *A Small Place*. New York: Farrar Straus Giroux, 1987. Although Kincaid's scathing nonfiction essay is about the ruination of Antigua, her island home, many of her targets are similar in Jamaica and other Caribbean islands.

Rapley, John. "Debating *Life and Debt*." *The Jamaican Gleaner* (online at www.jamaica -gleaner.com/gleaner/20010823/cleisure/ cleisure3.html). One Jamaican's view from the island's only morning newspaper: the film is a successful polemic, but there is irony in relying on Prime Minister Michael Manley as a spokesman for anti-globalization since "many argue that it was the policies of Michael Manley's government in the 1970s which first led Jamaica into the hands of the IMF."

Tate, Greg. "Journey Through Debtor's Prison." *Village Voice,* 13 June 2001. The film exposes "globalization as genocide by calculator."

▸▸▸

Lilya 4–Ever

SEX WORK/TRAFFICKING

2002, 109 mins., R, Sweden/Denmark, in Swedish and Russian with English subtitles
Director: Lucas Moodysson
Screenplay: Lucas Moodysson

In 2000 a Lithuanian teenager, Dangoule Rasaleite, threw herself from the window of an apartment in the Swedish city of Arlov where she had been imprisoned and forced to work as a prostitute. European sex trafficking doesn't receive the headlines of its Asian counterparts, but the global exploitation of girls and women there is no less fierce. Typically the girls come from the former Soviet Union or its satellites, often tricked into believing that a legitimate job lies at the end of the path of the faked passport and agreeable contact. A term for these East European girls has even evolved—they are "Natashas," a disturbing synonym for prostitutes.

Moodysson transformed Rasaleite's story—and perhaps that of hundreds like her—into the tale of Lilya, a teenager in a city in the former Soviet Union whose dead end life is further complicated when her mother abandons her and her aunt forces her out of her apartment. She befriends a pathetic neighborhood boy, is tempted into selling herself at a local disco, and is ultimately sold into sexual slavery. She ends up in a Swedish city and is forced along the same hellish path as Rasaleite.

This film is so brutal and disturbing (the point of view shots of Lilya during forced sex are un-precedented) that it will adamantly convince most viewers that there is little room to define prostitution as sex work as opposed to human trafficking. Even the slight indication of Lilya's assent and connivance in prostituting herself at first is no justification for what follows.

Recommended Reading

Graffy, Julian. "Trading Places." *Sight & Sound,* April 2003, 20–22. Discussion of the film in the context of other contemporary Russian films about "the suffocating tedium of provincial life and the dream of leaving" the country for a new life.

▶◀▶◀▶◀

The Little Girl Who Sold the Sun

La petite vendeuse de soleil

NEOCOLONIALISM

1999, 45 mins., Senegal/Switzerland, in Wolof with English subtitles

The Little Girl Who Sold the Sun: The Little Girl (Lisa Balera) and her friend (Tayerou M'Baye) selling newspapers on the streets. Courtesy California Newsreel.

Director: Djibril Diop Mambéty
Screenplay: Djibril Diop Mambéty
Distributor: California Newsreel

The economic background of all three of Djibril Diop Mambéty's films in this book is France's collusion with the World Bank, keeping former French colonies such as Senegal at the mercy of economic forces they cannot control. In *Le Franc* the French devaluation of the West African franc is literally the name of a lottery won by a the street musician; in *Hyenas* a billionaire somehow related to the World Bank buys a town's acquiescence in her vigilante justice. In *The Little Girl Who Sold the Sun* we see a headline that predicts an event that has yet to happen: "Africa Leaves the Franc Zone."

Mambéty begins his tale of the "global economy" (as the film refers to it) by tracking a diverse lot of Senegalese as they approach a central market: our little heroine, Sili Laam (played by Lisa Balera), is on crutches, a legless boy is in a wheelchair, and countless others use everything from horse carts to an unlikely Mercedes to make their way. In the background of a shot of a man splitting rocks with a hammer a jumbo jet takes off. The street market in Mambéty's world becomes metaphoric for the world market—free, seemingly uncontrolled, but at the mercy of ruthless competitors, whether they are teenage gangs or the World Bank.

We don't meet Sili at first. Instead we witness a disturbing incident: a woman is arrested by the police as a shoplifter, abused when she resists arrest, and taken off to the nearby jail. She insists that she is a princess, not a thief, but the crowd mocks her. When Sili herself is dragged off to the same police station because an officer thinks she has too much cash in hand, she bravely denounces him for, in effect, asking for a bribe, and wins not only her freedom but the freedom of the poor woman arrested earlier. Sili is a brave girl attempting to break through the forces that control the market, both literally (the police and gangs of rival salesboys) and metaphorically (the Western countries).

Sili, with the help of one sympathetic boy,

Babou Seck (played by Tayerou M'Baye), struggles to make a success of her newspaper sales. Babou sells *The Nation*, which Sili considers the establishment paper, while she sells *The Sun*, because "the people read it." If anyone could "sell the sun," this street child can. When a gang of rival street vendors steals her crutches, Sili's friend asks, "What can we do?" She replies, "We continue."

Recommended Readings

Ukadike, N. Frank. "The Hyena's Last Laugh." *Transition* 78 (1999): 136–53. Extensive interview with Mambéty, including a discussion of his use of nonprofessionals as his leading actors.

Verniere, James. "Girl and 'Sun' Are Glorious." *Boston Herald,* 31 December 1999. Calls the film "proof [that] neo-realism is as viable and useful a style today as it was in postwar Italy."

⊢⊢⊢⊢

Live Nude Girls Unite!

SEX WORK/TRAFFICKING

2001, 70 mins., United States
Directors: Vicky Funari and Julia Query
Agit-Prop Documentary

There is no doubt in my mind that this film gets a lot of attention for the wrong reasons. But if the viewer stays the course and is not offended by the subject matter, the lead dancer/organizer will soon convince you that she and her sister sex workers deserve to have a union local of their own. Unfortunately for Julia Query, dancer and filmmaker, her intention was to keep her job a secret from her mom, Joyce Wallace, a doctor who leads a crusade to bring condoms to sex workers on the streets and has a national reputation for her sex education work.

I won't spoil the moment of confrontation between Julia and her mother, but suffice it to say that mom, despite her vocation, is mightily surprised at what she learns. For Julia turns out to be lesbian stand-up comic as well as a peep-show dancer and union organizer.

Julia works and organizes at the Lusty Ladies, a North Beach peep-show house, where men pay to watch "the ladies" dance, originally through a one-way mirror but eventually—because the women complained that the men were filming their act—through a window.

The organizing campaign raised issues such as the preferential treatment of white dancers over black dancers, and blond, white women over dark-haired women. We are at the far end of the spectrum of sex work and trafficking in this film, where the women fight for—and occasionally gain—some control over their working lives.

Recommended Readings

Cooper, Marc. "The Naked and the Red." *Nation,* 21 April 2003, 21–23. Report on organizing efforts among Las Vegas exotic dancers (six thousand strong).

Ebert, Roger. "Live Nude Girls Unite!" *Chicago Sun Times,* 22 June 2001. "She's a spirited Union Maid, and she and her sister organizers make labor history. She's the kind of woman Studs Terkel was born to interview."

Thomas, Kevin. "Sex Workers Try to Unionize in *Live Nude Girls Unite!*" *Los Angeles Times,* 23 March 2001. Reviewer argues that "any consideration of sex work as a legitimate occupation deserving of the same protections and security as other forms of employment is inevitably controversial and ever the source of often stupefying hypocrisy."

ㅑㅑㅑ

Maid in America

TRANSNATIONAL MIGRATION

2004, 58 mins., United States
Director: Anayansi Prado
Traditional Documentary
Distributor: Women Make Movies

While the narrator, Latina actress Lupe Ontiveros (who has herself played too many stereotypical Latina roles in films such as *El Norte,* in *Working Stiffs*), stresses the sobering statistics on domestic workers in Los Angeles—over a hundred thousand of them, 70 percent Latina, earning $5 per hour with no benefits—Anayansi Prado's film is as much about hard work as it is about motherhood. Two of the three women featured in the film are also nannies for the families whose houses they clean. As Telma, who works exclusively for African American families, says about taking care of a little boy from infancy through kindergarten: "You start to love him as if he were your own." His parents relate their shock when their son began calling their nanny "Mommy." During one sequence with this family we see photographs of two or three generations of their ancestors with the white children they raised and the white women they cleaned for.

Prado's film is filled with telling moments like that. Another nanny/domestic, Judith, left four daughters behind in Guatemala whom she hasn't seen in two years; she uses the occasion of the birth of her fifth child, Everest ("like the mountain") as the occasion to journey home, well aware that she and her husband may not be able to get back to the United States. At one point she mentions, with only a touch of irony, that when Everest—an American citizen by virtue of his birthplace—is eighteen he can claim his sisters as legal immigrants and bring them to America.

The film also features two organizations that help domestic workers achieve some autonomy as workers: the Coalition for Human Rights in L.A. (CHIRLA) has a domestic workers unit and the organization called Strategic Actions for a Just Economy (SAJE) operates a cooperative owned and operated by the workers themselves. The film demonstrates that although domestic workers and nannies never have it easy, they are nonetheless attempting to gain a measure of understanding, if not control, over their work lives.

Recommended Reading

Milanovic, Anji. "Maid in America." *La Plume Noire* (online at www.plume-noire.com). Discusses whether the children in the film "will either grow up seeing Latinas as their servants or, hopefully . . . will grow up with an appreciation of another culture and language different from their own."

▶◀▶

Mandabi

Le mandat
The Money Order

NEOCOLONIALISM

1968, 90 mins., Senegal, in French or Wolof
with English subtitles
Director: Ousmane Sembene
Screenplay: Ousmane Sembene, from his
own novel, *The Money Order* (1966)

The great theme in many films by Ousmane Sembene from Senegal, one of the most influential African directors, is the distortion of communal or village morality by France's colonial legacy. *Mandabi*, unlike his earlier *Xala* (in *Working Stiffs*), which opens with an explicit transfer of economic power from the French colonial elite to the new national bourgeoisie, dramatizes only a seemingly small incident in postcolonial Senegal, but the corrupting power of the French franc is nonetheless common to both films.

In *Mandabi* the filmmaker leaves the world of Ibrahim Dieng (played by Makhouredia Gueye), an unemployed but moderately middle-class Muslim living in Dakar, only once: in Paris we see an immigrant worker sweeping the streets with what could only be described as a traditional African twig broom. His voice-over tells us that he saves his wages and sends them back to his people by *mandabi* (a money order.) It is Ibrahim who receives his nephew's money order from Paris, but he cannot cash it. He needs an identification card, but to get that he needs both a birth certificate, which the city hall workers won't give him because they are too busy discussing their own scams, and passport photos, which he tries to obtain but is swindled by men at a booth in the market. And on and on.

In the end another nephew, very middle class, suave, and friendly, cheats him out of the whole amount of the money order, only part of which—Ibrahim reminds this ruthless relative—was actually his: the rest actually belonged to his Parisian nephew. Although Ibrahim knows his nephew is lying, he is

helpless at this point. In Sembene's world the punishment rarely fits the crime: Ibrahim is a bossy, vain patriarch, with two wives, but he does not deserve the endless parade of beggars, con artists, and fawning friends that make up his community.

Since every Senegalese official is either bent or abetted by another corrupt go-between we must wonder if Senegal can survive this calamitous system. When the postman returns at the end of the film he tells Ibrahim that only he and citizens like him can change this system. It's only the faintest of hope for a formerly communal society where faith, respect for elders, and sharing were high values. Ibrahim's neighborhood grocer, initially very helpful, is hoping he defaults on his bills, because he knows someone who wants to buy his house.

Recommended Reading

Pfaff, Francoise. *The Cinema of Osmene Sembene*. Westport: Greenwood, 1984. An early appreciation of Sembene's films.

▶◀▶

Maquila: A Tale of Two Mexicos

OUTSOURCING AND OFFSHORING

2000, 55 mins., United States
Directors: Saul Landau and Sonia Angulo
Agit-Prop Documentary
Distributor: Cinema Guild

If there are two Mexicos, as the film argues and, I believe, successfully demonstrates, one is an overly compliant client-state of the United States hosting maquiladoras or sweatshops along the border, and the other is a rebellious political entity of the Global South, where the Zapatistas (the EZLN or Zapatista Army for National Liberation) have briefly seized towns and land in Chiapas, reprising their namesake's cry of "Tierra y Libertad" (Land and Liberty) during the Mexican Revolution in the early twentieth century.

The filmmakers' strategy is clear and direct: build into every sequence where possible the contrast between the Maya people of Chiapas attempting to regain their communal lands and the thousands of Mexican border workers, mostly young women, trying to survive in shantytowns. The filmmakers are astute enough to realize that there are some gray areas here: women working in the maquiladoras admit that they don't long to return to their rural roots, where the work was also very hard and in drought seasons, no harvests meant widespread hunger and misery. One even says: "Here we earn more and live better."

The film is punctuated by a soundtrack that uses popular forms—rap and the corrido or border ballad—to sing of the two Mexicos. In "The New World Order Rap" "crops are replaced with maquiladoras / Hundreds of peasants, señors and señoras / Gotta make their way to the city by the border." In "El Corrido de la Maquila" a worker leaves "the fields behind her / Hot sundried earth and *el patron*" for the "bright lights, robots, computers" of the factory.

Violence in various forms is not far from either Mexico. The commander of the occupying troops in Chiapas cries out to peasants that "we're all brothers, Mexicans," before his troops attack, and in the wastelands around Ciudad Juarez hundreds of young women are found dead, victims of unknown marauders taking advantage of their vulnerability.

In many of the sequences the filmmakers cut from donkeys to forklifts, from lush vegetation to sandy shantytowns. The filmmakers are angry and it shows. (Saul Landau also directed *The Sixth Sun*, 1996, exclusively on the Zapatistas, while Lourdes Portillo's film, *Señorita Extraviada*, 2002, chronicles the missing young women of the borderlands.) If there are crimes against humanity uniquely a part of globalization, this film will serve as partial documentation of them.

Recommended Reading

Bacon, David. *The Children of NAFTA: Labor Wars on the U.S./Mexico Border*. Berkeley: University Of California Press, 2004. Combining both his excellent photography and journalistic eye, Bacon explores the difficulties Mexicans and immigrants face when they try to organize on either side of the border.

▶◀▶◀▶◀
Mardi Gras: Made in China

CHINA

2005, 72 mins., United States, in English and
    Mandarin with English subtitles
Director: David Redmon
Cinema-Verité Documentary

In 1978 two seemingly unrelated but momentous events occurred: Deng Xiaoping put an end to Maoism by endorsing the "capitalist road" for China (although only old-line Marxists called it that) but said, "It doesn't matter if a cat is black or white as long as it catches mice" and women in New Orleans began flashing their breasts during Mardi Gras parades to score more beads from passing floats.

David Redmon's film is the clear and damning story of how Chinese capitalism and globalization have created the Tai Kuen Bead Factory in a tax-free Special Economic Zone in Fuzhou. Hundreds of teenagers, mostly girls, work up to sixteen hours a day for ten cents an hour to make the millions of beads that Mardi Gras revelers need for the bodacious New Orleans parade scene. The girls also make assorted other souvenirs, including little porcelain figurines with exaggerated sexual organs.

The teenagers get Sunday off but some days must work twenty hours in a row and then go back to work after four hours of sleep. The factory is a classic sweatshop: dangerous machines and high production quotas. We hear the owner, Roger Wong, cheerfully announce a 10 percent bonus if the girls exceed their quota and a 5 percent fine if they don't. One girl points to four open bags near her machines and says her quota requires her to fill all four but that she is likely to get only one done.

Back in New Orleans the filmmaker capture the frenzy of the crowds as more and more women lift their T-shirts and earn their beads. A handful of interviewees haven't the slightest idea where their beads come from, but one or two catch on only to remark that such information will inhibit their fun.

The owner is a cheerful Hong Kong capitalist who glows with confidence and patriarchal benevolence. One of the more revealing sequences contrasts his opulent American-style house with the cramped spartan dormitories of the girls and one girl's extremely modest family home.

The film is riveting as it reveals the dark side of globalized producers of goods for a less than wholesome set of consumers. I suspect that very few of the naughty frat boys and sorority girls who cram the French Quarter every February will see this film.

The film concludes with Wong's plans to make American holiday trinkets. He does sound like the kind of new Chinese capitalist who would not package an Easter bunny toy in a Christmas tree box, one of my purchases (Made in China) a few years ago.

In a coda to the film, one Chinese teenager reacts to takes from *Mardi Gras* screened for the workers when Redmon returns to the factory: "They remove their clothes? Because they like our beads that much?" Perhaps if they learn more about American capitalism Roger Wong won't always think that women are the better workers because, as he says, they are "easier to control." But their family loyalty, lack of education, and the widespread pressure to migrate for jobs remain strong.

Recommended Reading

Gonzalez, Ed. "Mardi Gras: Made in China." *Slant Magazine*, 2005 (online at www.slant magazine.com/film/film_review.asp?ID=1833). A very positive review: "If Redmon's disturbing interactions with some Mardi Gras partiers who'd rather see boobies than his Tai Kuen footage are any indication, the director's goal is simply to inspire empathy."

ᴴᴴᴴ

The Mark Thomas Comedy Product

ANTI-GLOBALIZATION

1996–2003, TV series, 46 episodes of 30 mins. each; 2 episodes of 60 mins. each, United Kingdom
Directors: Steve Connelly, Michael Cumming, Andy de Emmony, Jenny Morgan, Stephen Rankin, and Mike Warner
Principal Writer: Mark Thomas

Despite six different directors and a name change—"comedy" was dropped from the title in 2000—Mark Thomas's Channel 4 British television series stayed remarkably close to the vision of a chronicler of corporate misdeeds and government incompetence, rendered with the occasional one-two punch of socialism and anarchism. Like Michael Moore, Thomas is a guerilla documentary filmmaker: he would stage confrontations and film the result. In one notorious moment, he interviewed a Church of England investment manager who stated that the weapons industry was an acceptable account for the Church to hold; Thomas then rolled up to his office a missile launcher emblazoned with the slogan "Church of England—Killing Foreigners for Profit and Jesus."

Often Thomas's targets were transnational capitalists and global politics, as he fingered immigration laws, banking policies, and Big Pharma's "drug dumping" (selling out-of-date drugs to the Third World) as culprits. He took on "corporate killing," once part of an early Labour Party campaign for a law to punish executives and board members of companies whose workers die in industrial accidents that could have been avoided. For some reason Thomas could not get any execs to sign a corporate killing clause: "In the event of an employee being seriously or fatally injured, due to non-compliance [with safety regulations], I am happy to go to prison if convicted." On a more serious level, his show discussed the Simon Jones case, in which a day laborer died in the first hours of working on a container ship (*Not This Time*, q.v.).

One of Thomas's sustained campaign targets involved the British Export Credit Guarantee Debt (ECGD) office of the Department of Trade and Industry that would indemnify any company whose loans were not repaid when they invested in large-scale foreign project. Thomas investigated the construction of two dams in Turkey, financed by transnational corporate consortiums: the Ilisu Dam, which would displace about 78,000 Kurds, and the Yusufeli Dam, which would displace about 30,000 members of the Georgian minority.

In the latter case, the British partner wanted to pull its 46 percent share out of the construction consortium and be indemnified for its losses; in the meantime, it had an option to buy the French partner's 54 percent share at the same time. Thomas erected an ice sculpture of the Yusufeli Dam at the headquarters of the French company, no doubt to remind them of the insubstantial nature of their investment.

Thomas has said that his political orientation was launched by the 1984–85 miners' strike. As a satirist he could not help "drawing out the stupidity of the situation," whether it be sending a water tanker to drought-ruined Yorkshire "as a gift from the people of Ethiopia" (see Otchet) or sampling the earth along the rail lines that traveled through the region served by the Sellafield nuclear processing plant (see *Edge of Darkness*).

Recommended Reading

Otchet, Amy. "Mark Thomas: Method and Madness of a TV Comic." UNESCO, May 1999 (online at www.unesco.org). Both an interview and outline of some of his program's "high jinx."

▶▶▶
The Mattei Affair

HISTORY OF GLOBALIZATION
OIL

1972, 116 mins., Italy, in Italian with English
  subtitles
Director: Francesco Rosi
Screenplay: Tito Di Stefano and Tonino
  Guerra

In the public arena that has been Italian politics Enrico Mattei played a remarkable role. Partly because of his experience in World War II as a partisan fighter against the Fascists, Mattei was appointed the head of AGIP, the Italian Petroleum Agency, a formerly Fascist quango. Instead of dismantling it as he was supposed to he transformed it into an instrument of Italian policymaking on energy, the National Fuel Trust or Ente Nazionale Idrocarburi (ENI). He pioneered natural gas (methane) as a national energy source and sought to build an independent network of oil consumers and producers, in effect bypassing the Anglo-American cartel that dominated the postwar shaping of the oil industry, especially as it related to the Middle East.

Although his claims of vast reserves of methane under Italian soil proved somewhat

The Mattei Affair: Enrico Mattei (Gian Maria Volointe) cheers a successful but rare methane gas strike.

illusory, he soon brought Italy into the global competition for oil by making separate deals with a number of less prominent Middle Eastern countries and socialist states. He offered such countries as Tunisia and Morocco larger cuts in oil profits than other Western nations, prospected for oil in Iran and Egypt without charge if he didn't strike oil, and even (it has been asserted) financed the Algerian rebels against France in the late 1950s.

By 1960 this socialist in charge of an international capitalist operation announced that the Anglo-American cartel's days were numbered. Within two years he died in a mysterious plane crash that many believed was an assassination. Even one of the director's key sources for the film, Sicilian reporter Mauro De Mauro, disappeared. Mattei himself never trusted the Italian secret service and often used former partisans for bodyguards.

Rosi is attracted to film projects in which the investigation of an official government story is reviewed with suspicion: *Salvatore Giuliano* (1962) tells the complicated story of a folk hero and bandit whose career in Sicily was complicated with post–World War II politics and the mafia, while *Hands over the City* (1963) plunges into political patronage and the "clean hands" (free of corruption) campaigns of the 1950s and 1960s.

The truth of Mattei's death has remained elusive; like *Syriana* (q.v.), the contemporary political scene, oil, government investigations, international conspiracy, and the CIA seem to go too easily hand in hand.

Recommended Readings

Ginsborg, Paul. *A History of Contemporary Italy: Society and Politics, 1943–1988.* Harmondsworth: Penguin Books, 1990. Helpful short review of the historical context of Mattei's career.

Testa, Carlo, ed. *Poet of Civic Courage: The Films of Francesco Rosi.* Westport: Greenwood Press, 1996. Includes an extensive analysis of the film by Harry Lawton: Rosi "keeps the public mind riveted on issues which simply will not go away," especially in "a republic born out of the collapse of a totalitarian regime," which retains "a curious residue of monopolistic groups."

▷▷▷

McLibel: Two Worlds Collide

ANTI-GLOBALIZATION
INTELLECTUAL PROPERTY RIGHTS (FOOD)

2005, 53 or 85 mins., United Kingdom
Director: Franny Armstrong
Mixed Cinema-Verité and Postmodern
    Documentary
Distributor: Media Education Foundation

Why do American celebrities go to London to sue whenever they are insulted or maligned? British libel laws—unlike those in the United States—are structured in such a way that the person accused of the libel must go to court and prove that the alleged libel is not false.

Helen Steel and Dave Morris, by profession a gardener and postman respectively, were also Greenpeace activists, environmentally concerned Londoners with an agenda: make people aware of what supporting McDonald's really meant. When McDonald's took them to court for distributing a leaflet (*What's Wrong with McDonald's*) criticizing this sensitive multinational fast food chain, their difficulties were immense. With limited funds and legal access, they had to do battle with a corporation known for its threats of legal action and virtually unlimited funds to back up those threats.

McDonald's vs Steel and Morris began in 1994 and lasted three years, the longest running trial in British history. Steel and Morris, supported by volunteers and activists and exhibiting an almost stereotypical British pluck and stubbornness, fought McDonald's to a draw which, considering the odds, looks like a victory to most. The judge ruled that they had proved that McDonald's did in fact "exploit children," use false claims of nutritional value of fast food in their advertising, are "culpably responsible" for cruelty to animals, and are anti-union, but that the corporation was not guilty of rainforest destruction, food poisoning or heart disease and cancer, Third World hunger, and poor working conditions. (See Steel's and Morris's website, www.mcspot light.org, for full details and transcripts.)

In 2005 the European Court of Human Rights ruled that Steel and Morris did not get a fair trial and were eligible for compensation and a retrial from the British government, which "must consider the European court's rulings when making their own" (*New York Times*, 16 February 2005). McDonald's had never pursued the court's judgment of ninety thousand pounds the High Court judge had assessed the couple (which they said they would never pay), but other fundamental issues remain: the difficulty of defending against a libel suit and doing battle with corporate Goliaths.

Although McDonald's and Coca-Cola were perhaps the earliest standard bearers for American cultural domination on a global scale, they have been curiously absent from most critical cinematic representation. Franny Armstrong's film, however, explains this case admirably, using a number of reconstructions of court testimony (directed in turn by Ken Loach) that highlight some of the absurdities of McDonald's defense. Ed Oakley, European Head of Purchasing for McDonald's, was asked by Steel if he meant to testify "that as long as there is room in the dumps, there is no problem with dumping lots of McDonald's waste in the ground?" Oakley replied: "I can see it to be a benefit. Otherwise you will end up with lots of vast, empty gravel pits all over the country." In courtroom drama like this everyone will have a favorite moment, but consider Oakley's response to the accusation that McDonald's creates an inordinate amount of street waste: "Not a fact of life," he testifies. "I walked through Paddington this morning. I found one McDonald's package, which I disposed of. So, I think that is a gross overstatement." Poor Justice Bell noted that "there were two on Waterloo Bridge this morning, but I did not dispose of them, I am afraid." Oakley chastised the judge: "I would have done so."

Recommended Readings

Schlosser, Eric. *Fast Food Nation: The Dark Side of the All-American Meal*. New York: Houghton Mifflin, 2001. Includes a chapter on the case, placing it in the overall context of his broad critique of an entire industry.

Vidal, John. *McLibel: Burger Culture on Trial*. New York: New Press, 1997. Definitive account of the trial, the verdict, and the case (through 1997).

⋈⋈⋈

The Men Who Would Conquer China

CHINA
GLOBAL CAPITAL

2004, 79 mins., Australia
Directors: Nick Torrens and Jane St. Vincent Welch
Cinema-Verité Documentary
Distributor: First Run/Icarus Films

This foray into the new China could have been subtitled "Two Charming Capitalists Go to Beijing." Mart Bakal, head of the American

The Men Who Would Conquer China: Business partners (Vincent Lee and Mart Bakal) looking for investment opportunities in China. Courtesy First Run/Icarus Films.

investment group Crimson Capital, and his friend and occasional partner, Vincent Lee of the Hong Kong–based Tung Tai Group, are the kind of international businessmen who have an extra $100 million or so to invest somewhere but as people don't put on airs. They are fairly nice. Bakal knows poverty exists in China and he is sympathetic. He can't, however, quite disguise his amusement that Gucci has shops in China: where did all these wealthy people come from all of a sudden? he wonders. And how cute it is that a restaurant uses the Era of Chairman Mao Thought as its theme—the walls are decorated with Red Guard posters and the waitresses dress as Red Army soldiers, for example.

Their story is about how to find the right company to buy, modernize, restructure financially, and eventually sell for a significant profit to a multinational corporation. Will it be tires? Dairy products? These industries are likely prospects, but after six years of work, Bakal and Lee have a list of companies to choose for their investment target at last. In the end they make a remarkable deal with Northeast Securities, a Chinese company that specializes in companies judged to be bad assets by the Bank of China and in a sense repossessed for future sale. (But Bakal makes it clear that he will still keep an eye on tires and dairy products just in case.)

Unlike *From Mao to Money* (q.v.), which charts native capitalists and their seemingly easy ascendance, *The Men Who Would Conquer China* shows how hard it is for foreigners to make a deal in China, despite Deng Xiaoping's prediction, "All will get rich, [but] some must be first." I would bet on Bakal and Lee being successful even if they are not first. Having made (he tells us) a bundle in Czechoslovakia after the fall of communism, Bakal clearly knows what he is doing: the film distributor's website credits him with privatizing and restructuring six hundred companies there. He may not know everything about China, but when the tire manufacturer makes it known that it would be ideal if the government privatizes his company first and then purchase it for resale to Bakal, Bakal is suitably annoyed: they're just crooks, he implies.

Recommended Reading

McGregor, James. *One Billion Customers*. New York: Wall Street Journal Books, 2005. Insights into the "front lines of doing business in China" by a *Wall Street Journal* China bureau chief and experienced analyst of Chinese-American business relationships.

▸▸▸

Mickey Mouse Goes to Haiti

ANTI-GLOBALIZATION
EXPORT PROCESSING ZONES

1996, 17 mins., United States, English and
    Spanish with English subtitles
Producer: Rooster Crow Productions
Agit-Prop Documentary
Distributor: NLC

When the Disney film *Pocahontas* (1995) created an enormous consumer craze among tiny tots and their parents for T-shirts, pajamas, and other Indian princess apparel, the company took advantage of Haiti's Export Processing Zone to pay a Haitian worker about less than a dime for every pair of Pocahontas pajamas sewn. Since the average worker made about four of these garments an hour, the average pay came to about $3.00 a day. At the time that item sold at Wal-Mart for $11.97.

Subtitled "Walt Disney and the Science of Exploitation," this agit-prop documentary about the globalization of garment work was produced by the National Labor Committee, an "Education Fund in Support of Worker and Human Rights in Central America." Charles Kernaghan, the leader of the National Labor Committee, and a small film crew interviewed workers as they commuted to the Disney plant. Over and over the workers are amazed at what Disney charges for the clothing they are creating for literally a fraction of a cent. One of the most visually arresting images of the film is a shot of Haitian workers in a tenement wearing Mickey Mouse T-shirts and silly masks to protect their identity from company spies and others who might get them fired for talking to the film crew.

The NLC has been very successful in exposing the little known and carefully hidden indirect subsidies the U.S. government employs to bolster its companies in the global market. The Salvadoran Foundation for Economic and Social Development (FUSADES), which has received millions of dollars in American aid, ran this ad in a trade journal: "Rosa Martinez produces apparel for U.S. markets on her sewing machine in El Salvador. You can hire her for 33 cents an hour. Rosa is more than just colorful. She and her co-workers are known for their industriousness, reliability and quick learning. They make El Salvador one of the best buys."

The NLC has always taken the position that jobs in the globalized market are volatile and that any criticism of American-based multinationals must include the request that they not abandon one country as soon as their sweatshop practices are exposed. Otherwise Rosa from El Salvador, somewhat overpaid compared to the Haitian workers, will not likely be sewing any Pocahontas pajamas any time soon.

Recommended Readings

Kaufman, Leslie, and David Gonzalez. "Labor Progress Clashes with Global Reality." *New York Times*, 24 April 2001. Reviews the progress in monitoring labor conditions: "Competing interests among factory owners, government officials, American managers, and middle-class consumers—all with their eyes on the lowest possible cost—make it difficult to achieve even basic standards, and even harder to maintain them."

Klein, Naomi. *No Logo: Taking Aim at the Brand Bullies.* New York: Picador, 2000. Devastating critique of global corporations such as Nike and Disney, with some discussion of the film.

The U.S. in Haiti. New York: National Labor Committee, 1995. This National Labor Committee pamphlet is subtitled "How To Get Rich on 11 Cents an Hour." It documents in detail which American companies are part of this assertion: "Approximately 50 assembly firms now operating in Haiti are violating the [Haitian] minimum wage law."

ᖇᖇᖇ
Mine

HISTORY OF GLOBALIZATION
LABOR HISTORY
SCARCE RESOURCES (GOLD)

1991, 6 mins., B & W, South Africa
Director and Artist: William Kentridge
Animated Film

The animation in this short film tells an imagistic story of class and power relationships in apartheid South Africa. Using his own black-and-white drawings, filmmaker William Kentridge reveals the relationship between black workers and white owners in the gold mining industry. With tongue in cheek, he designates his identity as "part of a group of Jewish English-speaking European-descended South Africans" who happen to be Lithuanians and lawyers (see Sittenfeld). His father was Nelson Mandela's lawyer in his treason trial of 1956 and also represented Steven Biko's family at the 1977 inquest into his murder by the security forces. In 1978 Kentridge coauthored and performed in *Randlords and Rotgut*, a play based on an influential essay by the South African writer Charles van Onselen on the use of alcohol to control the goldmine workers in the Witwatersrand region.

Although most people think of animation as filming in succession a series of minutely detailed but slightly modified drawings or cels, Kentridge instead draws on a large sheet of paper, films it, adds details or erases something, films it again, and so on. The final film is often screened in a gallery installation that includes the original drawings.

Mine situates a capitalist he calls Soho Eckstein in his office and other private spaces; his gold mines are populated with African workers in scenes that are visual analogues to the respective holocausts of African enslavement and Nazi concentration camps. The bunkhouse of the mine workers is virtually identical to a concentration camp building, and Kentridge intercuts the notorious schematic drawing of slaves lined up like planks in the hold of a slave ship.

In a act of controversial animated "casting," Kentridge models his white capitalist and mine owner, Soho Eckstein, on a noted South African Jewish insurance czar, Shlomo Peer, who supported apartheid and believed Afrikaan nationalism was analogous to Zionism (see Pollack).

Although *Mine* is barely six minutes long, Kentridge manages to combine both the symbolic relationship between capital and labor and its realistic representation in the mines. As Eckstein plunges his French press coffeemaker on his desk, it is as if the camera plunges the viewer straight through the desk downward through geological strata to spectacular underground views of the gold miners at work.

Mine was followed by *Monument*, another set of "drawings for projection," as Kentridge called his approach. Loosely based on Samuel Beckett's play *Catastrophe*, *Monument* offers again the sharp contrast between an African worker carrying a heavy load and Eckstein, now labeled a "civic benefactor." When Eckstein unveils his monumental gift to his city, it turns out to be the laborer whose sculptured self soon comes to life as the film ends.

Kentridge's films touch sometimes lightly, sometimes strenuously, on the transition of South Africa from neocolonial outpost to globalized source of scarce resources. Excerpts from most of the films discussed above are available in an extremely well-done survey of Kentridge's work, including extensive demonstrations by the artist himself, in *Drawing the Passing*, directed by Maria Anna Tappeiner and Reinhard Wulf and produced by Westdeutschen Rundfunk (1999). It is distributed in the United States under the title *William Kentridge: Art from the Ashes* by Films for the Humanities and Sciences (at www.films.com). The complete films are also available in *9 Drawings for Projection*, produced by Gatehouse in South Africa (2006).

Recommended Readings

Christov-Bakargiev, Carolyn. *William Kentridge.* Brussels: Societe des Expositions du Palace des Beaux-Arts du Bruxelles, 2004. Detailed discussions of his films, with numerous stills.

Pollack, Barbara. "Art of Resistance." *Village Voice.* 30 May–5 June 2001. Documents the controversies in Kentridge's career and calls him "the most celebrated artist to emerge from South Africa in the post-apartheid era."

Sittenfeld, Michael, ed. *William Kentridge.* Chicago and New York: The Museum of Contemporary Art and New Museum of Contemporary Art, 2001. Excellent survey of Kentridge's films and career.

MM

HISTORY OF GLOBALIZATION

2002, 13 mins., United Kingdom
Director: William Raban
Structuralist Documentary

MM, the title of William Raban's follow-up to the visual themes and politics of his earlier trilogy, *Under the Tower* (q.v.), denotes 2000 in Roman numerals. Besides the millennium itself, it also alludes to the Millennium Dome, the symbol of Tony Blair's New Labour Party. As in the earlier films, Raban isolates the cold geometric cityscape to suggest a political critique of the economic development of London. Taking all of the films together, Raban points to a continuity of urban development that owes no allegiance to a particular party: Tory and New Labourite alike are blasting away the old and hyping the new as the inevitable (global) order of the day.

The Millennium Dome was architect Richard Rogers's radical postmodern building. Using his characteristic architectural signature, a structural exoskeleton (like his most famous buildings, such as Lloyd's in the City of London or the Pompidou Center in Paris, codesigned with Renzo Piano), Rogers moved the utilities, as well as the elevators and escalators, in what was traditionally the central building core to the outside of the buildings. In Raban's film the Dome seems, however, to be an alien presence on the landscape, looming over much smaller buildings with its external derrick-like supporting columns arranged in a halo or crown over the dome itself.

Like *A13* from *Under the Tower*, which represented the Thatcherite expressways cutting through the cityscape, *MM* uses black-and-white archival stills of the construction of the nearby Blackwall Tunnel, which connected the East India Docks with the port of Greenwich across the Thames River in 1897. Footage of the explosion in 1987 of the power station originally on the Dome's site continues his theme of destruction of the cityscape for political and economic ends.

The world's biggest dome was built on the meridian line (or prime meridian), reprising the dominance of the British Empire in earlier centuries. For contemporary British citizens it perhaps symbolizes lackluster exhibits that failed to draw crowds and a planned fire sculpture on the Thames on New Year's Eve that failed to ignite. The Dome itself remains empty, having failed to attract a corporate sponsor or deal.

Recommended Reading

Osler, David. *Labour Party PLC: New Labour as a Party of Business.* Edinburgh: Mainstream Publishing, 2002. Documents the transformation of the "labor" party into a mainstream "party of business," rendered ironically in the title as a PLC (in the United Kingdom, a public limited company; in the United States, a publicly traded corporation).

▶◀▶◀▶◀

Mojados: Through the Night

MIGRANT LABOR (UNITED STATES)
TRANSNATIONAL MIGRATION

2005, 65 mins., United States
Director: Tommy Davis
Cinema-Verité Documentary

Traveling for eight days and nights across the Mexican border into the desert wastelands of Texas, filmmaker Tommy Davis accompanied four men from Michoacan on their illegal journey toward American jobs. Traveling literally "through the night," these *mojados* or "wetbacks" endure risk of contaminated water, rotten food, and freezing temperatures to reach their goal. In a sense the men, nick-

named Oso (Bear), Tigre (Tiger), Guapo (Handsome), and Viejo (Old Man), really interviewed the filmmaker rather than the other way around: as Davis wandered about the town, advertising his interest in making the trip, word got to some of his potential subjects, who tested him by having him schlep up (and down) a mountain with his eighty pounds of equipment. He eventually bought back a revealing document of a harrowing passage and the honorary title of "the gringo mojado."

The route taken was the result of a conscious strategy by the U.S. Border Patrol in 2000 to "over man"—increase the number of patrol officers at—the urban crossing point for illegal immigrants, forcing them to go the back way across dangerous open territory. Davis intercuts interviews with one border rancher from Texas, sometimes at the same spot where he crossed with the four men, who recounts the dangers to both cattle (who choke on plastic tortilla bags left behind) and human beings. Bodies, the rancher attests, would often be found lying about, especially after a bad cold spell.

When the men finally make it to a safe house, viewers are relieved to see fast food packages and soft drinks piled up next to them as they sleep. But the men are soon forced out of this house when the Border Patrol is sighted. One eventually makes it to Austin, but the other three are caught and deported. They try again, but Davis is not with them this time. He concludes with newscasts about a sudden frost and wind chill that kills a number of migrants. Were the three remaining men among them? About this we are left in the dark.

This is a rare inside look at the migrant laborers' journey. Two of them are leaving home for the first time, hoping for jobs and money to send home. The others have made this harrowing journey every year.

Recommended Reading

Stevens, Dana. "Pilgrimage across the Border That Tempts but Dodges Fate." *New York Times*, 18 May 2005. "The film "manages to capture firsthand the danger, fatigue, and sheer tedium of an arduous illegal border crossing from Mexico without ever becoming tedious itself."

⋈⋈⋈

Mondovino

INTELLECTUAL PROPERTY RIGHTS (WINE)

2004, 135 mins., PG-13, France/United States, in English, French, Italian, Portuguese and Spanish with English subtitles
Director: Jonathan Nossiter
Cinema-Verité Documentary

Although wine is not by most standards a scarce commodity, the argument that it is a globalized industry limiting consumers' access to the incredible variety of traditional wines is made persuasive and even comical by Jonathan Nossiter in *Mondovino* (a title that plays on early exploitation documentaries like *Mondo Cane*, 1962, depicting the world's excesses and sordidness).

And while a visit to any wine store would convince most of us of the competition in this multibillion dollar industry, the film suggests that wine behemoths such as CK Mondavi Winery—like Wal-Mart—are muscling in on the locals' territory, adulterating the product by giving it an unpalatable (to many people) American or even Californian taste. And like the stock analysts who urged people to buy Enron, these wine companies use two of the most famous wine experts in the world, Michel Rolland of France and Robert Parker of the United States, to pump up the volume of the global companies.

Local in this context means France and Italy primarily, places where we think of wine as virtually identical to a nation's culture, but also other places such as Argentina, Brazil, and Sardinia, where we might be surprised to find a flourishing wine culture. And like many a Sprawl-Mart's tale of woe, Nossiter's documentary has a heroic town, Aniane in the Languedoc, which has fought off the attempts of the once Californian but now transnational Robert Mondavi Winery to replace a local forested mountain with a vineyard. Mondavi and its supporters blame a newly elected com-

munist mayor—we had a good relationship with the old mayor, Mondavi family members say on camera—for blocking their move. Viewers of the documentary, however, will realize that the real power is in the hands of small winemakers such as Aime Guibert, a crusty local who is one of the stars of the film and who believes that all good things—wine, fruit, and so on—are dying because of the Mondavis of the world.

Part of the reason *Mondovino* is such a captivating view of the globalization of the wine industry is that we meet not only chatty French winemakers and globetrotting wine consultants but also the aristocratic families who have dominated Italian wine making in Tuscany, in some instances, like the Frescobaldis, since the fifteenth century. Despite their incredible good looks and manners and their grandfathers' collective admiration for Mussolini and Italian Fascism (society was kept in order), these distinguished folk make some fairly classic globalized deals with the Mondavis, who sense that local partners make it a lot easier to infiltrate traditional markets outside of the United States. (That one aristocratic family sticks it to another reminds us of Machiavelli's *The Prince*: do unto others before they do it to you.)

In addition to a camera style that has his interviewees speaking to us quite intimately, like an Errol Morris film, Nossiter has a wry sense of humor and a good eye for telling compositions. Although it is of course not in the film proper, the advertising art that features a huge plane with its bomb hatch open dropping bottles of wine is a nice touch. The film does end with a visual joke: two dogs struggle for tenancy of an untilled patch of dirt in a planter. Who will be top dog?

By the way, Nossiter has been for many years a sommelier at exclusive restaurants in New York City.

Recommended Readings

Asimov, Eric. "Shake Wine, and Look What's Stirred Up." *New York Times*, 16 March 2005. "Like a modern Thoreau, [the director] offers a starkly divided world in which the monolithic forces of wealth, technology, and marketing are at war with a pastoral peasantry."

Hohenadel, Kristin. "The Wine Wars, Spilled Onto the Screen." *New York Times*, 2 January 2005. Another report on the wine establishment's outrage at the filmmakers' exposé.

Macauley, Scott. "The Terroirist." *Filmmaker*, Winter 2005. Taking his title from the French emphasis on the "terroir" or quality of the local soil and climatic conditions for growing wine, the reviewer says that the film "serves as a witty and effective treatise on the complex, crushing and ultimately very human relationship between economic globalization and those who fight to produce something—a film, a bottle of wine— that has its own unique character in an increasingly homogenous world."

▸┤◂┤

My Journey Home

TRANSNATIONAL MIGRATION

2004, 120 mins., United States
Director: Renee Tajima-Pena
Traditional Documentary
Distributor: PBS

The changes in globalized transportation and communications in the last twenty-five years have resulted in a relatively new trend in immigration: transnational families. Renee Tajima-Pena, codirector of *Who Killed Vincent Chin?* (in *Working Stiffs*) and director of *My America . . . or Honk if You Love Buddha* (1997) follows four Americans—two writers and two social activists—who explore and maintain their roots in other countries. The presence of a Little Saigon, a Koreatown, and Mexican barrios in many cities has created a multiethnic society in America, to be sure, but unlike most of the urban Little Italys or Chinatowns of the past, these communities have populations who move back and forth from the United States to their families' countries of origin.

The journeys documented in this film are complex and painful. Faith Adiele grew up biracial in Sunnyside, Washington, the daughter of a Scandinavian American mother and an absent Nigerian father. The film follows her visits to Nigeria and her search for the father she never knew. Her latest (to date unpublished) writing project, "Twins: Growing Up Nigerian/Nordic/American," will document her journey. Andrew Lam fled Saigon with his Vietnamese family just before the city fell to the communists in 1975. He returns in search of his relatives left behind.

Both Adiele and Lam are professional writers whose transnational identities and journeys inform their work, while the brothers Peña— Armando and Carlos—are community workers in Mexican American communities. Armand develops affordable housing and Carlos fights for migrant workers' rights. As children they worked in the fields in the Rio Grande Valley with their siblings. Their father had disappeared, perhaps a victim of the deportations of workers in 1954 in Operation Wetback, when both *braceros*, recruited legally, and other Mexican workers, were forced back across the border. They also take a painful journey home, accompanied by their mother's ashes.

Director Tajima-Pena has explored Asian American families and communities in her previous films, and she brings to this task an empathetic eye and a talent for revealing, sometimes comic, sometimes tragic, detail as she follows these transnational individuals around the world.

Recommended Readings

Adiele, Faith. *Meeting Faith: The Forest Journals of A Black Buddhist Nun.* New York: W. W. Norton, 2004. The writer takes on the role of a Buddhist nun in Thailand in her first book about exploring her identity.

Lam, Andrew. *Perfume Dreams: Reflections on the Vietnamese Diaspora.* Berkeley: Heyday Books, 2005. Writing as a *Viet Kieu*, or transnational Vietnamese, Lam explores in this collection of essays vexing questions of identity and homeland.

▸┤◂┤

Nalini by Day, Nancy by Night

OUTSOURCING AND OFFSHORING

2005, 27 mins., India and United States, in
  English and Hindi with English subtitles
Director: Sonali Gulati

Filmmaker Sonali Gulati was amazed one day to hear her name pronounced with precision by a VISA card phone solicitor. She realized eventually that the caller was Indian, one of the many thousands recruited to work at call centers for Fortune 500 and other companies. Although the caller said her name was Nancy Smith, Gulati soon learned that it was really Nalini. The workers often adapt such an alias, not only to pass as an American on the phone but also as a means of making them migrate to a convincing American personality and accent. And they work at night, when the United States is in daytime.

Gulati expected to find sophisticated sweatshops when she began filming on location. She discovered that the operators earn only seven dollars a day and that the jobs are extremely difficult to get. Not only are there millions of English speakers in India (one of the results of the old British colonial education system) competing for these jobs, but the perks are considerable: there is a ride service to and from work, working conditions are relatively pleasant, and the pay and other incentives are attractive. Gulati, with some reluctance, concluded that the call centers were "not quite the sweatshops I imagined them to be."

Joining a virtual subgenre of Indian-related films, Gulati's documentary successfully takes us on a street-level tour of the call centers. Her interviews and observations of English coaching classes open up a complex world. A typical call center with four thousand operators requires an additional support staff of four thousand to eight thousand workers (drivers, security guards, techies, cafeteria workers, and voice and accent trainers), one indicator of the economic value of this outsourcing industry. Their economic value for American corporations is also obvious: Gulati interviews a call center worker, "Anne," who collected a million dollars of late charges and property taxes for G. E. Capital in a month, while earning seven dollars a day.

Call center recruits practice on this tongue twister: "Betty bought a bit of better butter," a touch of humor in the relentlessly serious task of learning how to pass for an American operator. Gulati is careful to demonstrate, with archival footage, some of the same drills and regimentation that early American phone companies used to train their army of operators in one of the first attempts at global communications (cf. *The Phantom of the Operator*).

The film begins and concludes with some charming animated sequences involving phones. In the very last moments we hear an operator mangle Gulati's name in what we think is a blind solicitation call. But no, it is simply a "real" American calling her about a film transfer at a laboratory, and it is clear he

Nalini by Day, Nancy by Night: The self-contained world of the Indian call center. Courtesy Women Make Movies.

doesn't have the training to pronounce her name correctly.

Recommended Reading

Gulati, Sonali. "Artist Statement." Online at www.sonalifilm.com. Filmmaker's website: "My goal is to not only find innovative ways of storytelling, but also to create films as organizing tools, in the hope of making this a safe, sustainable, and just world."

▶◀▶◀▶◀
The Navigators

DEREGULATION AND PRIVATIZATION
THATCHERISM

2001, 92 mins., United
    Kingdom/Germany/Spain
Director: Ken Loach
Screenplay: Rob Dawber

Ken Loach's dramatization of a horrible accident on the privatized British Rail system of the 1990s is primarily a cinematic attack on Thatcherism. London *Guardian* columnist Ian Jack (see "Recommended Readings" below) suggests that most Conservatives never cared much about this piece of the Thatcherite campaign because the railroads weren't likely to be profitable enough for private industry. When commuting by car became more frustrating, however, and more people began taking the train, share prices for the Balkanized system rose. Over twenty-five separate companies were formed from the system regarded worldwide as an exemplar in its heyday.

In light of the subsequent deterioration in service and safety record, Jack recounted a chilling story he heard from "a senior figure in the railways" about foreign visitors to the United Kingdom: "The ones from Europe come because they want to discover how not to privatize a railway. The ones from the Third World come to see how it might be done because the IMF [International Monetary Fund] has sent them. Poor mugs."

In October 2000 a high-speed Virgin train derailed at Hatfield, killing four people. It was the fourth fatal train wreck since the privatization of British Rail in the early 1990s. What made it a greater scandal was that Railtrack, the authority in charge of rail maintenance, knew that the rails were damaged in this locale two years before the accident. Jack cites the sobering statistics that are the essential background to the film: between 1992 and 1997 the number of workers assigned to maintain the infrastructure of the rails fell from 31,000 to less than 19,000.

Loach dramatizes the deteriorating relationships among five Yorkshire railway workers who have been friends for years. Set in 1995 at a train yard, the men are told that British Rail, the nationalized system they have worked for, has been replaced by a private company. At first they are casual, assuming their jobs will last. But they take pause when they are told that safety is a priority and "death has got to be kept to a minimum"— only two a year. One of the men accepts a buyout and works for a contract agency making twice as much an hour but with no vacation and sick pay and no union. The film has a tragic and disturbing twist I will allow viewers to discover for themselves.

Rob Dawber, the screenwriter, was a railway worker, union activist, and columnist for almost twenty years. After losing his job because of privatization, he continued his writing career but turned to the courts when he discovered that he had been exposed to asbestos while working in a British Rails shed. Although he won a settlement he died of a tumor caused by the exposure.

Critic Kathleen Olmstead on *Exclaim!* (10 September 2001, online at www.exclaim.ca/index.asp?layid=22&csid=812,) wrote that the "depiction of the effects of privatization and destruction of the permanent workforce is both brutal and honest," although she admitted that she was "a sucker for a good Marxist kitchen sink drama." But the film is clearly much more than that.

Recommended Readings

Hare, David. *The Permanent Way*. London: Faber and Faber, 2003. Hare's controversial play on the Hatfield crash and the government's mismanagement of the railroad.

Jack, Ian. *The Crash That Stopped Britain.* London: Granta Books, 2001. A chilling short account of the dangerous dismantling of a once great rail system and the Hatfield crash.

Strangleman, Tim. *Work Identity at the End of the Line? Privatisation and Culture Change in the UK Rail Industry.* Basingstoke: Palgrave Macmillan, 2004. Surveys the national political scene that created the privatization schemes as well as the workers who live under it.

▶◀▶◀

Net Loss: The Storm Over Salmon Farming

INTELLECTUAL PROPERTY RIGHTS (GMOs)
SCARCE RESOURCES (FISH)

2003, 52 mins., United States
Directors: Mark Dworkin and Melissa Young
Distributor: Bullfrog Films

When the idea of salmon fish farming was floated in the 1980s it seemed, especially to leaders of the commercial fish industry, like a good solution to the depletion of wild salmon, particularly in the northwest region of North America. But independent fishermen, many of whom were coastal Indians whose historical and cultural identity was tied to wild salmon, were not consulted.

With the rise of biotechnology, the fish industry added another disturbing factor to the mix: genetically modified fish whose growth was accelerated. And since fish farms were often located on the migration routes of wild salmon, the likelihood grew that native fishes would be displaced or interbred with the GM fish.

The film begins with an extensive critique of the very concept of fish *farming*: it is a false analogy, critics assert, because this industry uses no private land but rather public waters. Furthermore, the cages confining the fish result in the deposit of old food pellets and fish waste, smothering the life below it. The economic success of the farms drives independent fishermen onto the seasonal labor rolls of the processing plants for the farms. Most processing plants worldwide employ women on twelve-hour shifts with rare union representation.

The film takes an unexpected turn when it examines the Chilean fish industry, which accounts for one third of all the salmon consumed in the world. Wastewater from fish farms are sprayed on oyster beds with good results. With its conservation of wastewater and protection of a single species, could this be a model to slow down global fishing scarcity and adulteration?

Recommended Reading

Woody, Elizabeth, Seth Zuckerman, and Edward C. Wolf, eds. *Salmon Nation: People and Fish at the Edge.* Portland: Ecotrust, 1999. Careful analysis of the role of salmon in the history of the Native American "first people," by an advocacy group for environmental and Indian rights.

▶◀▶◀

The New Americans

TRANSNATIONAL MIGRATION

2004, 408 mins., United States, in English, Arabic, Kannada, and Spanish with English subtitles
Directors: Susana Aikin and Carlos Aparicio (Dominican Republic), Jerry Blumenthal and Gordon Quinn (Palestine), Steve James (Nigeria), Indu Krishnan (India), and Renee Tajima-Pena (Mexico)
Cinema-Verité Documentary
Distributor: PBS

This ambitious project tracking transnational immigrants from five countries originates from Kartemquin Films, a Chicago-based co-op responsible for the *Taylor Chain* collective-bargaining documentaries (both in *Working Stiffs*) and *Hoop Dreams* (1994), an inner-city basketball documentary directed by Steve James, one of the filmmakers on this project.

Originally broadcast as a television series, the film cuts back and forth between the immigrants' native country and the United States, as well as back and forth among the five stories. The net result is not confusing but illuminating: we compare what has been lost and gained by the move to the United States as well as the differences among the experiences of the immigrants. This approach also helps to define the concept of transnational migration: in some instances people go back and forth (the Dominican Republic), in others the passage to the United States is permanent (Nigeria), and in still another members of the migrating family virtually end up with two homes (India).

Thus this film teaches us the incredible complexity of the immigrant experience in the age of globalization. While some individuals cut ties with their homelands and others either travel back and forth frequently or infrequently, strong connections usually remain. Whether workers decide to return or not, they consistently send money home to families (and, sadly, in many cases, to their own children's caregivers). They tend to cluster by home village even in the United States, and they retain a close identification with both countries. Their children, however, often begin the age-old American immigrant story: the first generation remains bilingual, but gradually English (despite the xenophobic campaigns) dominates their speech.

Probably one of the biggest messages of the film is how close these immigrants come to *not* making it to the United States. Israel and Ngozi Nwidor, the Ogoni refugees from Nigeria, are here only because they win a lottery in a refugee camp in Benin, their home because the Ogoni opposed Nigeria's military dictatorship and its support of Shell Oil Company, which had polluted (and coveted) their land. Of the two Dominican baseball recruits to the Dodgers, Ricardo Rodriguez and Jose Garcia, only one makes the final team roster cut, while the other goes home. Luck and chance play differing roles in the other stories as well.

Recommended Readings

Hale, Mike. "American Dreams, Not Made in the U.S.A." *New York Times*, 28 March 2004. Detailed interview with director and series producer Steve James emphasizing how honest and in some instances depressing some of the material is.

Martinez, Rubén. *The New Americans*. New York: New Press, 2004. Impressive companion volume to the series but with numerous addi-

tional essays and profiles by Martinez who wrote a classic of transnational experience, *Crossing Over: A Mexican Family on the Migrant Trail* (2003).

⋈⋈⋈
New Earth

HISTORY OF GLOBALIZATION
LABOR HISTORY

1934, 30 mins., B & W, Netherlands, in Dutch
  with English subtitles
Director: Joris Ivens
Social Realist Documentary

The "new earth" of the title is the land reclaimed for agricultural use after the spectacular Dutch re-engineering of the Zuider Sea dams in the 1920s. *New Earth* uses footage from *We Are Building* and *Zuiderzee* (both 1930), two of Ivens's earlier films on this massive soil reclamation project. But in this film he transformed what had been relatively neutral social-realism into a political statement. After the project was finished and the first fruits from the reclaimed land were harvested, the worldwide depression caused thousands of Dutch workers to lose their jobs, and speculation in the stock markets abroad caused crops to rot or be destroyed. As the voice-over narrator states: "But the grain is not for food, but for speculation. There is too much grain and not enough world."

Thus three-quarters of this film is, in Ivens's words, a "joke." "We show a tremendous engineering work that conquered the sea, that is going to bring happiness and prosperity to everyone concerned and then we say 'but,'" he says. After the brilliant montage of the final closing of the Zee in 1932, we see Ivens's "dialectical counterpoint to the visual footage" of the abundant harvest: "the slogans of hunger marchers in London, Berlin, and over the newsreel footage of the hunger march we hear the yells of farmers, 'We are being choked with grain.'"

French censors in the 1930s refused to license the film because, they explained, if poor people in Paris saw it "they would get ideas and march on the city hall and ask for bread." Thus did social realism become agit-prop. And what was an intensive nationalistic project became victim to market forces worldwide.

Recommended Readings

Ivens, Joris. *The Camera and I.* New York: New World Paperbacks, 1969. Reflections on his own history as a filmmaker and a detailed discussion of the draining and filming of the Zuiderzee project.

Rosenbaum, Jonathan. "Joris Ivens's Labor-Intensive Industrials." *Chicago Reader,* May 2002. Brief but helpful overview of Ivens's career, neglected because of his affinities with communist states and the lack of a single-country identity for his work.

ᑐᑐᑐ

The New Rulers of the World

ANTI-GLOBALIZATION
NEOCOLONIALISM
TRANSNATIONAL ORGANIZATIONS

2001, 54 mins., United Kingdom
Director: Alan Lowery
Correspondent: John Pilger
TV Documentary
Distributor: Bullfrog Films

Although the British filmmaker John Pilger is not well known in the United States, his investigative journalism and television reporting have consistently focused on the poor and working classes of Ireland, England, and the Third World. His films expose both neocolonial violence as well as governmental schemes and lies in some of Britain's sore spots, such as Northern Ireland or the recurring labor struggles on the Liverpool docks. Pilger's producer maintains a particularly extensive website (www.pilger.carlton.com) of his work in both print and televised media.

With a focus on Indonesia and the human cost of globalization, *The New Rulers of the World* principally targets the World Bank and similar agencies. At one point Pilger successfully corners a World Bank bureaucrat—Stanley Fischer, deputy director of the International Monetary Fund (IMF)—who loses his cool under Pilger's close questioning. (The same exec also appears in *Life and Debt,* q.v.)

Pilger documents the U.S. role in deposing Sukarno, the 1960s nationalist leader, in favor of the vicious anti-communist Suharto. The massacre of any opposing forces ensued, leading to the transformation of a neocolonial state into a globalized client of the West.

Recommended Readings

Hayward, Anthony. *In the Name of Justice: The Television Reporting of John Pilger.* London: Bloomsbury, 2001. An extensive record and analysis of Pilger's career and all of his film work through 2000 (and therefore does not discuss *The New Rulers of the World*).

Pilger, John. *Hidden Agendas.* London: Vintage, 1998. Essays on global issues with Pilger's own assessment of his approach to investigative reporting.

———. *The New Rulers of the World.* London: Verso, 2002. Essays on Indonesia and other victims of globalization.

ᑐᑐᑐ

Nightcleaners

CHANGES IN THE WORKPLACE: EUROPE
LABOR HISTORY

1975, 90 mins., United Kingdom, B & W
Director: Marc Karlin and the Berwick Street
    Film Collective
Postmodern Documentary

Nightcleaners is an important but rarely screened film focusing on a job that in the 1970s had already begun to tilt toward an almost exclusively immigrant work force in most Western countries. It was an experimental attempt to document the working lives of women who clean London's buildings at night, as well as to create an agit-prop leaflet to provoke audiences to re-examine their commitment to women's rights.

Filmed in various London office blocks at night without official permission, the filmmakers use a cinema-verité style but intended to use the film as an agit-prop documentary to raise funds for the nightcleaners' unionization drive as well as to raise issues of women's rights. At first, Karlin reports, the nightcleaners would "wave, or sign, or whatever" at him and his crew. In the next stage, the workers sneaked them into the office suites.

In one of the interviews with two nightcleaners, Karlin asks them, "What would socialism mean to you?" For Ann, it would be a "better life for the working class people, if that was possible, but that couldn't be, could it?" When Karlin replies, "Why not?" Ann says, "It's like asking for the moon, isn't it?" Jean, another nightcleaner, suggests that socialism might be possible "if people were strong enough."

In the end *Nightcleaners* is more postmodern than agit-prop in its exposition, since the first few minutes of the film (and self-referential sequences) involve repeating identical images and shots of the clapper board, which remind you that this is a film. The interviews and other sequences clearly have been edited heavily, using techniques such as black spaces between the shots. The film is therefore technically experimental, while its subject area—balancing the demands of union reps and women's activists—make it a challenging film all around.

Recommended Readings

Johnston, Claire, and Paul Willemen. "Brecht in Britain: The Independent Political Film." *Screen* 16, Winter 1975–76, 101–18. A very positive assessment (with remarks by the filmmakers) of this film as a "unique contribution towards the development of political cinema" in the United Kingdom.

Wright, Patrick. "A Passion for Images." *Vertigo* (London), Summer 1999, 4–10. "The film," Karlin suggests in this interview, "was about the distance between the women who organize—the Women's Liberation movement, who were there to leaflet on behalf of the trade union" and the nightcleaners themselves.

ΗΗΗ

Night on Earth

TAXI DRIVERS

1991, 128 mins., R, United States
Director: Jim Jarmusch
Screenplay: Jim Jarmusch

The ad reads, "Five Taxis. Five Cities. One Night." We might put it this way: five mostly

Night on Earth: Taxi driver (Armin Mueller-Stahl) with reluctant fare (Giancarlo Esposito).

comic encounters in what is by any standards a difficult and unfunny job in this single, globalized "night on earth." Some of the drivers are immigrants: Isaach De Bankolé plays an unnamed Ivory Coast driver in Paris, ferrying the Blind Woman (played by Béatrice Dalle) to the edge of a canal or river for no apparent reason after throwing out two earlier fares, a pair of fellow Africans, for being snooty. German immigrant Helmut Grokenberge (played by Armin Mueller-Stahl) tries to drive New Yorkers YoYo (played by Giancarlo Esposito) and Angela (played by Rosie Perez), but his skills are limited and YoYo volunteers to drive instead.

The other segments—with cabbies and customers from the same country—are comic encounters set in Italy, Los Angeles, and Helsinki. If the night belongs to the taxi drivers of the world, the best we can hope for them is a good tip.

Recommended Reading

Ebert, Roger. "Night on Earth." *Chicago Sun-Times*, 8 May 1992. Celebrates the filmmaker's characters who "seem divorced from the ordinary society of their cities; they're loners and floaters. We sense they have more in common with one another than with the daytime inhabitants of their cities. And their cabs, hurtling through the deserted streets, are like couriers on a mission to nowhere."

⊢⊣⊢⊣

No Logo: Brands, Globalization, and Resistance

ANTI-GLOBALIZATION

2003, 42 mins., United States
Producer: Kelly Garner
Traditional Documentary, based on Naomi Klein, *No Logo* (2000)
Distributor: Media Education Foundation

This film is primarily a one-woman show, starring Naomi Klein, the author of the bible of the anti-globalization movement, *No Logo*. This film is the ultimate talking head documentary, but its message comes from an articulate, intelligent, and charismatic activist who is "taking aim at the brand bullies," as the subtitle of her book states.

The film offers a clear and convincing gloss on Klein's principal message: by the 1980s corporations who sold products realized that their true product "was not the object they made but an idea, a lifestyle." Thus the early masters of corporate branding—Coca-Cola, Disney, and McDonald's—began selling happiness or world brotherhood or convenience to customers. Soon the field was crowded: Nike was selling sports excitement, Diesel was selling nonconformity, Starbucks presented itself as the "third place" or a community center that was neither home nor work, and even IKEA was selling democracy (it's up to *you* to decide how to assemble your home furnishings).

The ultimate brand maneuver was Disney's creation of Celebration, its planned community in Florida. The "first branded town" allowed citizens to live inside a brand, to have the first "fully privatized life"—Disney's "brand nirvana." Celebration allows, by the way, no franchise restaurants or advertising billboards within the city limits.

Klein traces the creation of branding as the dominant mode of corporate public life from its early comforting personal logos—like the Quaker Oats man and Aunt Jemima—through its contemporary manifestations, which are characterized by marketing to youth, reducing the range of choice to consumers, and downsizing unionized workers to temporary employees.

Although the film's subtitle is "Brands, Globalization, and Resistance," it delivers the goods mainly for the first and a little of the second. It leaves the third to other anti-globalization films to pursue (see *Showdown in Seattle* or *This Is What Democracy Looks Like*).

Recommended Reading

Klein, Naomi. *Fences and Windows: Dispatches from the Front Lines of the Globalization Debate.* London: Picador, 2002. Collection of journalistic pieces, many of them on anti-globalization protests worldwide.

▶▶▶
No Sweat

ANTI-GLOBALIZATION
SWEATSHOPS

2005, 54 mins., United States
Director: Amie Williams
Traditional Documentary
Distributor: Balmaiden Films (www.
   balmaidenfilms.com)

Los Angeles has almost five thousand garment contractors and untold numbers of Latino and Asian immigrant workers, most of whom are employed in sweatshops that pay low wages with no benefits. Into this highly competitive and generally unpleasant labor environment two companies with hip credentials, crusading CEOs, and financial backers with anti-globalization rhetoric promise to make cool T-shirts without sweated labor. Vermonter Ben Cohen, of Ben & Jerry's Ice Cream, and Canadian entrepreneur Dov Charney vow to treat their workers with respect, pay them decent wages and benefits, and build a successful garment factory from scratch in a world market that favors outsourcing when even U.S. sweatshops have trouble with the bottom line.

Sweat X was launched by Ben Cohen's $2.5 million investment that created a union-friendly shop (UNITE), hourly wages, new, computerized equipment, English-language classes for the workers, and an advertising slogan that boasted "clothes with a conscience." American Apparel was founded by the hyperkinetic Charney without any venture capital, using what he calls "vertical integration" (everything, from thread to finished garment, is made on site), offering shop-floor massage stations but not union membership, traditional piece rate (with the twist of competing in "pods" of workers rather than individually), and an advertising campaign that was sexy and daring (using real people who actually sweat, says one of his L.A. staff fashionistas).

Sweat X tanked and American Apparel thrived. Amie Williams, who directed, among other films, the exciting *One Day Longer: The Story of the Frontier Strike* (in *Working Stiffs*),

attempts to find out why. Dov Charney is sure he knows the answer: all that phony Ben Cohen talk about workers' cooperatives—Sweat X was inspired in part by the pioneering Basque Mondragon Workers' Cooperatives—doesn't cut it: "You gotta have a bleeping director." While Charney wouldn't support UNITE's union drive at his factory, he nonetheless organized a campaign, Legalize LA, which fought for citizenship for undocumented workers.

Ben and Dov make a great comedy counterpoint; not so funny are the lost jobs when Sweat X goes under and Dov receives sexual harassment complaints, even as his workers earn—he says—more than any other garment workers around. If you have a sense of humor you might find Ben's remark that his company failed because it was "too well financed" amusing, but when you see the whirling dervish known as Dov at work you might conclude that being laid back and from the People's Republic of Vermont may sell dessert but not T-shirts.

Recommended Reading

Bacon, David. Interview with Amie Williams. KQED (radio), 2005 (online at www.balmaidenfilms.com). The noted immigrant and labor photographer and writer and the director discuss the film in detail.

Wolf, Jaime. "And You Thought Abercrombie & Fitch was Pushing It? Everyone Knows Sex Sells Clothing, But No One Has Taken that Idea Further than Dov Charney of American Apparel." *New York Times Magazine*, 23 April 2006. The title says it all, but a few of Charney's problems come through as well as his assertion that he pays "an average of twice the minimum wage (and sometimes much more)."

▶▶▶
Not This Time: The Story of the Simon Jones Memorial Campaign

ANTI-GLOBALIZATION
CONTAINERIZED SHIPPING

2002, 25 mins., United Kingdom
Producer: Simon Jones Memorial Campaign
Agit-Prop Documentary

Distributor: Simon Jones Memorial Campaign (www.simonjones.org.uk)

This film documents an appalling result of what the British call the "casualisation" of the dockers' workforce. In 1998, Simon Jones was sent by an employment agency, Personnel Selection, to the Shoreham docks of the Euromin company to unload cargo in the hold of the ship. He had no experience on the docks and no training on site. He died of head injuries within an hour of starting work.

That unloading ships is difficult and dangerous work no person in their right mind would doubt: sending an untrained person to this job is probably nothing short of criminal. Certainly that was what Simon Jones's family and friends believed, as they soon realized that nothing was going to be done about Jones's death.

Through a campaign of civil disobedience and legal demonstrations, they forced the state to prosecute Euromin and its manager, James Martell, for manslaughter in 2001. After a trial revealing Euromin's participation in what was an ongoing campaign of their own to break the union and enforce casualisation on the docks, the jury nonetheless found the defendants not guilty (although it did find the company guilty of violating health and safety regulations).

A number of globalization films has focused on the role of container and other mammoth ships; very few convey the dangers and human cost of this labor-saving technology.

Recommended Reading

Pilger, John. *Hidden Agendas.* London: Vintage, 1998. Includes an essay on the history of dockers' disputes in the United Kingdom with an emphasis on casualisation and Thatcherism.

▷◁▷◁

Now or Never

Ora o mai piu

ANTI-GLOBALIZATION

2003, 96 mins., Italy, in Italian with English subtitles
Director: Lucio Pellegrini
Screenplay: Angelo Carbone, Lucio Pellegrini, and Roan Johnson

Judging from the number of Italian films made about the 2001 G-8 meeting and demonstrations in Genoa, which resulted in the death of one protester and the beatings of many others, it is clear than Italians in particular and Europeans in general have made this event their equivalent to the Seattle demonstrations against the WTO. Lucio Pellegrini has directed the first dramatization of the events, tucking the protests inside a romance between two University of Pisa students.

David (played by Jacopo Bonvicini) is a

Not This Time: Simon Jones Memorial Campaign demonstration at the Shoreham docks. Courtesy Simon Jones Memorial Campaign.

physics graduate student more interested in Viola (played by Violante Placido) than issues of globalization. One sight of Viola distributing leaflets and he's hooked on the cause, however. And although it turns out he is good at organizing, he soon has to choose between taking an important exam or taking part in the Genoa protest. Needless to say he goes to Genoa and witnesses the police riot. And while we might not know if what the older brother of a friend said earlier is prophetic— that the students will give up their high jinks and settle down eventually—certainly David throws himself into the immediate struggle wholeheartedly.

Recommended Reading

Tanzer, Joshua. "Endless Summit." *OffOffOff Film,* 1 June 2004 (online at www.offoffoff.com/film). Film proves that "far from being an abstract academic subject, global economics has become a street-level conflict in which secret meetings are held behind closed doors and heads are cracked in the streets."

Off the Clock: Bill Moyers, producer and host of *Now.*

▸◂▸◂▸◂

Off the Clock

WAL-MART

2002, 60 mins., United States
Producers: Bill Moyers and Now
Correspondent: Andrea Fleischer
TV Documentary

Bill Moyers's *Now* and *Frontline* are both ideally situated to pursue allegations of corporate shortcomings because executives feel compelled to talk to their reporters. This *Now* program is no exception. The Wal-Mart execs don't come off well when discussing allegations that the company makes substantial profits by requiring its workers—oops, associates—to work off the clock. The *New York Times* reporter Andrea Fleischer interviewed forty current and former Wal-Mart and Sam's Club employees who worked overtime or through lunches and breaks without pay. Wal-Mart store managers were especially diligent about asking an associate to clock out just before logging forty hours to avoid paying overtime but then asking the employee to continue to work for a number of hours as a favor.

Although a class action suit is pending against the corporation for allowing this practice, corporate spokespersons maintain that any manager who exhibited such behavior could be terminated. (Not "would" but "could," although the practice is illegal.) When Steven Greenhouse, another *New York Times* reporter, pressed Wal-Mart execs on camera about how many managers have been disciplined for this behavior, they would hem and haw and only say "that it has been, um, taken care of on any issue that, that's been brought to us." What Wal-Mart means is that they have settled out of court with employees who have sued for loss of pay. It turns out that in Wal-Mart corporate culture store managers cannot allow or afford any overtime, so they resort to getting people to work off the clock to make their wage quotas.

After showing a clip from the agit-prop film made by the United Food and Commercial Workers (UFCW)—*Wal-Mart's War on Workers* (q.v.)—Fleischer discusses the Wal-Mart *Manager's Toolbox to Remaining Union Free*, a notorious anti-union document that highlights Wal-Mart's aggressiveness against unions and provides store managers with a direct phone number to alert corporate headquarters when any sign of unionism is spotted. Even the generally conservative National Labor Relations Board (NLRB) filed forty separate and specific complaints against Wal-Mart from 1998 to 2002. Cole Peterson, executive vice president in their "people" division, stated that "not one single allegation was substantiated in terms of Wal-Mart having terminated someone for union activities," although Wal-Mart is appealing some of the decisions. Fleischer then concluded: Wal-Mart was found guilty of dozens of violations in ten of the complaints, but there is "not a single store in the [American] Wal-Mart empire [that] has a union."

Recommended Reading

Greenhouse, Steven. "Forced to Work Off the Clock, Some Fight Back." *New York Times,* 19 November 2004. Extensive analysis of off-the-clock allegations and lawsuits involving Wal-Mart and other employers.

▶▶▶

The Oil Factor: Behind the War on Terror

OIL

2005, 93 mins., United States
Director: Gerard Ungerman and Audrey Brohy
Traditional Documentary
Distributor: Facets (www.facets.org)

Is oil the key factor in the Middle East wars of the last ten years? If it is, then the ostensible purpose of this documentary is to argue that the U.S. wars against Afghanistan and Iraq are driven by the politics and economics of oil. Fair enough. But the documentary covers these wars, the U.S. corporations like Bechtel and Halliburton who profit from them, and some of the notorious scandals in

the news, such as the Abu Ghraib prison abuses in Iraq, with ambitious and sweeping scenarios that sometimes take our mind (and eyes) away from oil.

Of course these sequences are all important, but they do move us away from the doomsday predictions about the end of oil that the filmmakers also provide. The filmmakers to a certain extent had already made their film about the wars and their horrors: *The Hidden Wars of Desert Storm* (2001). Depending on your tolerance for information on how the U.S. will run out of oil in five years and how oil policy affects the world's food chain—the opening subjects of the film—*The Oil Factor* may have just the right balance. But many other documentaries about oil and scarce resources (see topical index) cover this ground more adeptly.

Recommended Reading

Gates, Anita. "Fierce if Familiar Arguments about Iraq and Other Topics." *New York Times,* 15 July 2005. Filmmakers "never make a coherent case" as they pursue too many albeit "well researched" topics.

▶▶▶

Oil on Ice

OIL

2005, 60 mins., United States
Directors: Bo Boudart and Dale Djerassi
Traditional Documentary
Distributor: Zeiden Media (www.zeiden media.com)

Films against drilling for oil in the Arctic National Wildlife Refuge in Alaska, like this one, almost always ask the same question. Why should we exploit the 3.2 billion gallons of oil there if they can power America through only two hundred days of its usual consumption? Shouldn't we turn to solar power, wind power, and hybrid automobiles instead? Why not leave these nineteen million acres to the caribou herds, the polar bears, and the Arctic Circle sea creatures that the native populations have depended on for so long?

This film tries to answer these questions

with a straightforward pitch: the diversity and beauty of nature and the independence of native peoples, especially the Gwich'in Indians and the Inupiat, demand protection against drilling. And although the film does raise the issue of our national energy policy that favors oil and more oil, it may miss the agenda of the U.S. oligarchs who dominate the geopolitical or globalization struggle for energy. That agenda is relatively simple: if the United States is to control or at least consume the majority of the world's oil reserves then it must flex its political muscle in its own backyard. Never mind that the Arctic oil supply does not rival Iraq's.

The cinematography is superb. But so is the Refuge and as of 2006 it is still up for grabs.

Recommended Reading

Bass, Rick. *Caribou Rising: Defending the Porcupine Herd, Gwich-'in Culture, and the Arctic National Wildlife Refuge.* San Francisco: Sierra Club Books, 2004.The noted environmentalist and novelist reviews (and reinforces) the case for protecting the Refuge wildlife.

▶◀▶◀

Our Friends in the North

THATCHERISM

1996, TV series, 9 episodes of 70 mins. each, United Kingdom
Directors: Simon Cellan Jones, Pedr James, and Stuart Urban
Screenplay: Peter Flannery, from his own play, *Our Friends in the North* (1982)

In this extraordinary television series tracing the political and personal fortunes of four close friends over a thirty-one-year period (1964–95), the "north" is Newcastle-Upon-Tyne in the United Kingdom. The titles of all the episodes are simply dates: six of the titles designate General Election years. A number of the principal characters are Labour Party activists, and election campaigning and political fallout when the Tories win are especially highlighted in almost all of the episodes. The 1984 episode is, for example, not about an election year but the year of the miners'

strike, the pivotal event in Prime Minister Margaret Thatcher's career.

Although their relationship will be tested many times over thirty years, Nicky Hutchinson (played by Christopher Eccleston) and Mary Soulsby (played by Gina McGee) are soul mates: he's more than a little arrogant, fired up by some slight participation in the U.S. Civil Rights Movement in 1964, tries politics of both the left and far left, and in an important subplot works as a PR man for Austin Donohue (played by Alun Armstrong), a former Newcastle council Labour stalwart who turns to a shady (and shoddy) developer, John Edwards (played by Geoffrey Hutchings) to get some high-rise council flats built.

Mary's common sense deserts her when she takes up with Tosker Cox (played by Mark Strong), who with Geordie Peacock (played by Daniel Craig) round out the original group of four friends. Mary and Tosker have a son, Anthony (played by Daniel Casey), who will become a policeman required to put down a picket line of miners in the strike of 1984. Mary herself will go on to become a lawyer and a member of the county council, while Tosker is taken up by the Thatcherite Tories as a fine example of the ambitious new businessmen they wish to cultivate. Geordie runs away to London and becomes the right-hand man to Benny Barratt (played by Malcolm McDowell), a Soho porn and nightclub czar.

Even this relatively brief summary does scant justice to a complicated plot line, which recapitulates the highlights of thirty years of contemporary British history and politics. The scandals over poorly built high-rise apartments, the corrupt vice squads of the London Metropolitan Police Force, the anarchists and other political types who led demonstrations and dabbled in terrorism in the 1960s, the increase in the numbers of homeless during the Thatcher years all establish the baseline for the crises of our four heroes and heroines. None of them acts particularly heroically, by the way, and in fact all of them are seriously flawed personally even as they on occasion try to do the right thing politically.

It took the BBC more than ten years to

bring the original play to the screen because the high-rise construction scheme was based on actual Newcastle figures and their Tory parliamentary patron—whose daughter in the film defeats Nicky when he runs for the Labour Party in 1979—was also an actual government minister. Because of the delay, Flannery was able to make his screenplay current through the mid-nineties, just before Tony Blair's New Labour Party regained the government.

Recommended Reading

Eaton, Michael. *Our Friends in the North.* London: British Film Institute, 2005. Close analysis of the film and its major political themes.

⋈⋈⋈

Outrageous Fortunes

WAL-MART

2004, 6 episodes of 60 mins. each, United
   Kingdom
Producer: BBC Three
Correspondent: Emeka Onono
TV Documentary

Although this long-running BBC television program is not readily available outside of the United Kingdom, its 2004 survey of some of the world's "outrageous fortunes" and the people who control them deserves to be seen. In addition to Sam Walton's billionaire heirs, the series looks at the families behind Disney, Bacardi, Nintendo, Guinness, and De Beers, all global companies selling culture, rum, games, beer, and diamonds, to put it (too) simply. (Only the Nintendo episode was available online at Google Video.)

For the Wal-Mart essay correspondent Emeka Onono visited the United States and discovered more than just a rich family: he found donations to charity, stock options for executives, and even a couple who were married in the store during the obligatory employees' Wal-Mart cheer (give me a W . . .). He also discovered the indictments against Wal-Mart for employing illegal immigration and their fierce campaign to undercut prices

of the competing food chains, especially in California in 2004 during the United Food and Commercial Workers' strike.

Onono also interviewed supermarket experts who explain why Wal-Mart was so successful. And in keeping with the quest motif of the series, he pursued but did not actually speak to Alice Walton, the daughter of Sam Walton and reputedly the richest woman in the world, to find out what she spends her money on.

It is hard to say whether the BBC believes Wal-Mart's hype about its benefits package, but here is one of the producer's comments about "making money the Wal-Mart way": "Make it company policy that unions are unnecessary with welfare schemes such as [Wal-Mart's]; if you say it enough and make a company video all about how much money unions waste, your staff may begin to believe it" (www.bbc.co.uk/bbcthree/tv/outrageous_fortunes/walmart.shtml). Maybe.

Recommended Reading

Huey, John, and Sam Walton. *Sam Walton: Made In America.* New York: Doubleday, 1992. The true story: how to become a billionaire if you don't inherit wealth. Used copies sell for one cent on Amazon.com.

⋈⋈⋈

Outsource This!

OUTSOURCING AND OFFSHORING

2004, 4 mins., United States
Producer: Communications Workers of
   America (CWA)
Online Mock Documentary
Distributor: CWA (www.outsourceoutrage
   .com)

In this brief but charming online mock documentary, Jason Alexander, who starred as George Costanza on *Seinfeld*, plays a representative from the imaginary National Job Registry Program who visits a classroom of young children and urges them to accept job placement in Pakistan and other outsourcing locales. During this light but telling agit-prop exercise, one child asks, "Where's Pakistan?"

The representative explains that Pakistan is not technically in the Bush Administration's Axis of Evil—running his hand across a map from the Middle East to North Korea—because we wouldn't want to send anyone "in harm's way." A title at the end reinforces what Susan George calls the "debt boomerang": "Outsourcing destroys jobs and drives down wages."

Recommended Reading

George, Susan. *The Debt Boomerang.* London: Pluto Press, 1992. Concentrates on "how Third World debt harms us all," that is, the economy of the First World.

ᗴᗴᗴ

The Phantom of the Operator

LABOR HISTORY
WOMEN WORKERS AND CHILD LABOR

2004, 65 mins., Canada
Director: Caroline Martel
Structuralist and Postmodern Documentary

Using about half of the two hundred public relations, advertising, and industrial films made by Bell Telephone and Western Electric in the twentieth century—some as early as 1903—Canadian filmmaker Caroline Martel has created a remarkable portrayal of one of the first public voices of globalization: the telephone operator. This film, beautifully edited and scored (using one of the first electronic musical instruments, the Ondes Martenot, or Martenot Waves, still in rare use today), gracefully hovers between the pure visual forms of a structuralist or art documentary and the more historical material offered by clips from archival and feature films.

Martel makes a persuasive case that telephone operators were the "first agents of globalization," in the words of her narrator who calls herself the ghost of the "invisible women workers" who created the first worldwide telecommunications net. The ghost comes to her role as narrator, she tells us, as if the sound waves of her voice were retrieved from outer space. This science fiction premise is

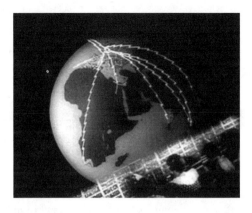

The Phantom of the Operator: Telephones, the first globalized communications network. Courtesy Women Make Movies.

one of the ways Martel holds her documentary together.

Although she uses mainly archival footage, she occasionally excerpts an obscure feature film or two, as well as brief footage of what looks like the great French dancer Lois Fuller in a semidiaphanous and hence ghostly gown, but she turns out to be an anonymous visitor from one of Eadweard Muybridge's experimental motion films.

Although the phone companies wanted to project a feminine, homey image of their "girls," the work was hard and stressful. It also served—and was touted to a certain extent—as a class conveyor belt moving the girls out of clean working-class homes into the world of business and middle-class customers, especially in the early days when phones were not yet a mass market item.

Recommended Readings

Debray, Regis. *Des machines et des ames: trois conferences.* Paris: Descartes & Cie, 2002. In one of the director's sources of inspiration (English translation not yet available), Debray defines the "mediosphere" in which "each historical period is governed by major shifts in the technologies of transmission" (according to a review in *Wired*, January 1995, online at www.wired.com/wired/archive/3.01/debray_pr.html).

Franklin, Ursula. *The Real World of Technology.* Toronto: House of Anansi Press, 1998. Cited by the director as her second source of inspiration, this book is an analysis of the interaction of technology and culture.

▶▶▶
The Ploughman's Lunch

THATCHERISM

1983, 107 mins., United Kingdom
Director: Richard Eyre
Screenplay: Ian McEwan

In England tourists and locals alike often order a ploughman's lunch at urban and rural pubs, confident that they are eating the traditional fare (bread, cheese, Branston pickle) of the farm workers of yore. Richard Eyre's film has a go at debunking this minor myth in its zeal to attack Thatcherism as an ideology of deception and betrayal. Although farm workers no doubt ate bread and cheese, the director uses the public's gullibility to symbolize their ignorance of the real reasons behind the Falkland Islands War and its continuity with the same colonialism that led a Labour government in the 1950s to conspire with France and Israel to invade Egypt to keep the Suez Canal out of Egyptian control.

BBC radio journalist James Penfield (played by Jonathan Pryce) is an opportunist, a product of the Thatcherite ethos: he ignores his dying mother, is ashamed of his working-class roots, but has a fierce drive to write a "true history" of the Suez Canal War, which will establish the secret British diplomacy as meritorious. His pursuit of two women—a historian, Ann Barrington (played by Rosemary Harris) and her daughter, Susan Barrington (played by Charlie Dore)—is an obviously unsavory business, because he pursues the older woman who has researched the Suez issue and he wants to use her notes. (He lies to her about his politics.)

This intellectual rogue's progress ends at the 1982 Conservative Party Conference in Brighton where Thatcher tells her cheering followers that she intends "to tell the people the truth, and the people will be our judge," as

The Ploughman's Lunch: Journalist James Penfield (Jonathan Pryce) flatters historian Ann Barrington (Rosemary Harris).

she celebrates the victory over the pathetic Argentine armed forces. Penfield is soon betrayed by the daughter just as he has betrayed her mother.

Although his rewriting of the history of Suez is a hit, he comes across as a hollow man. When he enters the conference he ignores a group of antinuclear protestors who had befriended him earlier. He marginalizes even further the only anti-Thatcher forces the film offers.

Recommended Reading

Brown, Simon. "The Ploughman's Lunch." *British Film Institute Screen Online* (at www .screenonline.org.uk/film). "The film presents a bleak Britain with little hope for the future."

ᕼᕼᕼ
Il Posto dell'anima

The Place of the Soul
The Soul's Haven

CHANGES IN THE WORKPLACE: EUROPE
OUTSOURCING AND OFFSHORING

2003, 106 mins., Italy, in Italian with English
  subtitles
Director: Riccardo Milani
Screenplay: Riccardo Milani and Domenico
  Starnone

When Italian workers at a tire company in a small mountain town (Campolaro in the Abruzzi mountains) begin chaining themselves to the gates because the U.S. owners have announced the company's closure, Riccardo Milani's film takes the industrial struggle of the Carair Tire Factory into a spirited celebration of Italianness—family stresses and joys, food obsessions, and operatic confrontations. The film attests to the resilience of a recurring Italian cinematic tradition, that of "rosy realism" or *commedia all'italiana*, in which serious subjects are given a light touch with Italian stereotypes lovingly portrayed. (See Marcus in "Recommended Reading" below and the film *Bread and Chocolate*, in *Working Stiffs*.)

What might be only a local blip on the global screen turns into national story when shots of the workers in chains make the television news. Three leaders emerge, with one agenda—saving the factory—but conflicted personal lives. Antonio (played by Silvio Orlando) has illusions about his girlfriend returning to him from the big city (Milan). Salvatore (played by Michele Placido) is the leading militant but his son is more interested in computers than tires. Mario (played by Claudio Santamaria), meanwhile, really enjoys organizing the workers' wives into a fresh pasta coop business.

Films about Argentine workers occupying their closed and abandoned factories because of the demands of deregulation and privatization imposed by transnational organizations such as the World Bank are available—see *The Take* and the *Grupo Alavio Films*—but a similar takeover in an advance industrial nation like Italy is news. And because Italian films often cater to operatic stereotypes, we follow a delegation of Campolaro workers to American for a comic confrontation with their parent corporate executives.

Recommended Reading

Marcus, Millicent. *Italian Film in the Light of Neorealism.* Princeton: Princeton University Press, 1986. Discusses "rosy realism" and *commedia all'italiana* in the context of the better-known tradition of Italian neorealism.

ᕼᕼᕼ
Power Trip

GLOBAL CAPITAL
PRIVATIZATION

2003, 86 mins., United States, in English and
  Georgian with English subtitles
Director: Paul Devlin
Traditional Documentary
Distributor: Films Transit International (www
  .powertrip-themovie.com)

The breakup of the Soviet empire made for interesting new comrades. A U.S. multinational corporation, Applied Energy Services (AES) of Arlington, Virginia, purchased Telasi, the power company of the former Soviet satellite, Georgia, at (surely) the bargain price of $28 million in 1998. With the collapse of their mother ship and the beginning of national independence in 1991, Georgians had begun to rewire their homes—how shall we say?—innovatively, bypassing any meters and tapping into tram lines, street lines, and already wired buildings. As a result, when the U.S. company entered the market, nonpayment of bills was at an astonishing 90 percent. What's a good U.S. company to do? Invest in more infrastructure, bill customers, and cut off their power when they don't pay. Start with the capital city airport: no pay, no electricity.

In this documentary we see that a different kind of chaos ensued. Since monthly incomes averaged fifteen to seventy-five dollars, charging a typical household twenty-four dollars a month fueled public outrage. Piers Lewis, the British-born projects director for AES, who speaks Georgian, is the central figure of the documentary as he tries to enforce a version of market capitalism on a edgy nation that is not too many street demos away from anarchism and after a foray into civil war. On Lewis's side are a group of Georgian investigative television reporters who expose government corruption. When one of them is murdered, Georgia's president Edward Shevardnadze (the former Soviet leader) suggests, unconvincingly, that it was not a political murder. The film's credits add that an AES-Telasi executive was also murdered, after filming was completed.

As a case study for First World investors moving into what we used to define as the (Soviet) Second World, rewiring Georgia can only be classified as scary. The AES people remain cheerful for a time, even though the Georgian elite, both officials and their friends, do everything possible to sabotage this power trip into monopoly capitalism. We don't find out enough about the worker bees of this industry, although the accidentally electrocuted body of an ex-customer who failed to jerry-build his own electrical bypass system is sobering. In the meantime we see a fascinating assortment of television commercials, cartons, and archival footage about a culture clash that would be a globalization comedy if it were funny. *Electricity Today* (online at www.electricity-today.com),

an industry magazine, was not amused: "It's a must-see for any utility manager still dreaming of fat offshore profits."

Recommended Readings

Holden, Stephen. "American Know-How Can't Prevail Nohow." *New York Times*, 10 December 2003. A "superbly balanced and organized documentary about the politics of electricity" that "underscores what became painfully evident at the height of the Enron scandal: political power and the distribution of energy are intimately connected."

Stratton, David. "Power Trip." *Variety,* 14 February 2003. The film "provides unique insights into the role played by a major American company in an impoverished, corrupt, almost Third World country."

⋈⋈⋈

Profit & Nothing But! Or Impolite Thoughts On the Class Struggle

ANTI-GLOBALIZATION
BANKING AND GLOBAL FINANCING
GLOBAL CAPITAL
HISTORY OF GLOBALIZATION

2001, 52 mins., France/Belgium, in English
  and French with English subtitles
Director: Raoul Peck
Postmodern Documentary
Distributor: First Run/Icarus Films

Raul Peck, who was born in Haiti but raised and educated in Zaire (the Democratic Republic of the Congo), is best known for two highly political feature films, *Lumumba* (2000) which dissected with great verve the probable CIA assassination of Patrice Lumumba, the Congo's nationalist leader in 1961, and *Sometimes in April* (2005), which dramatized the Rwandan genocide of 1994.

Although *Profit & Nothing But!* may represent his "impolite thoughts on the class struggle," I would characterize it as an extended and open-ended visual and verbal meditation on a quotation (given on an opening title) from Gerard Debreu, who won the 1983 Nobel Prize in Economic Sciences: "Every economist has the duty to inform his fellow man that the right to live cannot always be vouchsafed for reasons of cost." For him, globalization means the apparent triumph of the wealthiest 2 percent of the rich countries over the poor.

Using a series of remarkably similar speeches by eminent talking heads (such as Immanuel Wallerstein, the former president of the International Sociological Association, who regards modern capitalism to be in crisis), Peck juxtaposes their sometimes finicky analyses of capitalism with footage of Haitians trying to cope with their notorious history (archival footage of dictator François "Papa Doc" Duvalier handing out banknotes to the poor) and their improvised attempts to make do (a worker at a wood lathe powered by a man on a bicycle). He visits Duvalier's notorious prison on the Haitian coast while singers chant "Hell is on earth."

But Duvalier is long gone and capitalism remains. Footage of Nelson Rockefeller and Duvalier is replaced with shots of Thatcher and Reagan. Peck even concludes that "capitalism has won," although he wonders for how long. One of his experts bemoans the fact that "people who have hammers in their heads see nails everywhere," and capitalism offers us only an "economic hammer."

Like the woman in *The Girl in the Café* (q.v.), Peck is obsessed with the fact that thousands of children in the world die every day. One of Peck's undocumented cinematic quotations features a surrealistic funeral of a child: that image seems to have more power for Peck than economic analysis.

Recommended Reading

Kehr, Dave. "Haitian Capitalism and a Hunt for Diamonds in the Sea." *New York Times*, 8 May 2002. Although Peck is "a sloganeer, given to voice-over statements like 'capitalism has succeeded in buying our silence' . . . he is also a filmmaker with a fine eye for people and landscapes."

▸◂▸◂

Railroad of Hope

CHINA
MIGRANT LABOR (OTHER THAN THE
 UNITED STATES)

2002, 56 mins., China, in Mandarin with
 English subtitles

Director: Ning Ying
Cinema-Verité Documentary

Every year thousands of Sichuan Province peasants head to the railroad station and wait—sometimes as long as two days—for an overcrowded train to take them to Xinjiang, an autonomous region two thousand miles away, where they will help harvest cotton. This is a contemporary Chinese phenomenon and paradox: peasants who form a migratory labor force after their own mountainous farming duties are finished at home. These migrants will return home each year, but they are just a tiny subset of the millions of rural Chinese who migrate to the cities, sometimes to stay.

They are packed into trains after entering what are virtually cattle chutes at the railhead. The unseen narrator asks one of them, "Are you happy?" The reply: "Happy people do not have to go far away for a job." Why do they put themselves through this? In part to earn money to pay for education for their children. Others answer indirectly: the ideogram for peasant is a yoke.

But still others told the director, Ning Ying, a slightly different story. She recounted that "most began this journey not only, as one could assume, for economic reasons, but also with the desire to extend their horizon and see a new world" (International Forum of New Cinema in Berlin, 2002).

Ning Ying, who was an assistant director for Bernardo Bertolucci's *The Last Emperor* (1987), has directed a number of feature films herself, including *On the Beat* (1994), which used actual policemen in the roles of policemen. That film is part of her Beijing Trilogy about changes in the ordinary lives of people during the contemporary era of capitalist development.

Recommended Readings

Vietor, Cory. "Interview: Ning Ying." *City Weekend*, 7 December 2004 (online at www.city weekend.com.cn/en/beijing/features/2004_19/ Movies_CW19Interview). Overview of her career.

Zhen, Zhang. "Woman with a Movie Camera." *Nieman Report*, Spring 2004 (online at www.google.com/search?hl=en&lr=&q=Zhen% 2C+Zhang.+"Woman+with+aMovie+Camera.

"++&btnG=Search"). Another overview of her career.

▸◂▸◂

Rancho California (Por Favor)

MIGRANT LABOR (UNITED STATES)

2002, 65 or 56 mins., USA
Director: John T. Caldwell
Mixed Traditional and Post Modern
   Documentary

This close scrutiny of a number of migrant labor shantytowns in San Diego and Orange counties in Southern California from 1995 to 2001 has a split personality—like the state itself, some may say. Somewhat traditionally filmed but no less shocking because of it, this film is a look inside the shacks of the Mexican Mixteca and Guatamalan Kajobal peoples who live alongside the rich estates they serve as maids, garden workers, and construction help. With a sideways glance at what director John T. Caldwell perceives as the hopelessly inadequate perspective of contemporary academic media specialists, he challenges the idea that one cannot film the Other, that is, cannot speak "with any voice other than autobiographical."

To illustrate the latter remark, he turns his camera over to a migrant worker, who leads us through a tour of his extended wooden shack. Except for a shaky camera, the footage is not so different from Caldwell's own, although at one point the worker refers somewhat positively to a local *padrone* or boss, a verbal gesture not likely to come from Caldwell, who believes that the shantytowns are a deliberate creation of California's elite to guarantee invisible but nearby cheap labor.

A few surprises punctuate this tour of shantytowns, some of which lie next to amusement parks or golf courses as well as private estates. Caldwell does find a nice landowner, who allows workers to camp on his land. And he learns that there is a regular Monday night prostitute service for the workers, who get condoms from an activist for the migrant cause.

These workers speak neither English nor Spanish. And they live among Californians who should know better. Caldwell, in one of his rare sick jokes, acknowledges this as he cuts from a golfer's practice stroke to a gold ball bouncing against a shanty wall.

Recommended Reading

Boyle, T. Corghessan. *Tortilla Curtain.* New York: Viking Press, 1995. Novel of the tragic interaction of Mexican migrants and residents of a gated California suburban community.

▸◂▸◂

Rebellion in Patagonia

NEOCOLONIALISM

1974, 110 mins., Argentina, in Spanish with
   English subtitles
Director: Héctor Olivera
Screenplay: Héctor Olivera, Fernando Ayala,
   and Osvaldo Bayer, based on Osvaldo
   Bayer's nonfiction book, *La Patagonia Re-
   belde* (1972–1976)

The film begins and ends with murder: the opening sequence briefly chronicles the assassination of an officer, who we later learn was responsible for the massacre three years earlier (1920) of hundreds of workers of the anarchist-led federation of Patagonia. The film then concludes with that massacre.

The unusual politics and demographics of the region are captured in the first meeting between the workers and their anarchist leaders in the city of Rio Gallegos. Above the speakers' table are crossed flags—red for syndicalism and black for anarchy. A portrait of the grand old anarchist Peter Kropotkin is on the wall. The workers are from Chile, Spain, Poland, Germany, and Argentina. One employer caves in to their demands right away.

This early success actually works to make the anarchists a target to be destroyed. The governor of the state jokes: "Even Lenin had to do away with twenty thousand anarchists." When small strikes soon lead to a general strike of both urban and rural workers, a local judge makes a plea for the ruling class to obey their own laws. Government leaders seem to sympathize with the workers and belittle the local elite. Even the commander of the army, Zavala (played by Héctor Alterio) appears to favor the strikers, eventually brokering a deal to have the workers give up their weapons to achieve a written agreement.

Needless to say the state does not eventually support the agreement and Zavala turns vicious. The syndicalist ideal—assemblies of all the workers voting to make decisions for their federation—seems hopelessly naive in the face of duplicitous state power.

Director Héctor Olivera completed this film during the 1970s, an era of still another Argentine right-wing government. One of his final scenes, in which the Argentine ruling elite are led by a U.S. aide in a round of "For he's a jolly good fella" for Commander Zavala, alludes to the neocolonial situation, for the American is clearly intended to be an analogy for the CIA.

Richard Porton's important study, *Film and the Anarchist Imagination,* emphasizes a number of the strengths of the film—the alliance between rural and urban workers, for example, and the provocation of tackling such a political subject—but his summary of the end of the film, which describes the execution of two leaders (Antonio Soto, played by Luis Brandoni, and "the German," played by José Soriano,) is not supported by at least one version of the film that shows Soto galloping away towards Chile (although we never find out if he made it).

Recommended Reading

Porton, Richard. *Film and the Anarchist Imagination.* London: Verso, 1999. Very fine analysis of the film, but Porton worries that the film "ends with such tragic finality that a resuscitation of bygone Argentine militancy becomes too difficult to imagine."

▶◀▶◀▶◀

Re-Code.com Commercial

WAL-MART

Re-Code.com Commercial, 2004, 5 mins., United States
I'm Not Stealing . . . Don't Put Me Behind Bars, 2004, 10 mins., United States
Producers: The Yes Men
Online Film (www.re-code.com)

Re-Code.com is both the title of one of two related digital films and the name of the website by the Yes Men, globalization pranksters who offered potential Wal-Mart consumers bar codes to print for the low prices of their own choice.

"It is hard *not* to write satire," observed the great Roman poet, Juvenal. That is probably the appropriate excuse or context for the apology to Wal-Mart by the Yes Men for propagating their Re-code.com website, where visitors should "pay only what they want" for brand-name goods at Wal-Mart, using the business model Priceline.com made famous. After entering the bar codes of both the brand-name item they want and the code for the cheaper generic version—"pre-shopping" in Yes Men jargon—potential customers could "re-code" a bar code sticker, print it out (with labels available at an office supply store), go to Wal-Mart, attach the new label, and "buy" the item. (Use the electronic scanners, the site urged tactfully, since they tend not to notice price discrepancies.)

Wal-Mart of course went wild with cries of indignation and stop thief, sending cease-and-desist letters of such lawyerly impact that the Yes Men suspended their bar code data bank and edited their original *Re-Code.com Commercial* (which features *Star Trek*'s William Shatner singing—in karaoke style—about "the Age of Aquarius . . . a new era of consumer power") to emphasize its intention as satire. They added a second film, *I'm Not Stealing . . . Don't Put Me Behind Bars,* which uses an animated talking bar code head to plead their case for innocent high jinks at the expense of capitalist spoilsports who can't take a joke. They added some zingers as well: they urged switching the bar codes of Winchester Light Target Load Ammunition with Nerf Ballistic Balls because there "ain't no war like a Nerf war."

The Yes Men went on to much bigger and better things—see *The Yes Men*—but these early films set the tone for their successful satires to come. Trying to be serious, the Yes Men also asked if bar codes are in fact protected by copyright. We never actually stole anything, they cried, so Wal-Mart should not prosecute them. The Bentonville, Arkansas, corporation was not amused.

Recommended Readings

Mieszkowski, Katherine. "Steal this Barcode," 10 April 2003, and "Don't Mess with Wal-Mart," 17 April 2003. *Associated Press* (online at www.salon.com). A review of the controversy, featuring remarks by Tom Williams, Wal-Mart spokesman: "We were just concerned about what appeared to be an open invitation to steal from Wal-Mart and other stores. We can't let anything affect our bottom line."

▸◂▸◂▸◂

Red Desert

HISTORY OF GLOBALIZATION
OIL

1964, 120 mins., Italy, in Italian with English
   subtitles
Director: Michelangelo Antonioni
Screenplay: Michelangelo Antonioni and
   Tonino Guerra

Red Desert: The Ravenna gas works—industrial landscape as source of alienation.

The stunning industrial landscapes of Ravenna, Italy, photographed here by Carlo Di Palma, may not be able to compete with the city's legendary Byzantine mosaics in its medieval churches, but the filmmaker's fascinating mise-en-scène provides the viewer with a time machine to the Italy of Enrico Mattei, the controversial post–World War II energy czar whose career and mysterious death is the subject of Francesco Rosi's *The Mattei Affair* (q.v.). The industrial complex in the film is the petrochemical works of ENI, the Italian national oil company, which Mattei headed.

Antonioni's film dramatizes the neurasthenia of Giuliana (played by the inestimable Monica Vitti), the wife of a plant supervisor who treats her like a mental patient, and her lover, Corrado Zeller (played by an unlikely Richard Harris), the visiting son of the company's owner, who is trying to recruit Italian workers and engineers for a new plant in Patagonia (they can have Italian newspapers, yes, but wives, no). Add to this mix the striking workers at one of the refinery's units and assorted decadent friends of the estranged couple who occupy distant ends of the class spectrum.

For many viewers, not much seems to happen; for Antonioni the revelation of Italian society through its industrial pretensions and successes is obvious. The film is a foray into early-stage globalization filtered through a master of cinematic style whose trademark, world-weary angst shared by alienated lovers, is used here to reveal a precarious social and economic system that seems doomed. *Red Desert*'s mise-en-scène, which in the end includes a quarantined plague ship at canalside, has the look of a structuralist documentary perhaps because, as Nicky Hamlyn suggests in *Film Art Phenomena* (London: British Film Institute Publishing, 2003), in many experimental films "landscape forms an objective correlative of the protagonists' state of mind." They are victims of a plague of ill spirit.

Recommended Reading

Cameron, Ian, and Robin Wood. *Antonioni.* New York: Praeger, 1971. Detailed chapter on the film, charting Antonioni's ambivalent reaction to the industrial mise-en-scène: he films its beauty yet offers its poisonous smoke as an external manifestation of his heroine's neuroticism.

▶┤▶┤

The Revolution Will Not Be Televised

Chavez: Inside the Coup

HISTORY OF GLOBALIZATION
NEOCOLONIALISM
OIL

2003, 74 mins., Ireland, in Spanish with
    English subtitles
Directors: Kim Bartley and Donnacha
    O'Briain
Cinema-Verité Documentary

Venezuela, the fourth largest oil-producing country in the world, remained firmly in the American sphere of globalization until Hugo Chavez, a former paratrooper, was elected president in 1998. Although the oil industry had been nationalized, its profits still benefited mainly the Venezuelan elite, who conspired with members of the army, business leaders, and media executives (and possibly the CIA) to overthrow Chavez. Chavez's political friendship with Castro, his enthusiastic efforts to reach out to poor people, and his attempt to redistribute the wealth of the nation away from the elite led to a brief and successful coup against him in April 2002.

The private television stations celebrated his exit, while the state-run television outlet sympathetic to him was simply cut off the air. The new interim government soon faced more than a million supporters of Chavez in the streets of Caracas who demanded his return. Gunfire was exchanged between pro- and anti-Chavez supporters, and one of the fascinating aspects of this insider look is the manipulation of the television reporting, which tried to portray the Chavez protestors as the aggressors.

The filmmakers were able to have unprecedented access to these events because they had been on assignment to make a biographical documentary of Chavez when the coup developed. Literally caught in the crossfire of attackers and defenders of Chavez, the filmmakers televised the beginnings of a revolution, as Chavez remains an irritant in President Bush II's global strategy. In 2005 Venezuela's U.S. oil subsidiary, Conoco, announced it would sell heating oil to the poor families of Massachusetts who would be hardest hit by winter bills.

The film's title comes from proto-rap singer Gil Scott-Heron's hit, "The Revolution Will Not Be Televised" (1974), which concludes with this line: "The revolution will be live."

Recommended Reading

Ebert, Roger. "The Revolution Will Not Be Televised." *Chicago Sun-Times*, 31 October 2003. Detailed and very positive review.

▶┤▶┤

Rollover

BANKING AND GLOBAL FINANCING
GLOBAL CAPITAL
GLOBAL CATASTROPHES

1981, 118 mins., R, United States
Director: Alan J. Pakula
Screenplay: David Shaber

Although the chemistry between the stars in this political thriller is not very exciting, one shouldn't lose faith in the power of the eurodollar, the subject of the characters' business and romantic partnership. Eurodollars are U.S. dollars deposited by banks in branches abroad as a ready means of international financing; they can also be used as a way of determining interest rates for future fundraising.

Alan Pakula is capable of directing a thriller with an edge: his *Klute* (1971) explored a New York City exec's creepy pursuit of a hooker (played by Jane Fonda), and his *Parallax View* (1974) set the standard for conspiracy films on presidential assassinations. And although the voyeuristic opening sequence of the murder of the president of a major New York bank successfully pulls the viewer in, the film soon veers into unconvincing boardroom and bedroom chatter.

Rollover: Banking execs (Jane Fonda and Kris Kristofferson) approach rich sheiks for loans.

The murdered exec's wife, Lee Winters (played by Jane Fonda), a former film actress, is tempted to become chairman of the board of her husband's company. In a parallel plot, hotshot banking consultant Hubbell Smith (played by Kris Kristofferson) is brought in to rescue another bank that looks like it's heading into the East River. The banker makes a deal—and a date—with the widow: I'll figure out a way to make you chair if you let me play with any commission we realize from my maneuvers. Suffice it to say that they also play some other games, which will not raise anyone's temperature, much less a bank balance.

The plot actually gets complicated now: a Saudi Arabian bank will lend Winters the money to make the deal that will give her the chairmanship and Hubbell gets the 5 percent he needs to protect his other bank. The Saudis, however, have much bigger plans: they are lending millions like this left and right so that when the right moment comes they'll call in all these loans and bankrupt the West.

How they do this may require us to bone up on ECON 101. But before you can say "Pay at the pump," all the commercial banks in the Western world have collapsed and anarchy rules the streets of every metropolis. The ending of the film looks like a postapocalyptic city as imagined in one of the nonfiction books about global disaster written by Mike Davis or any one of a number of films in the

aftermath of a nuclear or climactic catastrophe. In this ending the globe, much less globalization, doesn't survive.

Recommended Reading

Maslin, Janet. "Kris Kristofferson and Jane Fonda in *Rollover.*" *New York Times,* 11 December 1981. Scathing review calls this an unsuccessful love story, satire, and thriller: "If the worldwide monetary situation is indeed as bad as the screenplay makes it out to be, movies this extravagantly silly only make it worse."

▸▸▸

Rouch in Reverse

NEOCOLONIALISM

1995, 51 mins., United Kingdom/United
   States, in English and French with English
   subtitles
Director: Manthia Diawara
Traditional Documentary
Distributor: California Newsreel

As one of the most influential Western ethnographic filmmakers in Africa and a leading progenitor of the French New Wave, Rouch and his reputation are secure. Manthia Diawara's film offers a critical but respectful attempt at reverse anthropology: Rouch is now the subject and Diawara the investigator, rather than Rouch the investigator and the people of French West Africa the subjects.

As Diawara flies into Paris to film Rouch, we see a clip from *Petit a Petit* (a Rouch film from *The Jaguar Quartet*, q.v.). Rouch's subject, a migrant worker, is also flying into Paris. His goal is to see how the French build tall buildings; Diawara wants to see how Rouch represents French attitudes toward West Africans. Diawara makes films in America, but he is from Mali. He wants to discover how imperialism, colonialism, and racism shape French society and interviews French citizens of African descent who do not really feel French.

But as Diawara is led through Rouch's Paris, he realizes that Rouch, too, is probing him. Rouch encourages Diawara to recite a French poem he had memorized in school. Learning French, Diawara reminds us, was the way the colonized thought they would become "black Frenchmen." Thus Rouch reminds Diawara of his complicated French roots.

The urban uprising of African and other Muslim immigrants in 2005 in Paris and other French cities would not have surprised Rouch, who tells Diawara of the heroic black soldiers of the Free French Army who contributed so much to the liberation struggles against the Nazis. Desecrate their Muslim graves, Rouch told audiences in the 1990s when anti-immigrant hostility swept through France led by right-wing politicians, and you desecrate the graves of heroes.

Diawara also appreciates Rouch's *Chronicle of a Summer*, his cinema-verité breakthrough in 1960, because the topics raised by the youths in the film—both black and white—included Algerian independence from France and the rebellion of the Belgian Congo.

Has the legacy of colonialism changed, Diawara speculates, since Rouch began his career in the 1950s? He shows a clip from *Le maitres fous* (*The Mad Masters*) of the Hauka sectarians who imitate their colonial masters in a trance. Rouch comments on his old film: the European elite *are* African's "mad masters."

Recommended Readings

Smith, Craig S. "France Faces a Colonial Legacy: What Makes Someone French?" *New York Times*, 11 November 2005. "The concept of French identity remains rooted deep in the country's centuries-old culture, and a significant portion of the population has yet to accept the increasingly multiethnic makeup of the population."

Stoller, Paul. *The Cinematic Griot: The Ethnography of Jean Rouch*. Chicago: University of Chicago Press,1992. A very sympathetic, convincing account of Rouch's career and his ethnographic work, both in print and on film.

⊣⊢⊣

Saaraba

NEOCOLONIALISM

1988, 86 mins., Senegal, in Wolof and French with English subtitles
Director: Amadou Saalum Seck
Screenplay: Amadou Saalum Seck and Deba N'Diaye
Distributor: California Newsreel

The Wolof word *saaraba* refers to a mythical land of trouble-free existence, probably best translated in English as "utopia" (which plays on Thomas More's famous Greek pun on *eu* and *ou*, both a "happy" place and a place that is "nowhere").

Many of the characters in Amadou Saalum Seck's world are driven by quests for material wealth. Only a few mavericks hold out for the old ways, for a happier place, whether at home or in *saaraba*. Our hero, Tamsir (played by Abdoul Aziz Diop), has returned to Dakar after seventeen years in Paris and receives a patronage job from his uncle, who, we later learn, is using milk powder from the Red Cross and donated German ambulances as graft. After a visit to his ancestral village, Tamsir falls in love with Lissa (played by Fabiene Joelle Felhio). She becomes pregnant with Tamsir's child, although her parents have promised her to a member of parliament as his third wife. Tamsir runs away to join the youth of Dakar who are experimenting with sex, drugs, and Rastafarian pipe-dreams. He returns to his uncle's office to rip up the MP's plans for building a salt factory and driving off the farmers and shepherds from Tamsir's home region.

This summary does not do justice to this complex and intriguing exploration of traditional rural life and the corrupt urban world of Dakar. Only Demba (played by Diankou Bakhayayokho), an urban mechanic who has inherited a motorcycle from a French priest, is left to resolve the rootlessness of all the characters we have met. Demba is an innocent who is obsessed with the idea of saaraba, which he believes, at first, must be in France, where "machines work for people."

In an exciting finale, which I will not reveal, Demba teaches Tamsir that "if you fight for humanity and your fellow man, you'll go to saaraba." Like many other late-twentieth-century films from Africa, the struggle between the former colonial powers and the national ruling elite for the economic control of the former colony is a struggle for the metaphorical soul of its people.

The film dramatizes the transition between neocolonialism and globalization: besides the actual material remnants of the French influence, Dakar has a new international trade forum and a new stadium built with Chinese investment. The final motorcycle ride for Tamsir and Demba, who wish to flee Westernization and seek saaraba, is an appropriate nail-biter.

Recommended Reading

Martin, Michael T., ed. *Cinemas of the Black Diaspora.* Detroit: Wayne State University, 1995. Extensive collection of informative essays about African cinema, including a discussion of *Saaraba* and related films.

ᐅᐊᐅ

Savage Capitalism

HISTORY OF GLOBALIZATION

1993, 86 mins., Brazil, in Portuguese with English subtitles
Director: Andre Klotzel
Screenplay: Andre Klotzel and Djalma Batista

In a number of ways, the *Variety* reviewer captured the spirit of this film by calling it the "cinematic equivalent of a Brazilian soap opera." The intensity of the relationships and the improbable plot of this tale of greedy capitalists, environmental pillage, and the adulterous elite has some of the best mass media exploitation can offer. Occasionally, the savage capitalists take time out from profiting at the expense of indigenous peoples to attack each other.

But there is even some soft focus romance with a touch of flesh. The hero, Hugo Assis (played by Jose Mayer), a major land developer in search of gold, realizes that he is a descendent of Indians from the Amazon interior, and he falls in love with a lefty reporter, Elisa (played by Fernanda Torres). This unlikely turn of events is eclipsed by the arrival of some Indian headmen in Hugo's boardroom. They accuse him of murder after one of the Indians dies there. He survives the accusation because the moment his Indian mother dies elsewhere, the dead headman revives.

Logic is not the issue here; magic realism is. Hugo's Indian name is Ubirata, and he is the secret offspring of his father, who was head of the mining company, and Donna Eduarda (played by Maria Luíza Castelli) of the Caetes tribe. This union has given Hugo some schizophrenic moments, since he occasionally is spirited off to the jungle when he is otherwise occupied in a corporate boardroom.

But true love seems to win out, and Elisa joins him in his ancestral village. Unfortunately, Elisa is also transformed into Lara, "mermaid of the river" (and also the title of a film Dona Eduarda likes to watch), and sucks poor Ubirata underwater, presumably forever.

Although at the end we are a long way from the international capitalist exploitation of native lands for mining rights it is an unusual vision of the national bourgeoisie's exploitation of its native peoples.

Recommended Reading

Levy, Emanuel. "Capitalismo Selvagem." *Variety,* 29 November 1993. Enjoys the sexiness of the film but finds its success "as a political metaphor for modern-day Brazil" limited.

ꔷꔷꔷ

Save the Green Planet

EARTH AS COLONY

2003, 118 mins., South Korea, in Korean with
  English subtitles
Director: Jun-hwan Jeong
Screenplay: Jun-hwan Jeong

The original Korean title of this startling film translates as "Take Care of Earth," which is the final message from the mother of Byeong-gu Lee (played by Ha-kyun Shin) before she dies of chemical pollution at a factory. Byeong-gu decides that her mother actually died of a failed genetic experiment, since the earth (the green planet) is currently a colony of a planet in the constellation Andromeda controlled by Kang Man-shik (played by Yun-shik Baek), the CEO of his mother's factory, himself an Andromedan (of course). But his mother's dog was named Earth, so perhaps her last words were meant to be taken literally. (Byeong-gu's father died in a mining accident, but that apparently is not that important.)

Byeong-gu takes nothing literally, however, and after kidnapping the CEO proceeds to torture him as a way of getting to admit that he is an alien. These sequences are very difficult to watch. While Korean audiences may have a higher tolerance for intense violence than others, as many critics have noted, most other viewers, I believe, will find themselves flinching more than once. The film is part of the popularly known Asia Extreme genre of hyperviolent films from South Korea, Japan, Hong Kong, and Thailand. (See Olaf Blecker, "Mr. Vengeance," *New York Times Magazine*, 9 April 2006.)

The kidnapping is necessary because at the next lunar eclipse the Andromedans will arrive in force to take over the planet as planned. Our hero has a girlfriend/sidekick, Su-ni (played by Jeong-min Hwang), who is a circus acrobat, and he has a nemesis, Inspector Choo (played by Lee Jae-yong) who is on his trail. This film is not so much viewed as endured, but of course it would not be in this volume if Byeong-gu Lee didn't turn out to have a fair amount of truth on his side. Akira Kurosawa filmed the volatile mixture of corporate skullduggery and kidnapping in *High and Low* (q.v.), and perhaps this sick but fascinating film is a parody of that realistic drama. It certainly goes as low as it can go.

If the earth is colonized by aliens on a mission of (literal) globalization, it might be helpful to have Byeong-gu in our corner. We could do without the torture, of course, but our space enemies might not.

Recommended Readings

Dargis, Manola. "In a Beanie and on a Mission." *New York Times*, 20 April 2005. This is "a welter of conflicting tones, dissonant moods and warring intentions (conscious and perhaps unconscious)," but Dargis quotes sci-fi novelist Philip K. Dick approvingly: "The positive little figure outlined against the universal rubble is . . . gnat-size in scope . . . and yet in some sense great."

Russell, Jamie. "Save the Green Planet." *BBC*, 13 August 2004 (online at www.bbc.co.uk), "This energetically inventive, off-the-wall outing conceals a surprisingly powerful story about bereavement, corporate corruption and one man's sense that the whole world is going to the dogs."

ꔷꔷꔷ

Save the Tiger

HISTORY OF GLOBALIZATION
OUTSOURCING AND OFFSHORING

1973, 100 mins., R, United States
Director: John G. Avildsen
Screenplay: Steve Shagan, from his novel,
  Save the Tiger (1972)

Filmed on location in the Los Angeles of small dress manufacturers, John Avildsen's film captures a remarkable moment as the generation of World War II meets—and fails to understand—the hip world of the 1960s. Jack Lemmon won an Oscar for Best Actor for his role as Harry Stoner, world-weary co-owner of a dress business that is having trouble making its sales volume. Harry and his partner, Phil Greene (played by Jack Gil-

When Myra discusses a *National Geographic* article about tigers who "return to places of remembered beauty" to die, Harry fantasizes about the perfect Brooklyn Dodgers team of the 1940s and all but ignores a sidewalk table where collections for endangered species are being solicited. Of course Harry and his industry are both on the endangered species list, but he has yet to accept that.

Although Avildsen is known for a number of other popular films, such as *Joe* (1970) and *Rocky* (1976) (both in *Working Stiffs*), he rarely equaled the moment in this film when Harry, addressing a gathering of buyers and dress industry pros, sees them transformed into the weary and hurt soldiers of his old World War II unit.

The film, like its source novel, is chaotic in spots, but it rings true a number of times. When Phil asks his partner, "What the hell is going on? Fraud, arson, hookers. What the hell has happened to us?" Harry replies, "Nothing's happened. It's business."

Save the Tiger: Two species faced with extinction, the tiger and the ethical businessman.

ford) try everything—using hookers, love bombardment of the buyers, and even consider arson—to balance the books. But the future is now, and neither the dress industry nor the endangered species of tigers can be saved.

Save the Tiger is a brilliant look at one of Los Angeles' former premier industries at the moment just before offshoring of garment manufacture began in earnest, but it is also a sensitive portrait of a man coming apart at the seams. Harry takes up with Myra (played by Laurie Heineman), a hippie hitchhiker, whose attitude toward casual sex (which he takes advantage of) amazes him. He fantasizes about bluesy singers, old baseball players, and a world where the Good War meant something. Lemmon as always captures this cynical character to perfection, as in this exchange: *Harry:* "How old are you?" *Myra:* "Twenty." *Harry:* "Nobody's twenty."

Recommended Reading

Ebert, Roger. "Save the Tiger." *Chicago Sun-Times*, 2 March 1973. Argues that the numerous cultural issues are less important than the virtuoso acting performances of the leads.

ᐅᐅᐅ

Sex Slaves

SEX WORK/TRAFFICKING

2006, 60 mins., United States
Director: Ric Esther Bienstock
Correspondents: Ric Esther Bienstock and
    Felix Golubev
TV Documentary
Distributor: Frontline

It takes a daring filmmaker to set a scene at the Odessa Steps, the monumental staircase in the Ukrainian capital where one of the greatest film sequences, Sergei Eisenstein's massacre of civilians by marching soldiers in *The Battleship Potemkin* (1925), takes place. But if you are going to make a documentary about human trafficking with a hidden camera, you already have lots of nerve. A *Frontline* team, led by director Ric Esther Bienstock, makes a series of daring forays among unsavory and dangerous characters in Odessa and in the Russian quarter of Aksaray in Istanbul, Turkey, in an attempt to get the goods on sex traffickers in general and to help Viorel, a distraught husband from Moldova, locate Katia, his missing (and pregnant) wife.

In one of the hidden camera sequences, Frontline follows "Olga," who leads a small covey of mostly very naive women who have been promised jobs in Istanbul on a Black Sea voyage. Olga is able to pass through customs with remarkable ease—bribes?—and delivers most of the women to legitimate jobs. For the others, it's a quick sale to some pimps for a thousand dollars each and sexual slavery. Olga's favorite market is where migrant workers gather for jobs.

In another hidden camera sequence at Odessa's McDonald's, Viorel meets "Maria," the wife of the pimp, Apo, who purchased Viorel's wife, Katia. This woman is a piece of work, and without further commentary I leave viewers the dubious pleasure of seeing her. We track the *Frontline* team's attempts to help Viorel secure Katia's release, as the Americans debate the ethics of their participation in various schemes to rescue her. In the end the *Frontline* team may have succeeded simply because Apo and Maria either tire of Katia or worry that there is too much noise around to make her a safe commodity for them.

At this point in history no one needs to be reminded that human (sex) trafficking is a consequence and feature of globalization. The director was moved to work on this project by an experience she had while filming another story in rural China in 2002. The best hotel in this remote village was also the local brothel, staffed with young Chinese girls and two Natashas, who had been trafficked from remote Siberia to remote China. (See the director's notes at www .frontline.com.) One of the terrible ironies of the industry, the *Frontline* film demonstrates, is that "trafficked women are treated as illegal immigrants," not victims of a crime.

Unlike some films about this global industry, *Frontline* is not visually disturbing but the information is certainly R-rated and designed to destroy any illusions about sex work as an occupational choice.

Recommended Readings

Malarek, Victor. *The Natashas: Inside The New Global Sex Trade.* New York: Arcade Publishing, 2004. Incredibly detailed account of the Soviet and Eastern European trade in women and teenagers, whose value as commodities is exceeded only by drugs and weapons. Malarek analyzes this situation as a result of the collapse of the Soviet empire (one of the procurers in the film agrees that this is the reason he turned to the trade).

▶◀▶◀

Showdown in Seattle: Five Days That Shook the WTO

ANTI-GLOBALIZATION

1999, United States
Seattle Prelude, 25 mins.
People Unite, Police Riot, 28 mins.
Occupied Seattle, 28 mins.
Unwilling Captives, 28 mins.
What Democracy Looks Like, 28 mins.
Producers: Independent Media Center and Big Noise Productions, Changing America, Headwaters Action Video Collective, Paper Tiger TV, VideoActive, and Whispered Media.
Distributor: Whispered Media

What may become the turning point in the level of protest against the World Trade Organization is documented in this five-part, day-by-day video broadcast of the demonstrations in Seattle from November 30th through December 4th, 1999. Numerous video activists joined in an unprecedented collaboration to get the news out about the WTO, its policies, and the broad coalition of groups protesting its power. Labor unions, environmental activists, anarchists, and politicos of all stripes joined to challenge the global business-as-usual habits of the WTO.

The documentary is divided into five sections or daily broadcasts: 1) *Seattle Prelude*, with commentaries on the issues; 2) *People Unite, Police Riot*, with demos and counterattacks, including a working alliance of labor and "turtles" (environmentalists); 3) *Occupied Seattle*, documenting the abuse of civil liberties by the police; 4) *Unwilling Captives*, featuring "environmental hostages of WTO economic policy" in jail; 5) *What Democracy Looks Like*, with protestors celebrating and planning for the future and a review of the success of the video activists' collaboration.

The second part, *People Unite, Police Riot*, epitomized the broad coalition of forces joined in protest. Many of the leaders of the (then) major AFL-CIO unions held their own rally and march. In addition to the president and vice-president of the Federation—John Sweeney and Linda Chavez Thompson—the presidents of the United Steelworkers (USWA), the Teamsters (IBT), garment workers (UNITE), and government workers (AFSCME) all participated and spoke. The president of the West Coast dockworkers, Brian McWlliams, also announced a one-day shutdown of the ports on the West Coast. Since the latter carry the majority of the containerized shipping that services America's part of globalization, the gesture was significant.

This part places the unionists' rally and march within a sequence showing demonstrators other than unionists being attacked by the police in the daytime intercut with an interview with a carpenter who explains how he crafts perfect police batons for crowd control. The part concludes with night sequences of what seem to be anarchists and other street-fighting cells amidst police tear gas barrages.

The fifth part, *What Democracy Looks Like*, was released with a similar title (*This is What Democracy Looks Like*, q.v.) but is a different and longer final cut.

Recommended Reading

Rose, Cynthia. "WTO, The Movie, Plays to Packed Screenings." *Seattle Times,* 18 December 1999. "Despite its weighty subject," the film "is not melodramatic. While it covers almost all the issues raised by protesters, politics are balanced by humorous vignettes."

▶◀▶◀▶◀

A Single Spark

CHANGES IN THE WORKPLACE: WORLDWIDE LABOR HISTORY

1996, 96 mins., South Korea, in Korean with English subtitles
Director: Kwang-su Park
Screenplay: Chang-dong Lee

South Korea in the 1970s was under the control of dictator Park Chung Hee. Labyrinthine sweatshops with unsanitary facilities dominated the garment industry, staffed with teenage girls who were especially susceptible to diseases such as tuberculosis. Although sufficient laws to protect these girls were on the books, the dictator's hostility toward trade unions made enforcement unlikely.

On one level Kwang-su Park's *A Single Spark* focuses on the popular political martyr Chon Tae-il (played by Kyoung-In Hong), who worked alongside the girls in the sweatshops and who—when his efforts at calling attention to their sufferings proved futile—immolated himself in Seoul in 1970, probably inspired by the suicides of the Buddhist monks who protested the South Vietnamese dictatorship in the 1960s. He drenched himself in gasoline and started the fire that killed him by first lighting his labor law book, an image Park recreates in disturbing detail, including his shouts, "Comply with the labor laws! We are not machines!"

Park alternates black-and-white sequences of Chon's life with the story, shot in color, of Kim Yong Su (played by Sun-Jae Kim), a law student who challenges the dictatorship by writing a biography of Chon. Although Kim is an intellectual, he is also seen as a risk-taker. He is constantly on the run from the authorities who wish to suppress his work, and he must visit his pregnant girlfriend, also a labor organizer, secretly.

While a number of economists have celebrated the successes of the Asian Tigers—Malaysia, South Korea, Taiwan, Hong Kong, and Singapore—for their rise in the global economy, anti-globalization critics have pointed to the exploitation of labor forces that in part powers these economic miracles. Although its distribution has been limited, *A Single Spark* reveals to audiences outside of South Korea one of the reasons that now—long after the military dictatorship that seized power after Park Chung Hee's ouster in 1979—there is a robust labor union movement, built in some part on Chon's self-sacrifice.

Park's earlier film, *Black Republic* (1990), unfortunately not available, uses another activist on the run to expose the conditions in South Korean coalmines after the Kwangju Uprising in 1980 led to the killing of perhaps two thousand citizens by the government for protesting the dictatorship. *A Single Spark* has, however, a more optimistic ending: Kim sees a young man, who resembles Chon, carrying his finally published biography of the hero. And Park follows this consoling image with end-credits of the seven thousand individuals who contributed their money to make the film possible.

Recommended Readings

Chun Soon Ok. *A Single Spark: The Biography of Chun Tae-il.* Seoul: Dolbaegae, 2003. A biography of Chun Tae-il by his sister, with an analysis of the South Korean labor movements of the 1960s and 1970s.

Eungjun Min, Jinsook Joo, and Han Ju Kwak. *Korean Film: Resistance and Democratic Imagination.* Westport, CT: Praeger, 2003. Includes an analysis of the film and appreciation of its value as sociology.

Kyung Hyun Kim. "Post-Trauma and Historical Remembrance in Recent South Korean Film." *Cinema Journal* 41, no. 4 (Summer 2002): 95–1115. Argues that the film actually "demystifies the heroic representation of the political martyr."

▸◂▸◂

Songs from the Second Floor

GLOBAL CATASTROPHES

2000, 98 mins., Sweden, in Swedish with
English subtitles
Director: Roy Andersson
Screenplay: Roy Andersson

What are we to make of this poetic meditation on modern Scandinavian life and the collapse of capitalism? Will we understand its title or its poetic epigraph from poet Caesar Vallejo: "Beloved be the one who sits down"?

Not really. But it is a fascinating non-narrative film nonetheless, with a series of forty-six one-shot scenes (the camera itself is unmoving as the action unfolds), a number of which are clearly related and some of which are clearly symbolic or at the very least ambiguous. A few plot lines emerge. Pelle (played by Torbjorn Fahlstrom) is downsizing his middle-class workforce. Kalle (played by Lars Nordh) has torched his own store probably for the insurance money (but just as likely simply because all businesses in this film are failing). A number of individuals get interested in selling crucifixes. A girl is sacrificed by what appears to be the leaders of a corporation or similar organization or perhaps even the government itself, and a massive eight-hour traffic jam causes some human flotsam and jetsam to pile up in the streets.

Are these plot lines related? Cinematically, the answer is yes, in terms of characters with ashen appearances, cryptic but revealing dialogue, and sudden, disturbing bouts of action. Overall they seem to represent the decay of capitalist society, perhaps even society itself. An immigrant is severely beaten in front of a line of commuters on a bus queue. Men in suits whip themselves in a procession outside the torched furniture store in a scene reminiscent of Bergman's *Seventh Seal*. The crucifix salesmen give up: "How can you make money with a crucified loser?"

At one point the arsonist says, "It's not easy being human." True enough, the film argues, especially if the watchword of society is the following advice: "Try to find something you can sell with an extra zero at the end." Most of the souls in this film are lost but their decay is attractive. Perhaps more of Vallejo's poem ("Stumble between Two Stars," from *The Black Heralds*, 2003, translated by Rebecca Seiferle) should have been quoted: "Beloved be . . . the one who goes, ordered by his hands, to the movies, / the one who pays what he lacks."

Recommended Readings

Ebert, Roger. "Songs from the Second Floor." *Chicago Sun-Times,* 1 November 2002. "The movie argues that in an economic collapse our modern civilization would fall away from us and we would be left wandering our cities like the plague victims of old, seeking relief in drunkenness, superstition, sacrifice, sex and self-mockery."

Mitchell, Elvis. "Where Drama and Farce Meet Like Old Friends." *New York Times,* 3 July 2002. "The picture's mordant, almost ghoulish tone suggests Odin [the Norse god of war, death, and culture] watching the failures of modern society—and its alienating effects on the human race—through a snow globe."

▶◀▶◀

Squaring the Circle

HISTORY OF GLOBALIZATION
LABOR HISTORY

1984, 80 mins., United Kingdom
Director: Mike Hodges
Screenplay: Tom Stoppard

Tom Stoppard's successes—on stage (*The Real Inspector Hound*, 1968, and *Arcadia*, 1993) and on film (*Rosencrantz and Guidenstern Are Dead*, 1990)—are much better known than *Squaring the Circle*, his earlier film about the Polish Solidarity union leadership, which was released only with great difficulty and without much circulation nor recognition.

What Stoppard does best in *Squaring the Circle* is the comic deflation of communist bureaucrats and party leaders. The film is punctuated three times by cuts to an artificial-looking set signifying a Black Sea resort. The film opens in 1980, when Leonid Brezhnev (played by Frank Middlemann), first secretary of the Communist Party of the Soviet Union, is meeting Edward Gierek (played by Tom Wilkinson), his counterpart in the Polish United Workers' Party, who has been in power since quelling a workers' rebellion in 1970. We first see Brezhnev and Gierek meeting formally in suits on the beach. The narrator announces that it didn't really happen that way and we cut to the same beach, but now

Gierek and Brezhnev are wearing Hawaiian shirts and drinking little umbrella drinks, whereupon Brezhnev yells at Gierek "like a gangster" for using too many foreign loans to prop up his failing economy.

We return to the beach two more times, once when Brezhnev is meeting with Stanislaw Kania (played by Roy Kinnear), Gierek's replacement the same year, and then with General Jaruzelski (played by Richard Kane), Kania's replacement a year later. Jaruzelski has the dubious distinction of being the only communist head of state who was also the head of the party and the army. Stoppard can't resist a joke at his expense, as Jaruzelski examines his new uniform and says: "You don't think the effect is . . . a bit South American?"

The reason for the changes in leadership is, of course, the rise of the Solidarity trade union with ten million members under the leadership of Lech Walesa (played by Bernard Hill). In addition to wage increases and improved work conditions as items of negotiation, Walesa is demanding the erection of the Gdansk Memorial, a forty-meter-high "monument to the dead of 1970," which, when it is finally built, represents the first monument to rebelling workers in a so-called workers' state. By the end of the film, Solidarity is outlawed, its leaders arrested, and Jaruzelski seems in control.

In geometric terms, a circle cannot be squared, that is, one cannot construct a square with exactly the same area as a given circle. Stoppard's film uses this mathematical impossibility as a metaphor for the political situation in Poland in 1980–81: "Was freedom as defined by the free trade union Solidarity reconcilable with socialism as defined by the Eastern European communist bloc?" he asks in the introduction to his screenplay. Stoppard is a Czech, only occasionally turning to political issues in his work, but, in addition to *Squaring the Circle*, *Every Good Boy Deserves Favor* (1977) features an orchestra that silences dissent and discombobulates the Soviet empire with metaphorical irony and wit.

Recommended Reading

Stoppard, Tom. *Squaring the Circle.* London: Faber & Faber, 1984. The screenplay, with a history of the production and difficulties in distribution, especially in the United States.

►I◄►I◄►I◄
State of Play

OIL

2003, TV series, 6 episodes of 57 mins. each,
   United Kingdom
Director: David Yates
Screenplay: Paul Abbott

Combining investigative journalism with a political fix by an oil company makes *State of Play* exciting viewing, with an added bonus of an attractive newsroom team and a crusty chief editor. The mysterious deaths with which the series begins—a young woman working for a British MP goes under a subway car and a young black man is gunned down on the street in broad daylight—establish an anxious rhythm that each episode sustains.

It also provides a counterpoint between emotional and scary sequences and sardonic and occasionally sick humor. It turns out that the MP was on the very train that killed the young woman (Did she fall? Was she pushed?) and that he was having an affair with her. Anyone who has ever been in a crowded subway car stopped for unforeseen circumstances, according to the conductor over the p.a. system, will get guilty pleasure from the sequence in which the conductor announces, "Well, there's a body on the line at Green Park." And the passengers (including the MP) groan.

The MP in question, Stephen Collins (played by David Morrissey) is heading up a parliamentary Energy Select Committee in the midst of an inquiry into the oil industry. When he hears of his assistant's death, he breaks down in public and begins a rollercoaster ride that ends his marriage and puts his old campaign manager, Cal McCaffrey (played by John Simm), now an investigative reporter for the independently minded major newspaper, on the case. It will come as no surprise to viewers of political thrillers, not to

mention readers of the news, that a fix must be in.

This political thriller is not only a mystery—the two deaths in the first few minutes of the first episode are obviously related—but a condemnation of the ways of secret government business-as-usual, and like *A Very British Coup* (q.v.), which it resembles in many ways, the primary enemy is the upper-crust establishment types that dominate the government regardless of the political stripe of the party in power. In this film it is New Labour, mocked by Cal at one point for its Millennium Dome fiasco (*MM*, q.v.), while in *A Very British Coup*, the Tories don't like being upstaged by the old Labour Party, especially with a union leader as prime minister.

The politics of oil and brilliant newsroom performances by a cast, especially Cal's workmate Della Smith (played by Kelly Macdonald) and boss Cameron Foster (Bill Nighy), make this a must-see; globalization may have found its genre after all—the petro-thriller (*Syriana*, q.v.).

Recommended Reading

Goodman, Tim. "Two Reasons You Shouldn't Watch Sopranos on Sunday Nights." *San Francisco Chronicle*, 16 April 2004. Says that the film "gives credence to the idea that there may not be any better format for telling an impact story than over the course of four to six hours."

►I◄►I◄►I◄
Store Wars: When Wal-Mart Comes to Town

WAL-MART

2001, 59 mins., United States
Director: Micha X. Peled
TV Documentary
Distributor: Bullfrog Films

The subtitle of this PBS documentary is "When Wal-Mart Comes to Town"; the subtext is "Does Wal-Mart always get what it wants?" The answer is no. But in this film, after the planning commission in Ashland, Virginia, changes its vote, and their affirmative vote is ratified by a lame duck city council, we realize that Wal-Mart gets some of what it wants. Despite most of the evidence that Wal-Mart will not help the local community in any appreciative way, it will still get to come to town.

The surviving members of Sam Walton's family are billionaires, five of the richest people in the world. The film partly answers how they got that way: low wages. The film does not discuss the exclusive contracts with sweatshops all over the world, especially China, and the monopolistic drive by which it replaces every major local (small) competitor.

Even though 160 other local communities nationwide voted against Wal-Mart, Wal-Mart's low wages, and its billionaire owners (Sam Walton's heirs), Wal-Mart does come to Ashland. Class issues simmer just below the surface: the leaders of the anti–Wal-Mart faction, organized under the unlikely logo of a pink flamingo, are clearly middle class and are predominantly "come here's," as opposed to the working-class, sometimes black, "born here's."

Wal-Mart may lie with its statistics—70 percent of the 350 new jobs will be full-time, but the latter is defined as only 28 hours a week—but some locals like the lower prices, the convenience of one-stop shopping, and the jobs, however unrewarding they often turn out to be.

The antidevelopment forces seem to have a good shot, despite the fact that the town's elite (insurance people, bankers, and mayor) are lined up against them. They argue persuasively that local businesses invest their profits in local banks and business, and in any case there is another Wal-Mart just ten miles away. But their consultant, Al Norman, of Sprawl Busters, points out that once Wal-Mart clears out all the opposition it is relatively easy to close down one store and become king of all they survey.

Even the local teens are in a bad mood. Wal-Mart is the largest seller of pop music in America, but all they sell has to pass their own censoring mechanism to become "clean." Although the film does not raise it, Wal-Mart is viciously anti-union and has become the poster child for the mistreatment of low-wage workers in the retail industries.

Recommended Reading

Norman, Al. *Slam-Dunking Wal-Mart!* Atlantic City: Raphael Marketing, 1999. An activist explains "how you can stop superstore sprawl in your hometown." Includes detailed analyses of big box stores and their detrimental effects on local communities.

ЖЖЖ

Syriana

OIL

2005, 126 mins., United States, R
Director: Stephen Gaghan
Screenplay: Stephen Gaghan, based on *See No Evil* (2002) and *Sleeping with the Devil* (2003) by Robert Baer

Politics, oil, the Middle East, and the CIA are a volatile mix, and *Syriana* has them all. Loosely based on the provocative memoirs and geopolitical analyses of Robert Baer, a former CIA agent whose job description involved the other three categories, this political thriller sees globalization as an oil industry plot supported by the United States government and staffed with crooked people and an occasional villain out of a James Bond film.

The film has four major players in its exciting and converging plotlines. Bob Barnes (played by George Clooney) is the CIA agent. Bryan Woodman (played by Matt Damon) is a Switzerland-based oil adviser to Prince Nasir (played by Alexander Siddig), one of two sons of an aging emir whose country is up for grabs between American and Chinese interests. Bennett Holiday (played by Jeffrey Wright) is a Washington lawyer in charge of applying an objective due diligence review of the merger of two oil companies but who secretly supports one side. Wasim Ahmed Khan (played by Mazhar Munira) is a pipeline worker who has lost his job with Connex, one of those oil companies, and who takes on a suicide bomber's mission after indoctrination at a madrass or Islamic school. All plotlines converge after the emir announces which son will inherit his kingdom. Beyond the politics from today's headlines, the film uses the relationships of fathers and sons to make the four converging plotlines somewhat psychologically symmetrical.

Living and working in a world of deceit and betrayal has made Bob Barnes as weary as one of John Le Carre's great cold war spies, such as Alec Leamas in *The Spy Who Came in from the Cold* (1965) or George Smiley in *Tinker, Tailor, Soldier, Spy* (1979). Bob is the operational center of a conspiracy that even he is at a loss (sometimes) to understand. Securing the right son of the emir to lead an United States–friendly country will, not so coincidentally, be very profitable to a newly merged oil company, Connex-Killen. Whether the merger will be approved by the feds turns out to be one of the many subterfuges in the plot. Since Bob eventually realizes that he's become the fall guy for a scheme so labyrinthine that most viewers may well need to take notes, he falls back on his trade craft to try to regain his dignity.

The title of the film alludes to Pax Syriana, the occupation of Lebanon by the Syrian army from 1976 to 2005. If peace comes at that price—murder, torture, and betrayal—the film suggests, François Chateaubriand was probably right: "Forests precede civilizations and deserts follow them."

Relatively few globalization dramas are as explicit as this one about the collusion of the American government and oil corporations: *The Girl in the Café* (q.v.) set at a G-8 summit comes close, albeit without the betrayals and intrigue. Stephen Gaghan won an Academy Award for the screenplay for the global drug thriller *Traffic* (2000); he employs the same strategy of converging plotlines in *Syriana* and adds what can only be taken as a direct swing at the association of vice President Dick Cheney and his former company, Halliburton, as the latter cleans up on contracts awarded in Bush II's new desert war.

Recommended Reading

Scott, A. O. "Clooney and a Maze of Collusion." *New York Times*, 23 November 2005. The film "succeeds in being one of the best geopolitical thrillers in a very long time."

ᗏᗏᗏ

The Take

CHANGES IN THE WORKPLACE: WORLDWIDE DEREGULATION AND PRIVATIZATION

2004, 87 mins., Canada, in English and
    Spanish with English subtitles
Director: Avi Lewis
Mixed Agit-Prop and Traditional
    Documentary
Distributor: First Run/Icarus Films

Avi Lewis's documentary on the recuperated factories' movement in Argentina is too comprehensive to be purely agit-prop. Rarely veering from the strong, well-argued politics of writer Naomi Klein's anti-globalization perspective (*No Logo*, q.v.), the film is a careful examination of the economic woes of Argentina, the disruptive policies of the IMF, and the manipulations of the national capitalist elite.

Argentina is a textbook case of failed globalization policies. To secure IMF loans, the Argentine government, led by president Carlos Menem, drove a relatively satisfactory economic system into collapse in the late 1990s. The deregulation and privatization of both private and public industries, as well as of the currency market, increased unemployment and public debt. After receiving government loans and subsidies intended for their factories, some factory owners pretended to disappear.

After participating in demonstrations, riots, and bank runs, Argentine workers began seizing factories and running the enterprises on their own. The film focuses on a number of recuperated factories—especially factories making clothing (Brukman), ceramics (Zanon), and cars (Forja)—and studies in detail how the workers organized themselves and the obstacles they faced and still face. Over two hundred factories were occupied and run by the workers as coops. (*Grupo Alavio Films*, q.v., for further instances.)

The filmmakers take us inside a number of factories, and in fact the director was concerned that viewers might accuse him of

The Take: Forja workers in Argentina celebrate the takeover of their factory. Photo by Andres D'Eliua. Courtesy First Run/Icarus Films.

"soft-focus romanticism for heavy industry" because of an appearance of "a kind of industrial retro aesthetic." In fact, he suggested in an interview (see Rogge) that in his search for anti-globalization activism—to present positive alternatives to capitalism, if you will—they ended up "in the heart of the old economy," checking out traditional factory work. Nevertheless, if they had discovered that a group of bakers had seized their workplace then the film would have had a lot of bread in it instead of clothing, ceramics, and cars.

Recommended Readings

Holden, Stephen. "Fixing Argentina: One Grass-Roots but Uphill Approach. *New York Times*, 22 September 2004. This "stirring, idealistic documentary" clearly takes the side of the workers "determined to take their livelihood against overwhelming odds," although "the movement still faces an uphill battle."

Jordan, John, et al. *We Are Everywhere: The Irresistible Rise of Global Anti-Capitalism.* London: Verso, 2003. Jordan from the filmmaking team joins a group that documents the worldwide anti-globalization movement on a street level, emphasizing direct action and protest over electoral politics.

Rogge, Malcome. "Resolutely Hopeful." *Znet,* 8 August 2004 (online at www.zmag.org/content/showarticle.cfm?ItemID=6002). Interview with the director, who places the recuperated factories in the context of Argentina's overall economy and the movements to reform it (including the "union of unemployed workers" and the "neighborhood assembly movement" or "street corner democracy").

ЬΗЬ

Talking to the Wall

WAL-MART

2003, 60 mins., United States
Director: Steve Alves
Agit-Prop Documentary
Distributor: Hometown Productions (www
  .talkingtothewall.com)

To a filmmaker like Steve Alves the only thing scarier than *The Amityville Horror*, the horror film based on his Long Island home town, is Wal-Mart possessing his newly adopted home of Greenfield, Massachusetts (pop.: 18,000). "The horror is real," Alves says in his narration, because bucolic Long Island was destroyed by housing tracts, malls, and shopping centers. And if the residents had let it happen, Greenfield would have been destroyed too. If . . .

Greenfield fought back and organized a committee to defeat the planned store. Not the least of its arguments was the number of Wal-Mart stores in the area: within thirty-five miles there were ten Wal-Marts. Many commentators have noted this aspect of Sprawl Mart: two Wal-Mart stores don't cancel each other's sales but actually end up carving out more sales than the stores might individually get. Furthermore, if this growth doesn't happen, Wal-Mart simply closes one of the stores down and often the shell sits unused for years.

The Greenfield victory in 1993 was an extremely narrow one: Wal-Mart was only counted out by nine votes. Two years later the neighboring small town of Orange (pop.: 7,500) succumbed, losing its downtown and, according to Alves, its soul. Alves develops the history behind communities and legislators who tried to protect small businesses. His cinematic essay into the history of expansion of the chain stores of the 1930s—A & P, Woolworth's, and Sears—looks remarkably like Wal-Mart's contemporary history. Then the chain stores won: the American citizen was defined as a consumer who needed to have his freedom to shop at chain stores. Low prices and one-stop shopping were the mantras then as well.

Recommended Readings

Mead, Julia C. "Longing for an Island without Any Walls. *New York Times*, 24 April 2003. In-depth discussion of the filmmaker and his handling of Wal-Mart as a target of satire à la Michael Moore.

Norman, Al. *The Case Against Wal-Mart.* St. Johnsbury, Vt.: Raphel Publishing, 2004. The leading Wal-Mart buster explains how to do it and why.

Quinn, Bill. *How Wal-Mart Is Destroying America (and the World) and What You Can Do about It.* Berkeley: Ten Speed Press, 2000. Another broadside attack with suggestions on how to fight Sprawl Mart.

ㅐㅐㅐ
The Tank Man

CHINA
HISTORY OF GLOBALIZATION

2006, 90 mins., United States
Director: Antony Thomas
TV Documentary
Distributor: PBS

Frontline makes an extraordinary claim in its documentary about the "Tank Man," the Beijing man who stepped out in front of the Red Army's tanks as they rolled in to Tienanmen Square in 1989 to crush the New Democracy movement that was sweeping the nation. The photograph and video footage of his courageous and foolhardy act became an inspiration for many people to resist oppression in other countries. He disappeared after his moment of fame, but because he symbolized the resistance to state control, *Frontline* argues that in effect the entrenched Chinese leadership made an implicit deal with its own people: we will give you economic freedom but not political freedom. That is, there will be a Starbucks on the corner, but you cannot use the Internet without censorship.

Frontline demonstrates how, in just seventeen years, this strange pact with the devil seems to have come true. At the top China's economy is booming, people in Beijing now have incomes and consumer goods that were dreams in 1989, and capitalism is thriving. At the bottom millions of rural folk have been displaced, desperate for jobs in the new industrial economy, and are treated like second class citizens. Many Beijingers nevertheless remember how their fellow citizens were murdered by the Red Army the day before the Tank Man made his move. Some wonder if the cost of globalization for China's economy has been too high.

Of course capturing footage of such an event today is routine by cell phone and then web- and podcast around the world in seconds. In 1989 capturing this moment before widespread digitalization was lucky: the photographer, Jeff Widener of the Associated Press, hid his roll of film in his hotel toilet bowl tank because he knew the security people had spotted him photographing Tank Man from his balcony. (This is the most often reproduced Associated Press photo, en .wikipedia.org/wiki/Tiananmen_Square _protests_of_1989.) Live footage of Tank Man moving about to block the tank and even climbing aboard to converse with the driver is compelling viewing. To my eye the people rushing to lead him away were sympathetic fellow protestors, not security men, but others think he was arrested and murdered.

One man and one tank carry a big message for *Frontline,* but their evidence of a globalized China launched in part because of political oppression is nonetheless convincing. In one sense the students and others who demonstrated for continued economic reforms and political liberalization ended up with half of the loaf at a very great cost.

Recommended Readings

Martel, Ned. "Mystery of One Man's Act of Defiance on One Day in Beijing." *New York Times,* 11 April 2006. Although the reviewer is also captivated by the mystery of the Tank Man's disappearance, he finds some of the documentary "rambling" and overambitious in its scope. The film "reintroduces a frustratingly faceless enigma and teases a viewer with the hope of a resolution that never arrives."

Wong, Jan. *Red China Blues.* New York: Doubleday, 1996. Memoir, subtitled "My Long March from Mao to Now," by a Canadian of Chinese origin, who went from a pure red Maoist during the Cultural Revolution to a horrified participant in the Tiananmen Square events.

Zhang Liang, Andrew J. Nathan, and Perry Link, ed. *The Tiananmen Papers: The Chinese Leadership's Decision to Use Force against Their Own People—In Their Own Words.* New York: Public Affairs Press, 2001. Volume documents how both hardliners and reformers at the top levels of the Chinese Communist Party debated the fate of the student protests on the New Democracy movement; in the end it is economic reformer Den Xiaopeng who gets the credit for approving the military attack on the square.

⋈⋈⋈

Taxi Dreams

TAXI DRIVERS

2001, 120 mins., United States
Director: Joanna Head
Cinema-Verité Documentary
Distributor: PBS

Yellow cab drivers in New York City are almost always immigrants, often from the same handful of countries. The five cabbies profiled in this film are from very underdeveloped rural cultures: Om Dutta Sharma is from India; Sumon, Bangladesh; Rafik Bakayev, Tajikistan; Kwame Fosu, Ghana; and Rizwan Raja, Pakistan. A sixth, Robert Scott from Bolivia, the only cabbie not from the Third World, turns out to be a poet whose fares hear him recite as he drives.

The cabbies all rent their cabs from taxi fleet owners and out of their typically twelve-hour shift have to pay the rental and gas costs. Sumon quits after one day because he really didn't know how to drive a car and he never earned enough to meet expenses.

Yellow cab drivers barely make ends meet even after a twelve-hour shift. Although many of them go to such schools as the Taxi Academy and have to pass a city exam (not only on urban geography but also in English comprehension), quite a few of them encounter passengers who not only know the city much better than they do but in at least one instance recorded in this film volunteer to drive the cab.

The film does not cover the benevolent societies and taxi drivers' unions that help make their work bearable. Nor does it cover the political nightmare that is the New York City taxi rulebook (see Mathew).

Recommended Reading

Mathew, Biju. *Taxi! Cabs and Capitalism in New York City.* New York: New Press, 2005. A chronicle of a new union of mostly immigrant drivers—the New York Taxi Workers Alliance—and analysis of the taxi drivers' world of regulations and ownership.

⊢⊣⊢⊣

Tell Us the Truth

ANTI-GLOBALIZATION

2004, 97 mins., United States
Director: Gabriel Miller and Cecily Pingree
Agit-Prop Concert Documentary
Distributor: Artemis Records (www.artemis
   records.com)

It is unlikely that the AFL-CIO and the American Income Life Insurance Company (whose clients include labor unions and credit unions) have underwritten many concert tours or concert films. This film follows the concert tour of a number of performers who support a strong political agenda on issues of fair trade and media diversity. When the tour was in Miami in 2003, the AFL-CIO and other organizations were demonstrating against meetings of the Free Trade Area of the Americas (FTAA) organization. Although the protests had permits, they were attacked by the police, and footage of these incidents is included in this unusual film mix of protest rally and concert performance.

The performances of Billy Bragg, Steve Earle, Rage Against the Machine's Tom Morello, Jill Sobule, and other activist artists were staged to link issues of globalization with the control of the media, typified by Clear Channel's monopolistic acquisition of hundreds of local stations (made legal by the Federal Communications Commission's 2003 release of the cap on multiple media ownership) and Clear Channel's overt censorship of songs it deems unacceptable. Bragg's songs are as usual very specific: "The Price of Oil" points to the war in Iraq, while "NPWA" attributes lost jobs to the WTO: "No power without accountability!"

Tom Morello's message was more apocalyptic and pessimistic: "If you're feeling lucky, then hold your breath / And wave goodbye when nothing's left." Jill Sobule had already notched a double whammy when Wal-Mart banned her song "Kissed a Girl" for its gay content and her album cover showing two hands opening a Prozac capsule for encouraging drug use. Comedienne and Air America newscaster Janeane Garofalo was the tour's emcee and was joined onstage at the Washington, D.C., concert by the two dissenting FCC commissioners, one of whom played the harmonica.

The messages of both protest rallies and activists' songs are unified when Bragg sings about the IMF and WTO in "NPWA": "Who are these people? Who elected them?"

Recommended Reading

Lee, Jennifer. "Musicians Protesting Monopoly in Media." *New York Times*, 18 December 2003. Reviews the concert—"the raging was mainly against the star of media consolidation, Clear Channel Communications"—and discusses media ownership and censorship issues.

⊢⊣⊢⊣

They Live

EARTH AS COLONY

97 mins., 1988, R
Director: John Carpenter
Screenplay: John Carpenter, from Ray Nelson's short story, "Eight O'Clock in the Morning" (1963)

Director John Carpenter has always been an extremist. He created one of the greatest bogeymen of all time, Michael Myers, in *Halloween* (1978) and one of the scariest dystopian prison islands of all time, Manhattan, in *Escape from New York* (1981). The Los Angeles of *They Live* is also scary, and its wealthy ruling elite are control freaks and monsters. So what else is new? They enforce their power over the masses using subliminal ads and brainwashing slogans such as "Obey," "Consume," "No Independent Thought," and, my favorite, printed on paper money, "This Is Your God."

This elite, however, is literally out of this world. They are aliens who have colonized the earth as if it were a third world country, using select humans as their neocolonial lackeys, who are awarded special privileges.

They Live: Special sunglasses reveal the truth about the alien capitalists.

Globalization to them has a special and precise meaning: our blue-green planet is theirs to exploit.

Only the wonderfully named John Nada (played by Roddy Piper), an unemployed hunk who lucks into a construction job, can see the aliens' hideous faces and decode their subliminal messages (reminiscent of J.G. Ballard's classic short story, "The Subliminal Man," also 1963) by wearing a special pair of sunglasses he finds in a rebel hideout. Although this kind of maneuver is routine for sci-fi, here it joins a social protest agenda perhaps critical of Reaganomics.

Although the film begins with a gritty urban mise-en-scène—opening shots of the freight yards, graffiti walls (with "They Live" as one of the tags), and a view of Los Angeles from the bottom up—by the time Nada has discovered the aliens' secret, we drift into a vigilante film, with the human "terrorists" (as they are called) fighting both the aliens and the "human power elite" allied with them. Coincidences and shoot-outs abound. Nada kidnaps a producer who works for the very television studio that sends out the signal to make the aliens appear human. Betrayals both personal and global mark the film's end, but we suspect that the aliens—or "free enterprisers" as they prefer to be called—might end up like the ungrateful steel companies one of Nada's

human friends once worked for: "We gave the steel companies a break when they needed it," and after they took the money they closed the factories. The film ends metaphorically: an alien having his way with an easy earth girl loses his sexual edge when his cover is blown.

Recommended Reading

"They Live." *Variety*, 1 January 1988. "Conceived on 1950s B-movie sci-fi terms, *They Live* is a fantastically subversive film, a nifty little confection pitting us vs. them, the haves vs. the have-nots."

ᚼᚼᚼ

Thirst

SCARCE RESOURCES (WATER)

2003, 62 mins., United States
Directors: Alan Snitow and Deborah
    Kaufman
Traditional Documentary
Distributor: Bullfrog Films

Thirsty? Do you reach for a plastic bottle of spring water or turn on the kitchen tap? Which would you do if you knew that the former costs one thousand times the latter and that the privatization of the world's water supply—all the water, not just "spring" water—is the goal of numerous multinational corporations? Alan

Snitow and Deborah Kaufman, directors of *Secrets of Silicon Valley* (in *Working Stiffs*), believe that "water is the oil of the 21st century." Since the World Bank and the IMF often make the privatization of public water systems a requirement for loans, they may be right.

When representatives of the World Bank, water industry executives, and government bureaucrats assembled for the Third World Water Forum in Kyoto in 2003, Snitow and Kaufman filmed their speeches articulating a vision of the world's water supply behind huge dams, privatized, and controlled by, well, by themselves. This was their plan for Third World water.

These representatives did not seem surprised, however, when at the open forum for input from community organizations speakers argued for water as part of the "commons," a human right that should not be controlled by the marketplace.

Snitow and Kaufman follow the struggles of three areas whose leaders met at the forum. India's Rajasthan desert area; Stockton, California; and Cochabamba in Bolivia had their water supplies literally sold out from under them. All three then used mass community support to reverse the privatization of their formerly public systems.

In Cochabamba, the third largest city in Bolivia, Bechtel Corporation was given the city's water contract. In Stockton, OMI-Thames Water (a troubled British company owned by the German corporation RWE) purchased all of the city's wastewater utilities as a result of a narrow vote in the city council. And in Rajasthan, a desert region plagued by droughts, either Coca-Cola or Pepsi were prepared to purchase all the water rights of the local rivers, streams, and wells, the infrastructure of which had been patiently created or modified by hand by the local villagers.

All three struggles against privatization took on local or regional characteristics. In Bolivia demonstrators were attacked by the police and military in an incident that may have cost Bechtel the contract: we see a sharpshooter in civilian clothes, surrounded by uniformed officers, firing into the crowd. The killing of a demonstrator gave the antipri-

vatization forces a momentum for success they might not have had otherwise. In Stockton the proponents for overthrowing the councils' vote launch a massive campaign to put the matter up for public referendum. And in India, Rajasthan activists build a coalition of women who march to protect their water, using Ghandian nonviolence as their model.

Globalization, if thirsty capitalists have their way, may mean an Indian peasant buying a plastic bottle of Aquafina or Dasani filled with the water his family and ancestors helped to bring to the desert.

Recommended Reading

Forero, Juan. "Who Will Bring Water to the Bolivian Poor?" *New York Times*, 15 December 2005. Five years after their victory in the water war and a return to reasonable prices, half of Cochabamba's people still have no water.

▶◀▶◀

This Is Nowhere

WAL-MART

2002, 87 mins., United States
Directors: Doug Hawes-Davis and John Lilburn
Cinema-Verité Documentary
Distributor: High Plains Films (www.highplainsfilms.org)

Nowhere, to be more precise, is actually a Wal-Mart parking lot. No particular lot; any one will do. In this quirky documentary, working-class and middle-class retirees and other vagabond types drive their recreational vehicles from one Wal-Mart parking lot to another for various reasons—retirement, holidays, wanderlust. Most of the film consists of interviews with these happy campers as they sit in lawn chairs outside their RVs in Wal-Mart parking lots. One of them also demonstrates an RV which, at the flick of a switch, expands like an accordion and almost doubles the size of his living room.

Wal-Mart serves as an unofficial host to these couples because founder Sam Walton was an RVer and, more practically, although these itinerants don't pay to park—they call it boondocking—they buy virtually all of their food and supplies from the mother ship at the head of the parking lot. Wal-Mart even provides a special aisle with products chosen especially for RVers.

The travelers say they love America and love the vistas they get to enjoy after they arrive, usually after dark, although the lots are always extremely well lit. Since the film was made in Montana, they have a point. Take them to I-75 in Ohio, and they will probably agree that "this is (really) nowhere."

And it turns out that this is the final reason for choosing Wal-Mart and why the film ends up being an unsolicited ad for the company: anybody, the RVers say, can find a Wal-Mart, no matter where you are. The film makes an unexpected companion piece to Jem Cohen's *Chain* (q.v.), also a film about, in part, Wal-Mart and similar parking lots.

Recommended Reading

Chisholm, Colin. "This Is Nowhere." *Mother Jones,* March–April 2003 (online at www.motherjones.org). The film "explores the zany, postmodern subculture of travelers who wander the country in RVs," ending "with a montage of Missoula's strip culture, which might as well be Anywhere—or Nowhere."

◄►◄►

This Is What Democracy Looks Like

ANTI-GLOBALIZATION

2000, 72 mins., United States
Directors: Jill Friedberg and Rick Rowley
Agit-Prop Documentary

This is a smoother, somewhat more coherent, and somewhat more politically explicit documentary than *Showdown in Seattle* (q.v.), although both films share the footage shot by over one hundred videographers during the protests against the World Trade Organization at its Seattle meeting in 1999.

Although directors Jill Friedberg and Rick Rowley have stronger graphics, a terrific soundtrack (Rage Against the Machine, DJ Shadow, and Anne Feeney are featured), and celebrity narrators (Susan Sarandon and Michael Franti), the first compilation had a raw energy that comes from its lightly edited footage shot in the midst of quite violent demonstrations. It also intercuts a revealing interview with the craftsman who turns out wooden police batons with footage of the police using those batons to abuse protestors.

What Friedberg and Rowley bring to their film is a better feel for the complexity of the coalition of students, environmentalists (the "turtles"), anti-globalization activists, and trade unionists that were represented at the rallies and street demos. Some of the activists felt that the AFL-CIO pointedly avoided the more aggressive protest zones, even if some of their members—the United Steelworkers, for example—wanted to mix it up with the best of the demonstrators.

Certainly the film offers not only the excitement of those days in November when the delegates to the WTO summit could not reach their meetings, but also some of the reasons for the protest: virtually by definition, the film points out, any safety, labor, or environmental regulation in a member country will be ruled a barrier to trade and not permissible.

Recommended Reading

Yuen, Eddie, Daniel Burton-Rose, and George Katsiaficas, eds. *Confronting Capitalism.* Brooklyn: Soft Skull Press, 2004. Extensive collection of essays on the Seattle protests and other anti-globalization manifestations.

◄►◄►

Los Trabajadores

The Workers

MIGRANT LABOR (UNITED STATES)
TRANSNATIONAL MIGRATION

2001, 48 mins., United States
Director: Heather Courtney
Mixed Cinema-Verité and Traditional
  Documentary
Distributor: New Day Films

Austin, Texas, in the 1990s was a boomtown: not only computer hardware (Dell), but dot.coms and business software companies (Trilogy) whose names were not household words, were doing business in the hundreds of millions of dollars and attracting a new well-to-do population on top of the already considerably well-off communities based on the economic power of both the University of Texas campus and the state government.

Who was going to build all the new condos and homes and maintain all those improbable Texas lawns? The answer, of course, was day labor, whose ranks were swollen by the collapse of the Mexican peso in 1994 and the terrible hurricanes that devastated Nicaragua and Honduras in 1998. Immigrants, sometimes legal but often not, stood on one street corner in Austin and waited to be picked up for day labor. Sometimes they worked, sometimes they didn't. Sometimes they were paid, sometimes they were cheated.

Heather Courtney's film chronicles two illegal immigrants, Juan Ignacia Gutierrez from Nicaragua and Ramon Castillo Aparicio from Mexico as they attempt to survive in Austin when the site for day labor pickup changes from downtown (at First Street, site of a new high-rise) out to 51st Street amidst neighborhood activists whose signs proclaimed: "Not in My Neighborhood!" Besides antipathy to day laborers and Latino immigrants in general, the neighborhood firsters argued that homeless people and day laborers were indistinguishable, and that maybe some of them were criminals. Other community leaders saw the regularization of day labor as a way of protecting the workers from exploitation and making the access to jobs fair.

Courtney's film explains why work was plentiful. But both Juan and Ramon were forced to return to their homes. Both men, they themselves argue articulately, helped build the city of Austin and like generations of other immigrant workers before them, they deserved to stay.

Recommended Readings

King, Michael. "Los Trabajadores/The Workers." *Austin Chronicle,* 16 March 2001. Although the reviewer finds the film "rough-hewn and unpolished," it documents "the workers caught in economic waves they can't control" as it shows "the human underside" of Austin's "relentless growth."

Valenzuela, Abel, et al. *On the Corner: Day Labor in the United States.* Los Angeles: Center for the Study of Urban Poverty (University of California at Los Angeles), 2006. Based on surveying "264 hiring sites in 143 municipalities in 20 U.S. states," the report reveals "that the day-labor market is rife with violations of workers' rights. Day laborers are regularly denied payment for their work, many are subjected to demonstrably hazardous job sites, and most endure insults and abuses by employers. The growth of day-labor hiring sites combined with rising levels of workers' rights violations is a national trend that warrants attention from policy makers at all levels of government and the District of Columbia."

⋈⋈⋈

Trading Women

SEX WORK/TRAFFICKING

2003, 60 mins., United States
Director: David Feingold
Agit-Prop Documentary

Thailand has the well-deserved reputation as one of the centers of the global sex tourism industry, but perhaps inevitably the truth of the matter is more complex and much worse. The Thai government licenses twenty-four different kinds of establishments for sex workers, from brothel to karaoke bar. Virtually all of them now use girls and women from ethnic minority and hill tribes of the neighboring countries of Burma, China, and Laos. The economic pressures of globalization have either driven these tribes out of their homelands or deprived them of their sources of income (unfortunately, in many cases, growing opium). Thai sex workers, it turns out, are at a premium in Japan.

For the most part even using the term "sex workers" begs the question, for many of the young women are either tricked or coerced or even kidnapped into this profession. Many believe they are going to the big city to be waitresses. But waitresses at karaoke bars supplement their wages by turning tricks. Glossy tourist bars and brothels seem cheery enough, but backstreet brothels are virtual prisons for many of the girls.

A karaoke bar owner maintains that *her* girls occasionally date the patrons but don't have to have sex with them. Nonetheless she insists that her girls use condoms!

At one point the filmmakers take us on a tour with conservative senator Sam Brownback of Kansas, who joined with the late radical leader, Paul Wellstone, in pushing for a sex trafficking bill that would investigate the level of compliance with standards that sex work advocates found too restrictive as they left virtually no room for voluntary prostitution.

This important documentary attacks various myths in Western society about sex work—that families sell their girls because it is part of their culture to do so, that the trade exists because of Western tourists, and that sex work is a reasonable economic option during hard times.

Recommended Reading

Louie, Reagan. *Orientalia: Sex In Asia.* With essay by Tracy Quan. New York: PowerHouse Books, 2003. One might ask if photographers with beautiful picture books like this one and major museum exhibitions of their photographs of (mostly) very attractive Asian women have successfully tilted the debate about sex work and trafficking into the framework of a somewhat glamorous industry. Louie is widely exhibited and celebrated for these photographs.

Trinkets and Beads

OIL

1996, 52 mins., United States
Director: Christopher Walker
Mixed Cinema Verité and Traditional
    Documentary
Distributor: First Run/Icarus Films

The struggle between Amazon jungle tribes and multinational oil companies in Ecuador follows the pattern set in neocolonial

Trinkets and Beads: The Ecuadorian Huaorani demonstrate against the energy companies. Courtesy First Run/Icarus Films.

days and updated in the age of globalization. Missionaries come to a people in the service of the Lord but sponsored by a company from the mother country. "Savages" become Christians, a raw material is extracted, and diseases and subjugation follow.

Two tribes are at the center of this film, which documents the mostly successful attempts by multinational oil companies to tap an oil reserve in the Ecuadorean rainforest, a good portion of which is a national park. The Cofan people capitulated early on, in the 1980s, to Texaco's deal. But soon after they turned to the courts to undo the damage—disease and pollution caused by oil spills.

The neighboring tribe of the Huaorani, known as one of the fiercest in the Amazon because of their habit of killing missionaries at first contact, take longer to be persuaded to give up control of their land. But the oil companies have a formidable weapon of their own: Rachel Saint, an evangelical missionary whose brother was one of five missionaries the Huaorani killed in 1956. Forgiving them (for they knew not what they did), she succeeds in converting some of the tribe and covering up their pesky nakedness. It took a lot longer for the energy companies to enter Huaorani land, but in the end some of their leaders agree to allow drilling because of her support for the idea. The lead oil company is Maxus, based in Dallas. When all of the oil is processed, it will keep American cars on the road for about thirteen days.

The film's title comes from the celebration Maxus sponsors in one of the Huaorani villages. The daughter of Ecuador's president gracefully exchanges her earrings for an Huaorani woman's gift of a bracelet and a feather coronet. Was this a good deal, she asks a Maxus official, who says, "That's how we got Manhattan, with trinkets and beads."

One piece of archival footage is stunning: in 1957 Rachel Saint was the guest of the popular television show, *This Is Your Life*. She is accompanied by a young Huaorani woman who is one of those Stone Age people, the show's host observes, who don't live in communities, just family groups strung out in the jungle. It was the beginning of the virtual canonization of Saint. The tribal leader Moi—

who was opposed to Maxus' deal with his people—says Saint told his people lies: God was coming and the world was coming to an end. Unfortunately, not too long after their conversions, the Huaorani began to lose their children to polio and other diseases.

In this century the tribes of the rainforest are bringing lawsuits against the oil companies whose routine business involved excess oil that had to go somewhere. In one sequence we see it being spread on a road like tar, but it never dries. The hagiography of the Saint family continued in the feature film *End of the Spear* (2005), a missionary epic in which Rachel Saint's nephew is reconciled to his father's murderer. Oil seems not to have a role in this version of the story.

Recommended Reading

Spring, Rosamond Kilmer. "Trinkets and Beads." *Bridges*, Spring/Summer 2004 (online at www.bridges23.com/archives/vol_11_1_2.html). "An important film that should be seen by anyone concerned about the environment, first–third world relations, globalization, ethnology, and the role of missionaries."

▶◀▶◀

Under the Skin of the City

CHANGES IN THE WORKPLACE: WORLDWIDE MIGRANT LABOR (OTHER THAN THE UNITED STATES)

2001, 92 mins., Iran, Persian (Farsi) with English subtitles
Director: Rakhshan Bani Etemad
Screenplay: Rakhshan Bani Etemad and Farid Mostafavi

The new wave of Iranian films in the last ten years have opened up a virtually closed Muslim society dominated by the ayotollahs. How refreshing is it that this film focuses on a mixed working- and middle-class family in contemporary Tehran. The matriarch works in a textile mill, one son is a student dabbling in street politics, while another son is the personal assistant to a wholesaler of textiles, rugs, and similar items.

We see Tuba (played by Golab Adineh)

tending her machine at the mill, the family sharing a fast-food meal of pizza, and the son handling perks for his employer's mistress. But we also see one daughter brutalized by a vicious son-in-law and the other daughter's friend beaten by her brother for hanging out in ways he defined as offensive. In short, we have a very modern industrial society with a reactionary religious culture dominating certain aspects of daily life.

The details of Tuba's life in what must be the equivalent to an Iranian sweatshop make this film unusual viewing for most of us. We see the women tending large machines, each one buried in what has to be a sweltering but religiously correct garment. She has a serious cough, no doubt due to the particulate matter swirling about in her textile factory. It's a rare film from the Middle East which argues that religious and patriarchal harassment and industrial servitude are taken from the same page.

In a complicated denouement, the successful son decides to go to Japan to work, selling his family's house to buy a visa, which turns out to be the bait for a gigantic swindle. He tries to recoup his family's loss by an ill-fated smuggling operation.

Matriarch Tuba ends the film as it began, with what seems to be a film crew making a documentary of women's roles. Her first reaction? "I wish somebody would film what's going on right in here." Then: "Who the hell do you show these films to?" she asks both the director within the film and presumably Rakhshan Bani Etemad, not to mention us as well.

Recommended Readings

Scott, A. O. "An Iranian Family, Facing Conflict Within and Beyond." *New York Times,* 14 March 2003. Admires the way the film combines "the great deal of palpable political sentiment in this film: a quiet disgust at the way Tuba and her co-workers are exploited; a simmering contempt at the deeply ingrained habits of male domination; and a weary pessimism about the fantasy of cosmopolitan affluence that [one of Tuba's sons] finds so compelling."

Tapper, Richard, ed. *The New Iranian Cinema: Politics, Representation, and Identity.* London: I. B. Tauris, 2004. Although this helpful col-

lection of essays does not discuss *Under the Skin of the City*, it covers similar topics and films.

⋈⋈⋈

Under the Tower

THATCHERISM

Sundial, 1992, 1 min.
A13, 1994, 12 mins.
Island Race, 1996, 28 mins.
Director: William Raban
Structuralist Documentaries

The first two films of this trilogy use the development of Canary Wharf in the 1990s as the symbolic and actual centerpiece of the expansion of London's business center eastward into the formerly abandoned and (somewhat) derelict docklands. For William Raban this area is simultaneously a zone of cubistic structures (see Green) and a political/economic extension of Thatcherite politics. The renewal of the docks was a high priority of the unregulated economy Raban refers to as being "under the tower."

Sundial, the first film, is a montage of seventy-one shots in just one minute that situates the Canary Wharf Tower as an omnipresent sentinel and the dominant force in the cityscape.

A13, the second film, uses the construction of the Canary Wharf project and a nearby urban clearway, the Limehouse Road Link (aka the A13), as boundary markers in the transition from traditional London to chaotic London. Thus Raban cuts between men from the Victorian Billingsgate Market pushing meat on trolleys and men fishing on the equally old canal to an elaborate bank of CATV monitors keeping a camera eye on London traffic. In the meantime wrecking balls knock down neighborhoods in the path of the new road.

The investment of capital did not make the small and fairly impoverished local population in the Isle of Dogs disappear. These locals are the subject of Raban's third film in the trilogy, *Island Race,* which highlights racial and political tensions resulting in an antifascist march and the election of a member of the racist British National Party to Parliament.

The ultimate irony of the global investment in the Canary Wharf project (by the Toronto multinational Olympia & York) is that it displaced the remnants of the docklands, the former neocolonial shipping hub of the British Empire. But, as Bill Schwarz argues, that's imperialist biz.

Recommended Readings

Green, Darren. "William Raban: Profile." *Luxonline*, 2005 (online at www.luxonline.org.uk). Overview of Raban's career and discussion of his films.

Rees, Al. "Island Race." *Tate Magazine*, Summer 1996 (online at www.luxonline.org.uk). Stresses Raban's ability to use the "lyrical documentary" form which combines landscape (cityscape) and allusive content.

Schwarz, Bill. "Docklands and East London in the Thatcher Years." In *Enterprise and Heritage*, ed. John Corner and Sylvia Harvey. London: Routledge, 1991, 76–92. Reviews the transition in the docklands between neocolonialism and globalization.

▶◀▶◀▶◀

The Universal Clock: The Resistance of Peter Watkins

ANTI-GLOBALIZATION

2001, 77 mins., United Kingdom
Director: Geoff Bowie
Cinema-Verité Documentary
Distributor: First Run/Icarus Films

When is an hour not an hour? When it is on the "universal clock," or global standard broadcast schedule. Then the program or documentary must be 47½ minutes long (23½ if it is a half hour show). The extra minutes go to commercials, of course, and as Chris Haws, formerly of Discovery [Channel] International, explains, producers want a program for a global market that holds no surprises and will be processed to industry standards (Mitzi Goldman, "Round Docs in a Square Box," September 2003, online at www.ozdox.org/textz/round_docs.html).

Geoff Bowie's documentary is an extended critique of this notion of the universal clock and other manifestations of the globalized media conglomerates defined by Peter Watkins, the maverick filmmaker who refuses to be on anyone's clock and whose credo begins this film: "Making a film is a social act, a political act, a human act of work, love, and communication." Much of *The Universal Clock* consists of documentary footage of the making of *La Commune* (2000), Watkins' latest film, which at 345 minutes defies the universal clock.

Peter Watkins is the kind of filmmaker whose work—almost exclusively mock docs—gather high praise from film critics and film historians but whose box office receipts are low and whose pull among producers has been minimal. And the films are strenuously political and controversial: *Culloden*, a graphic (for 1964) depiction of the British troops massacre of Scottish defenders and civilians in the clearing of the Scottish highlands; *Punishment Park* (1970), which takes left-wing youths and hippies to the desert and allows policemen to hunt them down; and *The War Game* (1965), one of the first and most effective of the nuclear winter films.

Many of his films use the self-conscious man-on-the-street approach of the classic American television program, *You Are There*. We see action unfolding, and then one of the participants is interviewed by what appears to be a news team covering the event. As Michaela Poschi points out, interviewing participants is an "anachronistic strategy" that has the effect of "structuring the film around its 'collective protagonist' (the crowd)." This approach has become quite routine in anti-globalization filmmaking by independent videographers (*Showdown in Seattle* or *This What Democracy Looks Like*, q.v.).

La Commune refines this approach in a number of intriguing ways, despite the film's overall length. (You want me to stay within 47½ minutes? Well, then, here are 345!) He uses two film crews from opposite sides of the class struggle, one from a station called Commune TV, representing the Communards, the other called Versailles TV, representing the

The Universal Clock: Paris Communards (French actors) on break. Courtesy First Run/Icarus Films.

government and upper-class supporters, and we watch their crews work their respective constituencies and even see some of their broadcasts.

Peter Watkins's long takes are his response to another aspect of his critical engagement: what he calls the *monoform*, the tendency of traditional documentaries to use what he regarded as attention-friendly shots of just five to eight seconds each. (Both the monoform and the universal clock are the key limitations imposed on filmmakers by the American MAVM or Mass Audiovisual Media, discussed in detail in Watkins' *The Media Crisis,* 2003, available on line or in French.)

Bowie points to those aspects of Peter Watkins's style in *La Commune* that stymie the universal clock: his insistence on the crowd as protagonist (instead of the mainstream close-ups of stars or principal figures) and his process of employing nonprofessionals who research their own backstories. The film also acted as self-referential agit-prop because many of the Parisian participants in the film formed an activist group that challenged the industry's de facto censorship of the film (its length and topic) after its release.

Bowie is attentive to the radical critique of Watkins's enterprise. He merges an interview with one of the nonprofessional actors, an illegal Algerian living in Paris, with the story of the Communards, who were massacred by government troops in 1871. These same troops were sent to North Africa to put down a Berber insurrection in the Magreb. Those

rebels that survived were exiled to the same New Caledonian prison island to which many of the surviving Communards were sent.

Recommended Readings

Poschl, Micaela. "Beyond the Limits of the Rectangular Frame." Trans. Aileen Derieg. *Republic Art*, May 2003 (online at www.republicart.net/disc/representations/poeschl01_en.htm). Discusses *La Commune* as innovative in its form, its process of production, and distribution.

Welsh, James M. *The Illusion of Freedom: The Films of Peter Watkins.* Trowbridge: Flicks Books, 1998. Sympathetic review of Watkins's career.

ᕼᕼᕼ

Unknown Quantity

Ce qui arrive . . .

ANTI-GLOBALIZATION
GLOBAL CATASTROPHES

2003, 30 mins., France
Director: Andrei Ujica
Structuralist Documentary/Video Installation

Although this film may not have been released separately from its video installation organized separately, it is nonetheless a distinctive contribution to the cinema of globalization. It is an extended conversation between Paul Virilio, Parisian urbanist, technology critic, and futurist of disasters, and Svetlana Aleksievich, a chronicler of the victims and surviving witnesses of the Chernobyl nuclear plant disaster. Virilio investigates disasters that result from technological development (well-known ones such as Union Carbide in Bhopal, India, and lesser-known ones such as the dioxin gas leak from the Icmesa factory near Seveso, Italy, in 1976), apparently natural events (hurricanes), public health crises (mad cow disease in the United Kingdom), and even terrorist activities (such as the attack on the World Trade Center in New York).

Virilio's argument is convoluted and hyperbolic, but its essence is convincing: in the words of Hannah Arendt, quoted by one reviewer (Patricia Allmer), "Progress and catastrophe are the opposite faces of the same coin." Even if we accept only part of Virilio's claims, this potential builder of a "museum of accidents" has much to contribute to the analysis of the destructive power of one aspect of globalization, as the industrial disasters he exhibits are in large part attributed to the power of multinational corporations to proceed without controls or monitoring and to escape the consequences of their toxic oil, chemical, and gas releases. Virilio quotes a Swiss insurance company statistic: in the 1990s man-made accidents far exceeded all natural catastrophes by a ratio of seven to three.

Although the title of the film and installation in French is somewhat less elusive (*Ce qui arrive . . .* or "What Happens"), Virilio explains the English title in his companion volume this way: "The accident is what remains unexpected, truly surprising, the unknown quantity in a totally discovered planetary habitat."

One danger in this remarkable project is that the photographs of many of these industrial and other accidents are remarkably beautiful, but this is an occupational hazard of certain kinds of professional photography (witness Sebastio Salgado's photographic documentation of workers worldwide). Take away the elegant sluts of David Cronenberg's film, *Crash* (1996), a disturbing adaptation of the work of another catastrophist, J. G. Ballard, and we see in Virilio's compilation of photos mesmerizing, twisted piles of metal and concrete. More chilling, perhaps, is that "in most of these pictures, human beings have vanished" (Patricia Allmer), and we are left—in a physical sense only—with the intimations of catastrophe.

Recommended Readings

Aleksievich, Svetlana. *Voices from Chernobyl: Chronicles of the Future.* London: Aurum Press, 1990. Interviews with witnesses and victims of the disaster.

Allmer, Patricia. "Unknown Quantity." *Pop Matters Magazine,* 19 February 2003 (online at www.popmatters.com). Concludes that Virilio's work "is a work of mourning—mourning for a humanity, an earth which has lost control through globalization, through the irresponsibility of power-crazed politicians and businessmen."

Virilio, Paul. *Unknown Quantity.* New York and Paris: Thames & Hudson and Foundation Cartier por l'art contemporain, 2002. Trans. Chris Turner and Jian-Xing Too. With essays, stills from the film, photos of the installation, and numerous examples of "unknown quantities."

ᗊᗊᗊ

Unreported World

SCARCE RESOURCES (COLTAN)

September 28, 2001, episode: "The Real Mobile Phone War," 30 mins., United Kingdom
Producers: Channel 4

Most of the weekly episodes from 2001–5 of Channel 4's foreign affairs program, *Unreported World,* focus on trouble spots, mostly wars, that have not received enough attention in the media (online at www.channel4.com/news/microsites/U/unreported_world/index_old.html). This episode from the first season, "The Real Mobile Phone War," ignores the intense competition for consumers of cell phone services and focuses instead on what manufacturers all need: coltan. Coltan, the street name for the black mineral colombo tantalite, is an excellent conducting material—it can withstand severe temperature fluctuations—

and is universally used in cell phones, computer games and screens, and other digital devices.

Coltan mining has, therefore, special standing among scarce resources as one of the key indicators of globalization because it is one of the necessary building blocks for digitalization. It is unfortunate for the war-torn Congo that it has coltan in some abundance. Under a different peacetime regime, coltan could become a blessing. Now, however, it is a curse.

For years rebel and government forces have committed atrocities on the civilian population of the eastern provinces of the Democratic Republic of the Congo (formerly Zaire). Although tribal rivalries should never be discounted, the struggle is primarily over the profits to be gained from this resource-rich area. In addition to the control of coltan mines, multinational corporations, warlords, and government agencies are all vying for their share of the oil, gold, ivory, diamonds, and timber found in the region. The demand for coltan peaked in 2002 (although the United States remains the chief importer) to be supplanted by tin ore, as tin became another metal of choice in printed circuit boards, in addition to its common use as a packaging material (see Global Witness below).

The IMF and the World Bank were active investors in the Kabila government, as were a number of European countries and South Africa as well. Following a familiar pattern of neocolonial control, Belgium—whose King Leopold once ruled and exploited the entire country as his personal property for the purpose of extracting rubber and ivory—sent military advisers to the Congo in 2004 to train the government military and bolster their effectiveness against the rebels.

Recommended Readings

Global Witness. *Under-Mining Peace: Tin— The Explosive Trade in Cassiterite in Eastern DRC* [Democratic Republic of the Congo]. Washington, D.C.: Global Witness Publishing, 2005. Report by watchdog group (supported by government agencies in both the United States and United Kingdom) detailing the rise of tin ore (cassiterite) as the mineral now favored by

government and militia groups for international trade.

Werner, Klaus, and Hans Weiss. *Das Neue Schwarzbuch Markenfirmen.* 2nd ed. Vienna, Deuticke, 2003. Not yet translated into English, this "New Black Book on Brand Companies" charges the best-known branded companies with "exploitative practices, child labor, environmental destruction [and] cruelty to animals." The section on coltan, "Blood for Mobile Phones," focuses on Bayer as a major player among the competing forces in the Congo.

ㅐㅐㅐ

Up in Smoke

CHANGES IN THE WORKPLACE: WORLDWIDE NEOCOLONIALISM

2003, 27 mins., United States
Directors: Martin Otanez and Christopher Walker
Mixed Agit-Prop and Traditional Documentary
Distributor: Bullfrog Films

The southern African country of Malawi and its tobacco monoculture are a test case for the indivisibility of the colonial/neocolonial/globalization nexus. The British colony of Nyassaland began tobacco cultivation in the late nineteenth century. Upon independence in 1964, the country was renamed Malawi, and its tobacco cultivation increased when the unelected president-for-life Kamuzu Hasting became de facto owner of the tobacco plantations. After thirty years of his rule, multinational corporations such as Universal Corporation of America began to dominate the country's economy by purchasing more than 50 percent of the available tobacco through its subsidiary, Lime Leaf, which in turn ran the so-called free-market auctions in the country and sold 95 percent of the total crop to cigarette makers such as Philip Morris.

The Malawi labor force operates under the constraints of the same classic tenant farming system instituted in the American South after the Civil War. Whole families work the land

Up in Smoke: Tobacco tenant farmers in Malawi. Courtesy Marty Otanez and Bullfrog Films.

and turn over their crop to the landlords who, after deducting the costs of food, fertilizer, and whatever else is needed to maintain the tobacco drying sheds, pay the families virtually nothing or in fact compute their ever-deepening debt. In a related film, *Thangata* (2002), filmmaker Martin Otanez calls this system social bondage or forced labor, a practice outlawed by the United Nations.

An inevitable byplay of this system is not just debt peonage but also child labor. John Kapito from the Consumers Association of Malawi is interviewed for the film: "You'll find that minus what [the landlord] has been given [by the farmer] throughout the year, he has nothing left. And he cannot leave the farm. In fact, he owes you more."

The film also reviews the situation—and the deep ironies—of worldwide tobacco consumption. Tobacco sales in Malawi are set by auction, but the big buyers control the prices through their volume purchases and political connections. After purchase, the tobacco bales are trucked from Malawi to South African ports, loaded on container ships, and exported to seventy different countries, with the biggest shipments going to the United States, Japan, China, the United Kingdom, and Turkey. Marlboros are mostly Malawian tobacco, part of that transnational corporation's production of 5.5 trillion cigarettes a year.

When worldwide demand for tobacco lessens or auction prices fall, Malawians who service the debilitating monoculture are doubly oppressed. With no alternative forms of income, the economy suffers. Sustainable agriculture for food becomes threatened even further, and as farmers grow more tobacco in the face of declining prices more trees are cut down to build sheds and fuel the curing processes.

In a country that was once a major slave conduit from 1860 to 1890, labor union organizers now confront a situation that would violate most international standards, if in fact those standards had not slipped as a result of transnational trade agreements that often curtail discussions of environmental or labor issues. Malawian farmers must use their children to work, they drink water contaminated by fertilizer runoffs, and they are chronically short of food. Otanez's film *Thangata* supplies some vital background information that *Up in Smoke* takes for granted. When the British ended the slave trade in Malawi, they borrowed *thangata*, a local word for assistance, and used it to define a new system of forced labor. It created the most terrible of ironies for the Malawians, as one spokesperson for the government, confirms: while smoking may be death for many people worldwide, for Malawians "tobacco is life."

Recommended Reading

Muula, Adamson S. "The Challenges Facing Third World Countries in Banning Tobacco." *Bulletin of the World Health Organization* 79 (2001): 480. Discusses Malawi's dilemma, as "tobacco is the number one cash crop in the country" and "many people are afraid to attack this source of income. Talking against tobacco production is akin to promoting economic chaos."

⋈⋈⋈

Uprooted

MIGRANT LABOR (UNITED STATES)

2001, 28 mins., United States
Coproducers: Lilla Nilsen, Sasha Khokha, Francisco Herrera, and Jon Fromer
Agit-Prop Documentary
Distributor: Progressive Films (www. progressivefilms.org)

While most of us assume that immigrants to the United States are in search of jobs, this film demonstrates in three diverse stories exactly why globalization has driven three families from their homes and a reasonably secure economic life. Maricel from the Philippines, Jessy and Jaime from Bolivia, and Luckner from Haiti are direct casualties of their native countries' relationship with the World Bank and the IMF.

Ten percent of all Filipinos work abroad, and their remittances home are the largest single item in the plus side of the national budget ledger. On the minus side is the payment of interest on loans from the World Bank and IMF. Maricel responded to the government's campaign to send workers abroad by taking a domestic job with an American executive in Hong Kong. When the businessman moved to New York she went too, but here began what she considers ten years of low pay and insulting treatment.

Luckner in Haiti was making one dollar a day stitching baseballs for American professional leagues. He was stupefied when the American company left for China, where they intended to pay workers even less for the same work. He ended up in Florida picking oranges for Minute Maid.

The only middle-class people in the film are Jessy and Jaime, whose small Bolivian factory closed. One of the conditions for a loan from the IMF was an open market: cheaper electrical fixtures soon drove out their goods. They left for the United States, where, despite his training as an engineer, Jaime works as a janitor.

Since this film was sponsored by the National Network for Immigrant and Refugee Rights, it is not surprising that almost all its subjects have become organizers for various causes: Luckner is a farm worker organizer, Jessy teaches immigrant rights, and Maricel organizes minimum wage campaigns.

Recommended Reading

Dwyer, Augusta. *On the Line: Life on the U.S.-Mexican Border*. London: Latin American Bureau, 1994. Reviews the economic benefits to the multinationals and how they shift their costs from the United States to the maquiladoras.

⋈⋈⋈

El Valley Central

HISTORY OF GLOBALIZATION

2000, 90 mins., United States
Director: James Benning
Structuralist Documentary

The Central Valley of California supplies America with about a quarter of its food supply. James Benning makes its 26,000 square miles accessible in 35 shots (36 if you count the end credits), each exactly 2½ minutes long. His structuralist filmmaking is based in the precise timing of each shot, his stationary but strategically placed camera, and his mostly long shots of the landscape, in this case, an agricultural valley transformed by agribusiness into a mammoth machine for creating food and wealth.

The thirty-sixth "shot" is a kind of politicized credit sequence, because Benning lists where each shot was filmed and which agribusiness owns or controls that instrument or parcel of land or water. Thus one shot is identified as "Freight train, Southern Pacific, Bakersfield," and another "Freighter ship,

Naviera de Chile, Stockton Deep Water Channel."

El Valley Central is the first film in Benning's *California Trilogy*. The second, *Los* (2000) uses the vast urban sprawl of Los Angeles as a counterpoint to the third film, *Sogobi* (2001), which features mostly wilderness tracts. All three stick to his structuralist formula of 35 (or 36) shots 2½ minutes long. All three, but especially *El Valley Central*, are about the ownership of the lands, their physical exploitation, and those who labor on them.

What does Benning gain by his very formal and seemingly quite rigid approach? We must first of all note that his shooting ratio is probably ten times the length of the final film, so he is able to select particularly revealing moments in his exploration of the valley. Thus the backbreaking labor of a Mexican farm worker is followed by a shot of the relatively easy work of a man on a tractor. Or the opening shot of the water in a reservoir draining out of central hole is bookended with the final shot of the entrance gate of the city of Modesto which proclaims "Water. Wealth. Contentment. Health." And some of the shots are visual triumphs: we see a freighter crossing the frame but no water is visible; then a sailboat crosses its path in the opposite direction and, finally, a car goes in and out of the shot as well, but there is no road visible either. This is a minimal aesthetic with significant content nonetheless.

Recommended Readings

Alvarez, D-L. "Tortured Landscapes." *Filmmaker*, 6 March 2002 (online at www.filmmakermagazine.com). Very helpful overview of the director's career and his trilogy with an interview.

MacDonald, Scott. "Exploring the New West: An Interview with James Benning." *Film Quarterly* (Spring 2005): 2–25. "The whole trilogy is basically about the politics of water."

▸▸▸

Valley of Tears

MIGRANT LABOR (UNITED STATES)

2003, 82 mins., United States
Director: Hart Perry
Traditional Documentary
Distributor: Seventh Art Releasing (www.7thart.com)

Not many filmmakers have access to a community over four decades, plus the footage to show for it. *Valley of Tears* is a longitudinal view of Raymondville, a South Texas agricultural community—once the "Onion Capital of America"—from 1954 to 2000. The first third of the film uses director Hart Perry's footage from 1979 when, fresh from helping to shoot Barbara Kopple's award-winning *Harlan County USA* (in *Working Stiffs*), he worked for the Texas Farm Workers' Union, recording their mostly Mexican migrant worker strike against onion farm owners. The second part brings Perry back to the scene in the early 1990s when Latino parents are struggling against a white school board. The third part in 2000 features a Mexican American candidate running for district attorney. We see how far this community has come since 1954, when, the newsreels of the time show, it was a culturally homogeneous (white) community with its annual Miss Onion contest.

The farm workers lost their bitter 1979 strike, although the first round of scabs brought in went over to their side. Subsequent scabs (recruited from a rival farm owner's workforce), however, successfully broke the strike. Since many of the Mexicans soon became Mexican Americans the economic struggle also became a cultural one, as they had to confront a school system that did not adapt to Spanish-speaking children.

An unusual part of this story is the filmmaker's falling out with the union that brought him to Raymondville. "We did have a disagreement," Perry states on his website (www.perryfilms.com). "I thought the story of the town was far more interesting. It was not a black-and-white story of migrant farm workers being exploited. It was more complex than that. I thought it was about a community that was out of touch with each other." Whatever the dispute with the union might have meant, Perry has captured not only a difficult phase of migrant history but also, like the filmmakers of *My Journey Home* and *The New Americans* (q.v.), how they have adapted to becoming Americans.

Recommended Reading

Kehr, Dave. "A 1970's Farm Union Struggle Leaves a Broken Town Today." *New York Times*, 28 November 2003. "Another title for Mr. Perry's film might have been 'American impasse'; though truth and justice may lie on the side of the workers, the farm owners have a hammerlock on the real-world economy."

ᕦᕦᕦ

A Very British Coup

GLOBAL CAPITAL
THATCHERISM

1988, 148 mins., United Kingdom
Director: Mick Jackson
Screenplay: Alan Plater, based on Chris
    Mullin's novel, *A Very British Coup* (1983)

A Very British Coup: Sheffield union leader (Ray McAnally) becomes prime minister.

This television series about a former steel worker and union leader from Sheffield who becomes an openly socialist Labour Party prime minister offers a fictional but intriguing interpretation of Thatcherism. Both the television series and its source novel dramatize an upper-class shadow government of high-ranking civil servants and their lackeys who are Tory to the bone regardless of which party wins a general election. This group will do anything to keep Harry Perkins (played by Ray McAnally), a Labour Party prime minister, from staying in power and they attempt "a very British coup" (with very different results from the ending of the source novel), one—the title implies—that does not involve the vulgar use of actual weapons.

When Perkins ruminates about his working-class background, he recalls that his only inheritance was a shaving mug from his grandfather. But, after all, "what you do with your inheritance is what matters." At one point Perkins confronts Sir Percy, head of British intelligence service and his primary upper-class opponent, who has inherited fifty thousand acres from his family: "Do I frighten you that much, Harry Perkins, a

steelworker from Sheffield?" The answer is obvious, even to Harry, although he of course underestimates the dirty tricks that will victimize him in the future. And he seems only to have gradually realized that the United States would unleash its agents once it understood that he was going to sever the United Kingdom's traditional subservient ties, especially in terms of American missile placement, to the United States.

One of the substantial subplots involves the need to keep the pound afloat. Perkins selects as his chancellor of the exchequer Lawrence Wainwright (played by Geoffrey Beevers), whom earlier he had defeated for party leadership. Wainwright argues that only the IMF with its strict policy of "structural readjustment" of reducing social welfare expenditures can assure British solvency. Without telling Wainwright, Harry arranges for a loan from (of all places) the Soviet Union (not yet collapsed in this fictional world), who in turn has borrowed the money from oil-producing countries in the Middle East.

Three of Perkins's controversial "socialist"

planks in his platform are the removal of U.S. bases from British soil, the dismantling of British nuclear missiles, and the subsequent increase in public spending on social welfare programs, all of which would mark a decisive break with the Thatcherite ethos. When Harry's adviser on nuclear disarmament is murdered and an old love affair is exploited against him, it seems only a matter of time before Harry will capitulate. The last minutes of the series should have sympathetic viewers gasping with mixed awe and delight.

Chris Mullin, a Labour MP and author of the source novel, began writing his book in 1980 when Prime Minister Thatcher had not yet seemed so absolute. He tried to speculate what the Tories would do if a left-winger gained ground on them, but as he said in the preface to a later edition of his book (London: Politico's Publishing, 2001), he only learned after publishing his book of the allegations that there did exist a group of British intelligence officers who had plotted to undermine Labour Prime Minister Harold Wilson's government. Both his novel and the film develop a complex and fascinating story of intrigue among politicians, press lords, and just plain lords.

Recommended Reading

Birchall, Danny. "A Very British Coup." *British Film Institute Screen Online* (online at www.screenonline.org.uk). "In the end, *A Very British Coup* is perhaps best seen not as a conspiracy thriller, but as a political fantasy: a story of politicians, not plotting amongst themselves, but trying to do the best for their country and its working-class population, in a world increasingly hostile to the will of the people."

ㅐㅐㅐ

Wage Slaves: On Not Getting By in America

WAL-MART

2002, 100 mins., United States
Producers: Bill Kurtis, Erik J. Nelson, and Amy Briamonte
TV Documentary, based on Barbara Ehrenreich's *Nickel and Dimed* (2001)
Distributor: A & E Television (www.aetv.com)

This investigative report from the Arts & Entertainment Network confirms what Barbara Ehrenreich's best-selling book demonstrates and most intelligent commentators believe: minimum-wage jobs are just another way of doing poverty in America. Ehrenreich's provocative narrative account of one woman's attempt to survive in low-wage jobs—house cleaning, Wal-Mart clerking, waitressing—included her analysis of the economic and human costs of these non–living wage jobs.

Fortunately Ehrenreich's lively book inspired the producers to find five working stiffs (Sandra Gale Hurst, Ronald Rooney, Sofia Acosta, Virginia Perry, and Robert Nichols) who embody wage slavery. Unfortunately they padded what could have been a brilliant cinema-verité exposé into an over-long and repetitive documentary that sinks whenever the film leaves the five working stiffs and cozies up to the experts, who range from articulate (Robert Reich, secretary of labor under Bill Clinton) to unconvincing (Walter Williams and Donald Bordreaux, respectively, economists from George Mason University).

Even some of the revealing footage of the workers is repeated unnecessarily. We need to hear and see what frustrations they face, but once is usually enough for each of the subjects. The five are remarkably resilient, and while nobody would call them cheerful, they struggle on with high hopes and generally a positive attitude. They do the daily jobs—dry cleaning shop worker, home care worker, limo driver, receptionist, and temp worker—that simply never pay enough to give them the security they and their families need. They are part of the 24 percent of Americans who earn $16,000 or less a year.

Ehrenreich, who took on these kinds of jobs for a year to see how the working poor make it, concluded that they cannot. Unless they live with a relative (and not pay rent) or work a second job (equally bad paying) or do without necessities or health care, they are simply a paycheck or two away from welfare.

The film is a little stronger when it comes to analyzing contemporary trends and issues. The mythical solution to welfare called "workfare" is briefly but resolutely punctured. The successes of the living wage campaign in many cities are suggested. The student-worker alliance at Harvard, which doubled some of the campus workers' wages, is noted, as is the countertrend: Wal-Mart's apparent success to date in making workers come early and stay late without pay.

Recommended Reading

Wertheimer, Ron. "The Poor Who Work, Yet Live with Desperation." *New York Times*, 26 August 2002. "Despite its important subject, this [film] is no more than fast food for thought. You want fries with that?"

▶◀▶◀▶◀

Wall Street

BANKING AND GLOBAL FINANCING
REAGANOMICS

1987, 124 mins., R, United States
Director: Oliver Stone
Screenplay: Oliver Stone and Stanley Weiser

Two milestones of the Reagan Era are behind the plot of *Wall Street*: the Ivan Boesky insider trading scandals and the battle between Eastern Airline's Frank Lorenzo and the International Association of Machinists (IAM) in the 1980s (*Collision Course*, q.v.). The leading inside trader of the film is Gordon Gekko (played to perfection by Michael Douglas) and appropriately named after a lizard (although the gecko is not as scary as it looks). Gekko, as one character says, received an "ethical bypass at birth." He was invented so people could say he loves money more than sex. That Gekko is like an unstoppable male beast in rut is clearly Stone's metaphorical intention. Thus, the first time we see and hear Gekko he is on the phone making a deal and announces, "Raise the sperm count of the deal!" When he is asked to meet for a meal, he replies: "Lunch? You got to be kidding! Lunch is for women."

Gekko is trying to raid the Geldar Paper Corporation, at whose stockholders' meeting he makes his now-legendary "greed is good" speech and attacks the thirty-three vice presi-

dents on the dais as do-nothings with dubious job descriptions. Management, not Wall Street, he tells the stockholders, is the real enemy: "I am not a destroyer of companies. I am a liberator of them." That his lies seem to work for such a long time—he basically wants to hold on to a company only long enough to loot its cash assets and sell off anything that is left—is part of his attraction to other Wall Street hustlers.

In the second, Eastern Airlines–inspired part of the plot, Gekko's apprentice, Bud Fox (played by Charlie Sheen), uses insider information on Blue Star Airlines that he receives from his father, Carl Fox (played by Martin Sheen), the head of the airline's maintenance union. Gekko deceives Bud into thinking that the airline will be allowed to survive. Bud ends up in a secret war against Gekko to save the company by forming an alliance of the pilots' and flight attendants' organizations, his father's union, and Sir Harry Wildman (played by Terence Stamp), one of Gekko's chief rivals. Instead of a "garage sale at Blue Star," the company survives. Unlike Eastern Airlines, we might add.

Wall Street is a fable primarily because a potentially good guy realizes the error of his ways and uses a stock war between Wall Street velociraptors for a noble end. (Bud's parallel in real life, Boesky's apprentice crook, Martin Siegel, was also wired to trap others, but he had no altruistic goals.) Clearly Stone has a point here: the deals at the top can make or break the people on the bottom. Boesky did get caught; Gekko is captured on tape incriminating himself. But Eastern Airlines is long gone, and so are millions of dollars past accounting.

Recommended Readings

Canby, Vincent. "Greed." *New York Times*, 11 December 1987. A mixed review that describes poor Daryl Hannah as having "the screen presence of a giant throw pillow."

Robinson, Jack E. *Free Fall: The Needless Destruction of Eastern Air Lines and the Valiant Struggle to Save It*. New York: Harper, 1992. Discusses Lorenzo and the unions who squared off against him (ALPA, the pilots; TWU, the flight attendants; and IAM, the machinists).

Stewart, James B. *Den of Thieves*. New York:

Wall Street: Wall Street from the POV of Gekko (Michael Douglas).

Simon and Schuster, 1991. A detailed narrative of Boesky and his fellow inside trading swindlers.

▶◀▶◀

Wal-Mart: The High Cost of Low Price

WAL-MART

2005, 97 mins., United States
Director: Robert Greenwald
Agit-Prop Documentary

Robert Greenwald's *Outfoxed: Rupert Murdoch's War on Journalism* (2005) was a brilliant dissection of Fox and its relentless right-wing distortion of the news. Greenwald used the occasion of national campaigns against Wal-Mart organized by both anti-sprawl groups and labor unions as an opportunity to offer his critique of Wal-Mart. The film had an unusual distribution in that it was shown in cafes, homes, and halls across the nation at the same time it was released directly to DVD, bypassing both traditional theater and television broadcast release.

Greenwald tracks the misdeeds of Wal-Mart from one frustrated community of the United States to another and also includes stops in Honduras, Bangladesh, and China. The film follows a pattern domestically: the filmmakers visit a small business or group of employees whose grievances against Wal-Mart include not only the obvious ones—low pay, anti-unionism, and inadequate health benefits—but also touch on some other important and often ignored aspects. One of the ways Wal-Mart begins every new store almost in the black, for example, is getting its construction infrastructure paid for by the local county—tax abatements, road access, sewer and water lines, resulting in company savings from three hundred thousand dollars to more than a million dollars.

And when the parking lots are built, Greenwald's film documents relentlessly, they are terribly unsafe, with over 80 percent of all criminal incidents occurring in the lots with virtually no supervision of any kind. Furthermore, Greenwald documents a Belmont, North Carolina, Wal-Mart that stored pesticides, herbicides, and fertilizer bags on the periphery of the property, dangerously close to creeks and storm water drains.

When Greenwald documents Wal-Mart's tremendous reliance on Chinese and Bangladeshi sweatshops, his indignation boils over. In China, for example, he interviews workers forced to live in crowded dormitories, have rent taken out of their paychecks, and lie to inspectors about overtime and other harsh conditions. In the opening sequence at a Middlefield, Ohio, family hardware business that closed as a local Wal-Mart was opening (although this part of the film has generated a fair amount of controversy—see Featherstone in "Recommended Readings"), one frustrated family member says that Wal-Mart is like a Chinese company with American board members. This documentary shows the truth of this comparison. Wal-Mart has served as a means of giving Chinese industry a really good distributor for its goods.

Greenwald has two techniques he employs throughout the film. He lets Wal-Mart's CEO, Lee Scott, make endless self-serving remarks, which Greenwald easily contradicts. He also runs seemingly endless crawl titles listing Wal-Mart's sins of sprawl but reserves the final list for those communities who have succeeded in keeping Wal-Mart at bay.

Recommended Readings

Featherstone, Liza. "Watching Wal-Mart: Four Documentaries, Four Perspectives." *Columbia Journalism Review*, January–February 2006 (online at www.cjr.org/issues/2006/1/feathersone.asp). A helpful review of Wal-Mart documentaries; notes that the hardware store did close before Wal-Mart opened but that Greenwald's general analysis—while valid overall—suffers from a lack of attention to the whole issue of small business competition.

Gates, Anita. "A Look Inside the Company that is the Biggest Retailer on the Planet." *New York Times*, 4 November 2005. The film makes its case against Wal-Mart "with breathtaking force."

Spott, Greg. *Wal-Mart: The High Cost of Low Price*. Foster City: Disinformation Company,

2005. Companion book to the film, detailing the trials and tribulations of filming and taking the film on the road, as well as the idea of DVD as a mass medium. Written by the director of *American Job* (q.v.).

▶◀▶◀

Wal-Mart's War on Workers

WAL-MART

2002, 16 mins., United States
Producer: United Food and Commercial
    Workers (UFCW)
Agit-Prop Documentary
Distributor: UFCW

Although many unions produce agit-prop documentaries, I have included this particular UFCW film because Wal-Mart, one of the most resolute anti-union companies in the world, boasts that not a single one of its stores or divisions are unionized. (Germany, Japan, and China are partial exceptions to this rule.) This video in part explains why.

Wal-Mart has devised numerous means of remaining union-free. Its confidential handbook, *A Manager's Toolbox to Remaining Union Free*, is an exhaustive guide, rivaling even Borders' similar publication. (See *The Big One* in *Working Stiffs*.) The manual exhaustively documents the type of workers who might be tempted by the union: those who are "inefficient" and "low-productive" or "independent" and "happy-go-lucky" or "rebellious" and "anti-establishment" or the "something-for-nothing" type or the "chronically dissatisfied" or the "overly qualified."

The company provides its managers with a "union hotline" phone number: call immediately and identify any associates who look susceptible to the union message or tell us what union activity is brewing. The store has a "union probability index" rating which measures how happy the workers, uh, sales associates, are. Their training video stresses: "We are not anti-union. We are pro-associate."

But this video argues that there are six other reasons why Wal-Mart has been successful in remaining union-free: its employees are victims of interrogation, surveillance, brainwashing, intimidation, profiling, and termination. Even Sam Walton, a sales associate suggests, wouldn't recognize his own store anymore.

Talking heads of workers and former managers dominate this film, which is almost overwhelmed by the cunning and successful union-busting strategy of the company. By the end, the UFCW has mounted solidarity demonstrations and offered suggestions for viewers to help them unionize Wal-Mart. Besides buying union and buying American, the UFCW asks union members to wear their union buttons and to tell Wal-Mart workers about the advantages of unionization.

More than this strategy may be necessary. As Bill Moyers's exposé, *Off the Clock* (q.v.), makes clear (and Stephen Greenhouse's article supports), Wal-Mart will spend millions paying off plaintiffs (individually or in class-action suits) who contend they worked off the clock without pay.

Recommended Reading

Greenhouse, Stephen. "Labor Opens a Drive to Organize Wal-Mart." *New York Times*, 8 November 2002. "Many labor leaders see" the UFCW "organizing effort as a test case of whether unions can succeed in the 21st century."

⋈⋈⋈
Water

HISTORY OF GLOBALIZATION
THATCHERISM

1985, 98 mins., United Kingdom
Director: Dick Clement
Screenplay: Dick Clement, Ian La Frenais, and
    Bill Persky

Broad satire is the polite phrase for this early globalization comedy, a colorful pastiche of British understatement, Monty Python high jinks, "Carry On, Nurse!" sexy foolishness, and anti-Thatcher barbs. Cascara is a British colony, a Caribbean island (played by St. Lucia) sleeping through the 1980s until an American oil company, drilling for black gold, hits a gusher of delicious Perrier-like water. Soon the scramble to make money on this well consumes American capitalists, the island's governor, Baxter Thwaites (played by Michael Caine), jealous French politicians, and even Cuban mercenaries who have been sent to help the island's two rebels, who wish to end British colonial control.

As a satire on Thatcher's invasion of the Falkland Islands (defended by the Argentines) and Reagan's siege of Grenada (defended by Cubans), the film works fitfully. Prime Minister Thatcher is an arrogant (younger) lady who is concerned that any rebellious activity is a bad idea: "There was only one Gandhi. One anorexic little loony in a loin cloth and we lost an entire subcontinent." A concert at the UN to support the island's bid for independence (financially possible because the water gusher turns to oil) features Ringo Starr and George Harrison, about as close a Beatles reunion we are likely to see for a while.

Depending on one's tolerance for British blinkers on colonialism (the natives like to sing and dance) and funny, bad pop culture references (the Cuban mercenaries are afraid to "face Fidel after this fiasco" and decide to go to Miami to "deal coke like Al Pacino in *Scarface*"), this premature globalization comedy might be worth a visit.

Recommended Reading

Sutton, Mike. "Water." *DVD Times*, 22 April 2006 (online at www.dvdtimes.co.uk). It may be very British but it is not very good: "It's a comedy that isn't funny, uses well-known actors but gives them nothing to do, and aims at all manner of targets but hits none of them."

⋈⋈⋈
Waydowntown

CHANGES IN THE WORKPLACE: NORTH
    AMERICA

2000, 82 mins., Canada
Director: Gary Burns
Screenplay: Gary Burns and James Martin

Relatively low-budget but very captivating, *Waydowntown* and its hyperkinetic satire of Calgary's Plus 15 Walkway should join the

American film *Office Space* (in *Working Stiffs*), American television's *The Office* (2005–6), and British television's *Office* series (2001–2) as the Canadian entry in the competition for the best film about a toxic but funny office environment.

The Plus 15 perches fifteen feet above street level, a walkway connecting 100 office buildings and apartment complexes, covering 16 kilometers with 57 bridges. Calgary is proud of the "world's largest elevated walkway system."

Leave it to filmmakers, however, who find the walkway not a convenience but an invitation to expose corporate mayhem. Four office workmates bet a month's salary that they will not leave the enclosed zone, since they can walk from their apartments to work. To go outside means forfeiture.

Waydowntown never quite received the American distribution it perhaps deserved because its images of businessmen falling from office towers were not considered acceptable in 2001 when the film was supposed to reach the theaters. Nonetheless as a corporate dystopia its visuals are hard to beat. One interviewer suggested that it was a "dystopian space-station film," reflecting director Gary Burns's opinion that the walkway destroyed the city (Don McKellar, "Legends of the Mall," *Village Voice,* 23–29 January 2002).

Like *Chain*, its unfunny twin, *Waydowntown* is solidly—fifteen feet aboveground—a concrete symbol of many globalized cityscapes.

Recommended Reading

Holden, Stephen. "Struggling to Find Fresh Air Inside the Hive Incorporated." *New York Times*, 25 January 2002. The film offers "a meditation on passive-aggression in the corporate workplace," since we never find out what the business really does.

⋈⋈⋈

Where Do You Stand?

GLOBAL CAPITAL
GLOBAL LABOR

2004, 60 mins., United States
Director: Alexandra Lescaze

Traditional Documentary
Distributor: California Newsreel

In Kannapolis, North Carolina, the Cannon family and its textile mills ran a benevolent dictatorship from 1888 (the year its first mill was founded) to the 1970s when a series of former competitors took turns purchasing the company. From the 1930s through the 1990s, the Cannons and the other CEOs who headed up the company successfully resisted union challenges. The textile workers' union (under two different names, TWUA-CIO and ACTWU) lost union representation elections four times until UNITE! finally won a narrow victory (100 votes out of almost 2,300 cast) in 1997. In every major loss and even in the final victory, company coercion, a strong organization of anti-union workers, and the eventual departure of the CEO and/or sale to a rival company was the pattern up to the very end. The CEO always promised the moon to the workers on his side, and then immediately (in some cases just two weeks later after the union lost the election) sold them out.

Cannon became Fieldcrest-Cannon, which became Pillowtex, which became in the end the final victim of globalization. Jim Fitzgibbons, CEO of Fieldcrest-Cannon sold out to Pillowtex and later (after a brief retirement) re-entered the industry as the leader of a group of importers of the same goods he manufactured earlier but now made in the globalized sweatshops of Bangladesh. He smiles in the film when he lists about ten countries of origin of his new products.

In closing titles we learn that Pillowtex liquidated the company in 2003 and that 266,000 textile jobs have been lost in North Carolina since 1994. The filmmakers have deftly portrayed through archival footage, stills, and reminiscences more than a hundred years of textile workers' history, from company town to globalized loser. The lows and a few highs of the union organizers and their allies make up the roller-coaster action footage. The entry of such players as A and C Associates, an African American union-busting company, and the National Labor Relations Board, with its slow but surprisingly pro-union decisions, demonstrates the challenges of organizing industries under the relentless pressure of powerful corporate leadership and global initiative.

Recommended Reading

Byerly, Victoria. *Hard Times: Cotton Mill Girls*. Ithaca: Cornell University Press/ILR Press, 1987. Provides detailed portraits of working women in the mills in the South.

▶◀▶◀

Where's Rosie?

ANTI-GLOBALIZATION
CHINA
OUTSOURCING AND OFFSHORING

2004, 1 min., United States
Producer: National Labor Committee
Online Digital Film
Distributor: National Labor Committee
(www.nlcnet.org/campaigns/he-yi/rosie
.shtml)

"Rosie the Riveter, a symbol of working class dignity and women's rights, has gone missing!" This is the opening title of this online film, which uses the stop-action photography typical of short, agit-prop Web films. Rosie was the symbol of the American woman during World War II who entered male-dominated job categories in record numbers (see *The Life and Times of Rosie the Riveter* in *Working Stiffs*). The Rosie in this film is part of a line of action, celebrity, and campy action figures manufactured by Chinese sweatshops under contract with Accoutrements, a Seattle, Washington, company that prides itself as an "outfitter of popular culture." "Welcome to the cutting edge of cool," their website boasts, featuring such action figures as Luci (The Devil Girl Nodder), Jane Austen, and Albert Einstein.

This film from the National Labor Committee (NLC) tells us that Rosie was nabbed by Accoutrements and has now disappeared because she was "caught pushing for an end to sweatshops and child labor somewhere in China." Just before she disappeared, Rosie was seen at a rally holding a picket sign: "No more sweatshops."

Where's Rosie? is part of the NLC's campaign against what it calls the Toys of Misery, during which the economic activists have investigated the Chinese sweatshops that make bobblehead dolls for the National Football League, the National Basketball Association, the NCAA, and NASCAR, as well as small plastic cars for Wal-Mart, Disney, and Hasbro. As in their classic agit-prop film, *Mickey Mouse Goes to Haiti* (q.v.), the NLC argues not for the closing of sweatshops but their upgrading so that workers who need these jobs will be decently paid.

Recommended Reading

Toys of Misery 2004. National Labor Committee and China Labor Watch, February 2004 (online at www.nlcnet.org). Systematic catalog of Chinese sweatshops, with locations and number of employees.

▶◀▶◀

Where the Heart Is

WAL-MART

2000, 120 mins., PG-13, United States
Director: Matt Williams
Screenplay: Lowell Ganz, from Billie Letts's
novel, *Where the Heart Is* (1996)

Besides the obvious places, the heart also resides in Wal-Mart, as this sentimental valentine to trailer trash and true grit would have one believe. At first Wal-Mart is the unknowing participant in one young girl's journey from her Tennessee trailer and unpleasant boyfriend to a quirky and wholesome Colorado community. Novalee (played by Natalie Portman) is spectacularly pregnant but while shopping for slippers her boyfriend dumps her and she is forced to sleep every night—secretly of course—on a Wal-Mart sleeping bag. But it's just a matter of time that she gives birth to Americus, the "Wal-Mart baby," as the press anoints her.

In this pleasant fantasy Wal-Mart doesn't have her arrested but relishes the publicity, gives her money and gifts, and offers her a job. Eccentric and endearing characters abound, including her new friend, Lexie Coop (played by

Where the Heart Is: The Wal-Mart mom (Natalie Portman) finds out where the heart really is—in marriage.

Ashley Judd), who names her numerous off-spring after desserts (Brownie, Praline, etc.)

The film closes with still another example of Wal-Mart's big heart: Novalee and her new boyfriend, Foney Hull (played by James Frain), as well as Lexie and her latest guy all get married at her store, as a loudspeaker announces: "Attention Wal-Mart shoppers and wedding guests! The garden center is running a special on potting soil and rakes." The final credits thank Wal-Mart for its assistance. Some critics have wondered why Wal-Mart wasn't assessed for a feature-length promotional piece.

This is Wal-Mart as the company would like to see itself: proudly American, benefi-cent, a community center for all, especially the marginally successful.

Recommended Reading

Mitchell, Elvis. "Where the Heart Is." *New York Times,* 28 April 2000. "The cynical might say that Wal-Mart would happily extend its corporate arms for the kind of publicity it gets here, and even the most kindhearted may be rendered cynical by this movie."

⋈⋈⋈

Where the Rivers Flow North

HISTORY OF GLOBALIZATION
SCARCE RESOURCES (WATER)

1994, 106 mins., United States
Director: Jay Craven

Screenplay: Jay Craven and Don Bredes, from Howard Frank Mosher's novel, *Where the Rivers Flow North* (1978)

Vermont, where natural beauty and a pro-gressive, opinionated citizenry go hand in hand, has an even more idiosyncratic region of its own called the Northeast Kingdom. On the Canadian border in an even colder and more challenging environment than the rest of the state, the Kingdom also has its own writer, Howard Frank Mosher, whose novels have chronicled the history and folkways of a people who struggled on farms and logging camps to survive.

Craven's adaptation captures the essence of Mosher's original story. Noel Lord (played by Rip Torn) and his companion Bangor (played by Tantoo Cardinal) fight to retain his access to the land and the (log) driving dam soon to be literally swallowed by the waters behind a new hydroelectric dam being built by the Northern Vermont Power Company. In 1927 Lord and the kind of folk he represents stand little chance against the lawyers and money commanded by the power company. What Lord has, however, is the resilience and cunning of a survivor who has lived so long off the grid that what the grid has can never tempt him. He fights back, cutting a deal ("The way to beat a man in a horse trade is not to let that man know you got to have what he don't know you want"): he trades his logging access for a stand of a thousand ancient white pines that were once part of his family's land.

Noel's attempt to beat the company at its own game leads to unexpectedly tragic results, however. The film captures Noel's tragic death but omits much of the history of his people and the novelist's mythic celebration of Noel's anarchistic victory over the powers that have almost succeeded in forcing the Northeast Kingdom into the twentieth century.

Both novella and film deliver a violent tale, not flinching when Noel's hook (where his left hand, lost in an oxcart accident hauling moonshine, should be) pierces the hand of a Power Company man who calls Bangor a squaw and embarrasses her in public. Noel does have an escapist vision of running a sawmill in Oregon with Bangor. He would be a fitting companion to the feisty Stamper family of Ken Kesey's *Sometimes a Great Notion* (1971) but without the latter's anti-union message.

To steal a term from another of Kesey's novels (*One Flew Over the Cuckoo's Nest*, 1975), Northern Vermont Power is just another Combine waiting to take over the commons, in this case, the water, that at one time belonged to everyone.

Recommended Reading

Baumgartner, Marjorie. "Where the Rivers Run North." *Austin Chronicle*, 29 July 1994. Reviewer appreciates "this beautifully shot, low-budget independent film" but finds it relies "too heavily on our familiarity with these stock homesteader-developer conflicts and inserting one-note stereotypes in the villainous roles."

▶◀▶◀

The White Rose

Rosa blanca

HISTORY OF GLOBALIZATION
OIL

1961, 100 mins., Mexico, in English and
   Spanish with English subtitles
Director: Roberto Gavaldon
Screenplay: Roberto Gavaldon, Phil Stevenson, and Emilio Carballido, from B. Traven's
   novel, *The White Rose* (1929)

Toward the end of this adaptation of B. Traven's novel delineating the ruthless acquisition of The White Rose, an oil-rich Mexican hacienda, Collins (played by Reinhold Olszewski), the evil head of the American company Condor Oil, learns that the Mexican government may move to nationalize the oil industry because of the scandals he has created. He isn't particularly worried: he spins the globe in his office and announces that there are many more "white roses" in the world, specifically in Arabia.

Don Jacinto Yanez (played by Ignacio Lopez Torres) is the padrone of an extensive landholding in Vera Cruz in 1937, but he runs his hacienda in a benevolent and compassionate way. He is as much a product of Indian peasant stock as his many workers. When Condor Oil tries to buy him out because his land is on a rich reserve of oil, he refuses, citing his many dependent workers as his primary reason. Collins has him murdered and Condor Oil steals his land. He is literally "disappeared," while everything he has created is bulldozed. His peasants can choose: work for the new owners or disappear too. Most of them stay and work, although his son eventually leads a successful demonstration against Condor.

This radical critique of American imperialism was banned from Mexican screens for many years. Too many Mexican officials would have been embarrassed and too many sensitive issues raised if this cinematic critique of Mexican-American partnerships became well known. The film ends with a celebration of the union's campaign against the oil company because it refused to pay death benefits for workers killed in an oil derrick accident. Even the Mexican supreme court and the president are moved to support the workers.

Director Roberto Gavaldon used his renowned cinematographer Gabriel Figuera to great effect in a number of symbolic shots: in addition to the spinning globe at the end, a bush of white roses is splashed by oil when a well is sunk, and Collins' mistress is given a diamond brooch in the shape of a sprig of white roses. Some hope, however small, is held out by Don Jacinto's son, who leads the demonstration against Condor Oil: "The time for justice is now."

Recommended Reading

Pranagua, Paulo Antonio, ed. *Mexican Cinema.* Trans. Ana M. Lopez. London: British Film Institute, 1995. Excellent survey of Mexican cinema, with a chapter on Gavaldon's career by Ariel Zuniga, who argues that, "in a country where film production was fundamentally linked to the state," being opposed to the state meant to commit suicide as an active director.

▸◂▸◂

Why Cybraceros?

DIGITALIZATION
MIGRANT LABOR (UNITED STATES)
OUTSOURCING AND OFFSHORING

1997/2002, 5 mins., United States
Director: Alex Rivera
Online Digital Film
Distributor: Invisible America (www.invisibleamerica.com/whycybraceros.shtml)

This satire on migrant labor, globalization, digitalization, and the original *bracero* (arms) migrant labor program of the 1950 was so successful that at least a few media outlets took its core suggestion seriously. Director Alex Rivera, using a website (www.cybracero.com) called Remote Labor Systems ("Market Driven Solutions for Today's World Order"), proposed in this online digital film that America can have "all the labor without the worker" by using robots in the fields controlled through cyberspace by Mexican workers who never leave their native villages. Rivera shows two robots picking oranges, intercutting what appears to be a Mexican working at a terminal controlling the robot. His use of footage from a 1940s Council of California Growers advocacy film *Why Braceros?* gives his own film an authoritative air.

This solution to "America's farm labor problems," the film argues, avoids the key problem with the old bracero program: some of the braceros ran away and stayed in the United States illegally and were even joined by other migrant laborers who were never braceros in the first place. The comic high point of the film comes in an animated sequence in which a Mexican worker jumps the fence on the U.S.-Mexico border—that's the old way. In the new way his arms detach and *they* clear the fence—that's the "remote labor solution."

Rivera uses a *New York Times* article about the call centers of American corporations in India ("Hi, I'm in Bangalore," 21 March 2001) as one of his resource links on the website: not only do the Indian workers not even come to America, they also pretend they *are* Americans. As the feature film *American Daylight* (q.v.) dramatizes, they are another successful remote labor solution.

Recommended Readings

Empire/State: Artists Engaging Globalization. New York: Whitney Museum of American Art, 2002. Catalogue with essays documenting the exhibition of Rivera's digital film, shown in installations in 1997 and 2002. Includes a related essay by Yates McKee, "On Counterglobal Asthetics," that challenges "the utopian stories corporate-driven globalization tells about itself."

Gonzalez, Miguel. "Cybracero: Telepresence of Farm Workers." *La Opinion* (Los Angeles), 27 April 2003. Reporter takes the project seriously but is surprised to find out that the United Farm Workers and the Los Angeles Corporation of Economic Development don't know anything about it.

▸◂▸◂

Why Wal-Mart Works: And Why That Drives Some People Crazy

WAL-MART

2005, 72 mins., United States
Director: Ron Galloway
Agit-Prop Documentary

Ron Galloway attempts a pre-emptive strike against the widely publicized *Wal-Mart: The High Cost of Low Price* (q.v.), but the film, directed by this Ayn Rand fan (see *The Fountainhead* in *Working Stiffs*), does not really succeed in what it promises. Instead it offers testimonials by happy Wal-Mart workers and managers, the opinions of a number of academics and free-enterprise experts, and some interviews with customers and just plain folks on the street.

A few of the workers were selected to make specific points that are clearly rebuttals to the charges raised by Greenwald and other Wal-Mart critics. Renata (first name only given) from the Owatonna, Minnesota, store is ninety years old, in her fifteenth year of employment, and currently handling the switchboard. She says a number of times that she always takes her lunch and two other breaks and that she never works off the clock. In a section devoted to healthcare, the filmmakers interview a worker whose close friend was born with spina bifida. Although one would think this anecdote might be about healthcare benefits for her parents or for herself, it turns out that all we learn is that she held a cashier's job at Wal-Mart until she died.

Interviews with potential customers and average citizens take place mainly in Boone, North Carolina, home of Appalachian State University and a main street whose small businesses all collapsed when Wal-Mart moved in nearby. Now main street is back, with numerous "funky" shops and hang-out spots more characteristic of college towns. Another bizarre moment occurs when a student complains that his favorite band, Nirvana, apparently allowed Wal-Mart to censor one of its albums so that it would be acceptable for sale. Did he realize, one of the filmmakers asks, that this issue is really "a double-edged sword," since Wal-Mart is responsible for one third of all album sales in America?

Under the rubric of globalization we learn that Wal-Mart is one of the first companies to understand the value of Chinese manufacturing and has been smart enough to figure out that all their communist talk was "malarkey" and that the Chinese were probably the best capitalists in the world.

In the Hurricane Katrina finale of the film, the attempt to make Wal-Mart a heroic company is also double-edged, perhaps unintentionally. At first we hear that the Waveland,

Mississippi, store gave water and food away to hurricane victims, but the longest sequence shows the temporary structures Wal-Mart erected to continue selling when customers had nowhere else to shop. Furthermore Wal-Mart was more efficient than FEMA in servicing its customer base. To which most of us should probably say, amen!

Can a film like this help Wal-Mart regain the public relations edge it needs? While the filmmakers never quite explain why Wal-Mart's success drives some people crazy, the film's opening titles, which lists complaints about a company that treats its workers unfairly, is taking over the world, and puts competitors out of business, turn out to be about Starbucks, another global economic player. Point made?

Recommended Readings

Featherstone, Liza. "Watching Wal-Mart: Four Documentaries, Four Perspectives." *Columbia Journalism Review*, January–February 2006. A helpful review of Wal-Mart documentaries that calls Galloway's film the most "amateurish of these efforts" and essentially a "lengthy infomercial" for Wal-Mart.

Soderquist, Don. *The Wal-Mart Way: The Inside Story of the Success of the World's Largest Company*. Nashville: Nelson Business, 2005. An insider's view, from a Judeo-Christian perspective, written by the former chief operating officer and explaining the twelve keys to the company's success, most of them not covered by *Why Wal-Mart Works*.

⊭⊭⊭
Winstanley

INTELLECTUAL PROPERTY RIGHTS (THE COMMONS)
LABOR HISTORY

1975, 95 mins., B & W, United Kingdom
Director: Kevin Brownlow
Screenplay: Kevin Brownlow, Andrew Mollo, and David Caute, based on the latter's novel *Comrade Jacob* (1962)

In the hippie sixties in San Francisco, a group called the Diggers gave food away and became irregular apostles of sharing. Not everyone realized that they had appropriated their name from one of the many religious/political groups that sprung up under Oliver Cromwell during the English Civil War that led to the execution of Charles I. Gerrard Winstanley was the leader of the Diggers of the 1640s, a group that believed that the king, the clergy, and the landowning class were equally responsible for the desperate lot of the poor. They were the first revolutionaries of "the commons," literally, common land not enclosed for private use but open to all.

This film dramatizes the moment in the career of Winstanley (played by Miles Halliwell) when he leads about twenty followers onto St. George's Hill and later to Cobham Manor Common to farm plots formerly considered common land. Winstanley's defense of their "manuring" or cultivating the land was, in Kenneth Rexroth's words, "the first systematic exposition of libertarian communism in English." After a hard slog in rain and muck, the Diggers were eventually run off their communal plot, the first time by the army, the second time by the authorities under the leadership of the local landlord, John Platt (played by David Bramley), who was also a clergyman (confirming, of course, Winstanley's rhetoric about who oppressed the poor).

Winstanley's mystical belief in the power of divinity in each person is close to Quakerism—like William Blake's poetry without the difficult symbols. Christopher Hill argued that Winstanley believed that "buying and selling, hiring wage labor, are all part of the fall of man" (lecture at Kingston University, 24 January 1996). To Rexroth it points to the utopians of nineteenth-century America, such as the Shakers.

The film is oddly compelling, although one needs a sixteenth-century scorecard to keep the factions straight—the Cromwellians or Puritan victors, the levellers (similar to the Diggers, but more middle class in their political goals, which included the abolition of the House of Lords), and the Ranters (sexual revolutionaries), who barge into the Digger encampment at one point and look decidedly unattractive as they help themselves to the food.

This is important labor history because the great wealth of the landed classes in England and elsewhere is based on private property—although for many generations it was not private—and the dispossession of many farmers from their lands. The commons has become a rallying cry for indigenous peoples and activists against globalization. Who owns the water? Fish? Other scarce resources?

Recommended Reading

Rexroth, Kenneth. *Communalism: From its Origins to the Twentieth Century.* New York: Seabury, 1974. A good, popular guide to the period of the Diggers from a poet with anarchism in his blood.

⋈⋈⋈

The Wire

CONTAINERIZED SHIPPING
SEX WORK/TRAFFICKING

2003–4, TV series, second season, 13 episodes of 60 mins. each, United States
Directors: Ed Bianchi, Elodie Keene, Steve Shill, Thomas J. wright, Dan Attias, Tim Van Patten, Rob Bailey, Ernest Dickerson, and Robert F. Colesbury
Writers: David Simon, George Pelecanos, Rafael Alvarez, Ed Burns, and Joy Lusco Kecken

They don't call Baltimore the Charm City for nothing. Despite the segregated neighborhoods, rampant drug use, and horrible public housing, we find Ukranian social clubs, crab shacks, and the Inner Harbor shops. While it is true that too many films that focus on dockworkers emphasize mob connections, the second season of *The Wire* looks at a union trying to keep its members working and not stealing.

Although television series such as *The Wire* are permeated by crime—cops and drug dealers usually—the second season of *The Wire* moved in a new direction—emphasizing the workers of a city, in this case Baltimore dockworkers. There is still lots of violence and crime, but the "argument" of the series, according to its chief writer, David Simon, is

The Wire: The Baltimore detective squad investigating crime on the docks.

"that raw unencumbered capitalism without any social framework around it is not a good thing for most people. It's a good thing for the few" (*City Paper* online, 28 May 2003). Simon, known for two other successful Baltimore-centered slices of real life, *Homicide* and *The Corner,* tells the story "we have not heard much of . . . [that] vast legions of union-wage and benefit citizens have disappeared from the Baltimore landscape over the course of a couple of decades."

In the first season of *The Wire* a Baltimore police task force pursued a local drug cartel. In the second season the same squad is assigned union corruption on the docks, but here the mix of characters is quite a bit more complex, since the plot mixes the cruel deaths of fourteen Natashas, or prostitutes, from Eastern Europe (one body found in the bay while the others died in a container left on the docks), the precise mechanisms for handling (and stealing) containerized cargo, and a union leader fighting by any means at hand, legal or illegal, to keep his men at work. In the end the union leader, Frank Sobotka (played by Chris Bauer), is the most sympathetic character in the series, as he attempts to balance the old ethnic workers from Poland and the new African American workers in the cargo handlers' local while trying to keep all the men working by any means necessary.

This is a series in which total attention to character and detail is necessary and in-evitable if you stick with all the episodes. Some of us might find it hard to return to real news off screen, so mesmerizing is the range of (some) good, (mostly) flawed, and evil (really evil) characters that abound in each episode. You will learn how containerized shipping works, how it has a global reach, and even how some people cheat by "hiding" a container or two. Baltimore takes a star turn, like Manhattan in *The Apprentice,* but maybe not quite as beautiful.

Recommended Readings

Barsanti, Chris. "*The Wire*: The Complete Second Season." *Slant Magazine,* 2005 (online at www.slantmagazine.com/dvd/dvd_review.asp ?ID=540). Reviewer celebrates the hugely ambitious and hugely successful crime epic whose plot tentacles just keep on spreading, wonderfully so.

Havrilesky, Heather. "Beyond Good and Evil in Baltimore." *Salon,* 7 July 2003 (online at dir .salon.com/story/ent/tv/review/2003/07/12/wire/ index1.html?pn=1). Appreciates the "kaleidoscope of different cultures and attitudes" in the series, "from union laborers to Greek criminals to Catholic priests to gay drug dealers" and notes that "the characters talk about each other in openly racist terms. Anyone who's familiar with hard-bitten industrial towns of the Northeast, where there are five different Catholic churches, two Jewish temples, a Pentecostal storefront and, these days, a mosque within a few blocks of each other, knows that this is how many immigrants explain their differences."

Women for Sale

SEX WORK/TRAFFICKING
TRANSNATIONAL MIGRATION

2005, 56 mins., Israel, in Hebrew, Russian,
 Ukrainian, and Uzbek with English
 subtitles
Director: Nili Tal
Cinema-Verité Documentary
Distributor: Ruth Diskin Films

The impact of moving to a distant land as a sex worker is more than personal. As this documentary demonstrates, the fallout is also generational and community-centered. When the four "Natashas" or former Soviet and Eastern Bloc women go to Israel to work as prostitutes, they discover not only the dangers inherent in their new jobs but also the pain of being an absentee parent—or child—whose main contact back home is too often the money they remit from their work. And then there are questions from neighbors and others about where this money is coming from.

Women for Sale is unusual among the mix of

Women for Sale: Two Natashas flank filmmaker Nili Tal. Courtesy Ruth Diskin Films.

films about international sex trafficking because of its intensity of focus on four women and their relationships back home. The filmmakers move back and forth between home country and Israel, asking in effect the same question: what is it really like to be a provider who happens to be a sex worker? Some of them pursue this line of work voluntarily, and others were deceived. One, Nargiza, had to work a year just to pay off her debt to her "transporter." In this group only one is on the receiving end of violence. After being smuggled from Egypt to Israel by Bedouins, Yulia from Moscow is harassed and beaten by policemen while working the Haifa Beach area. She gets a major share of screen time, partly because of her pleasant disposition and partly because of her wit: she refers to the beach scene as a "traffic jam of horny men" and agrees that the only good Russian men are already married—the rest are junkies or alcoholics.

Shahida from Tashkent, Uzbekistan, has another typical experience for these women: she is arrested, spends time in a detention home, and is finally deported. She is lost back home. It's bad enough, she notes, to be a Muslim and make the choices she did, but she cannot even find an odd job to support her children.

The filmmakers mention that these are only four out of fifty thousand in this particular route of human trafficking. It is a growth industry for globalization.

Recommended Reading

Kempadoo, Kamal, and Jo Doezema, ed. *Global Sex Workers: Rights, Resistance, and Redefinitions.* New York: Routledge, 1998. A helpful collection of essays, a number of which focus on the economic reasons for the transmigration of sex workers.

Workingman's Death: 5 Portraits of Work in the 21st Century

GLOBAL LABOR
LABOR HISTORY

2005, 122 mins., Austria/Germany
Director: Michael Glawogger
Cinema-Verité Documentary

Workingman's Death: The sulfur workers of Indonesia. Courtesy Lotus Film GmbH, Quinte Film, and Arte G.E.I.E.

Michael Glawogger's warm-up for this survey of five of the world's worst occupations was *Megacities* (2001), a perverse documentary travelogue of the dangers and difficulties of being poor in four cities, Moscow, New York, Mexico City, and Bombay. Like Pietra Rivoli's best-selling book, *The Travels of a T-shirt in the Global Economy* (2005), *Megacities* traces a T-shirt from a Bombay garment-worker's hand until it arrives for sale on a Manhattan sidewalk.

Workingman's Death is a global survey of some of the most difficult and dangerous jobs on earth presented in six self-contained episodes: "Heroes," in which Ukranian miners struggle in shafts less than a foot and a half high; "Ghosts," in which Indonesian workers clamber in the mouth of a volcanic basin, mining sulphur; "Lions," in which Nigerian workers make a slaughterhouse look like Picasso's painting *Guernica*; "Brothers," in which Pashtun workers in Pakistan dismantle tankers that have outlived their global usefulness; "The Future," in which Chinese steelworkers risk injuries in a blast furnace; and "Epilogue," in which a German blast furnace is lit up "artificially" as part of a theme park.

Glawogger uses no narration, preferring to let the footage—so reminiscent of the still photographs in Paul Virilio's film and installation, *Unknown Quantity* (q.v.) or in Sebastio Selgado's book, *Workers: An Archaeology of the Industrial Age* (New York: Aperture, 1993)—speak for itself. The film's subtitle reminds us that these brutal and unsafe jobs are really the wave of the globalized future in Third World countries, not a holdover from neocolonial control.

Recommended Reading

Felperin, Leslie. "Workingman's Death." *Variety*, 11 September 2005. Appreciates the filmmaker's "respect for the dignity of labor" but suggests that the "pic looks set to toil in festival mines only."

Sandhu, Sukhdev. "The Sheer Slog of Life." *New Statesman*, 24 October 2005. The film "refuses to trade in picturesque misery in order to strengthen its critique of the damage wrought by neoliberal economics. Rather, aided by a dynamic score by John Zorn, it is a document of ongoing defiance, a paean to workers around the world who continue to laugh, who refuse to be crushed by the heaviest load that capitalism places on them."

ᕯᕯᕯ

Working Women of the World

Ouvrières du monde

GLOBAL LABOR
WOMEN WORKERS AND CHILD LABOR

2000, 53 mins., Belgium, in French, Flemish, Indonesian, and Tagalog with English subtitles
Director: Marie France Collard
Traditional Documentary
Distributor: First Run/Icarus Films

Marie France Collard vividly demonstrates the effects of globalization by focusing on three women in different countries, all of whom work for the American-based transnational corporation Levi Strauss & Co. A fourth woman from the Philippines and a fifth country (without a specific woman) are also less thoroughly surveyed. The European sections of the film are set in factories in France and Belgium, both threatened with closure. The French workers are led by a militant union leader, Marie Therese, who has worked in the plant all her life. Similarly, we visit Rose's Belgian workplace and home, as she explains what her job has meant to her.

The director alternates the European footage with sequences set in the Third World countries Levi Strauss has already relocated in. In one compelling sequence, Yanti and other Indonesian workers watch with amazement the footage shot of Marie Therese's union activism. They marvel at the freedom of the union activity they themselves are forbidden to participate in.

The film concentrates on the human scale of globalization, how the women in Turkey, for example, travel long distances on buses to enter a fortress-like factory way out in the countryside, or how Rosario and other women in the Philippines are hectored by posted dos and don'ts: "Do not disrupt production. Do not listen to agitators." Despite living more comfortable lives, their European counterparts are nonetheless facing economic hardships as well.

Levi Strauss, which has been criticized vehemently in recent years for its sweatshop conditions, is a privately held company without any public oversight. (One of the members of the founding family bought back enough stock in 1996 to change it back to a private company.) Clearly a 300 percent markup on each item in France was not enough: 400 percent can be achieved in Turkey.

Recommended Reading

Howe, Ken, et al. "Levi Strauss & Co. On the Record: Phil Marineau." *San Francisco Chronicle*, 5 March 2006. Detailed interview with Levi

Strauss's CEO, who discusses outsourcing and other corporate decisions: "If you look at it from a justice standpoint, there's no reason to say that the person in San Antonio deserves that job versus the person in Pakistan."

ᴽᴽᴽ

The World

CHINA

2004, 133 mins., China, in Mandarin with English subtitles
Director: Jia Zhang-ke
Screenplay: Jia Zhang-ke

The Chinese suburban theme park outside Beijing called The World has a slogan: "See the world without leaving Beijing." Visitors can approach the Eiffel Tower, the Leaning Tower of Pisa, the pyramids of Egypt, and even New York's World Trade Center. The park is staffed by women who are dancers and models and men who act as attendants and security guards. A number of them are tired of China and want to see the real world; some of the visiting acts—a Russian dance troupe, for instance—looks like it is going to be stuck there for a long time. Romantic liaisons and family relationships all turn sour.

At first Tao (played by Zhao Tao) seems like a model citizen of this world. She has a job like a Rockette, wearing glammy costumes and looking sexy in ethnic garb. Her boyfriend, Taisheng (played by Chen Taisheng), is a security guard running one scam or another (such as fake IDs) for extra cash. Tao's younger brother, also just in from the provinces, tries to make a living in the booming construction trade. But Chinese prosperity, so the film (like others directed by Jia Zhang-ke) argues, is hollow and perhaps fraudulent. When Taisheng cheats on Tao it is with a women making knockoffs of western fashions.

Like The World, Jia's film goes global on occasion. When Tao text messages her friends, the film switches into lightweight animated sequences featuring cartoon versions of her and her friends. The travel that most of them seem to wish for is not in the future, despite the booming Chinese economy. The film ends with a grotesque tragedy, the result of the dilapidated housing provided for the employees, quite similar to that provided to the millions of provincial workers who have flocked to the new urban centers for sweatshop jobs.

There used to be two Chinas, mainland and Taiwan, provincial and modern. Now both Chinas exist in one new globalized "world." Jia's previous films, especially *Pickpocket* (1997) and *Unknown Pleasures* (2002) also chart this new China.

Recommended Reading

Havis, Richard James. "Illusory Worlds: An Interview with Jia Zhang-ke." *Cineaste*, Fall 2005, 58–59. Discusses how *The World* dramatizes China's illusion that it "is an internationally focused culture."

▶◀▶◀

Yang Ban Xi

The 8 Model Works

CHINA

2005, 90 mins., The Netherlands, in Chinese with English subtitles
Director: Yan-Ting Yuen
Postmodern Documentary

There is no more exciting way to trace the transition from Mao's bright red China to the contemporary country that dominates the manufacturing end of the spectrum of globalization than a viewing of the "eight model works" that epitomize the narrowness and, to our eyes now, deeply kitschy approach to mass culture.

When Madame Mao rose to the leadership of the Cultural Revolution in China in the 1960s, the former actress continued a campaign to tinker with a distinct Chinese form of performance, Peking opera, usually devoted to "emperors and kings, generals, ministers, scholars, beauties, lords and dowagers, young gentlemen and ladies," the very roles, ironically, she herself had played on stage and screen.

Yang Ban Xi: The Red Army puts on a show in a model opera. Courtesy Shadow Distribution.

The new revolutionary Peking opera and a number of related plays and films became hyper red in staging and in politics, celebrating a glorious coalition of workers, peasants, and soldiers engaged in revolution against ruthless landlords, corrupt officials, and the enemy (either the Japanese or the Nationalist Chinese).

A number of these operas were made into films. *The East is Red* was probably the most famous, but the most labor intensive was *The Docks*. In the end eight were collectively deemed "model works," templates for a new revolutionary socialist culture that would replace the decadent Chinese and Western classics. They must be seen to be believed, as they usually feature selfless heroines, bold Communist leaders, and squads of Red Army soldiers (sometimes only women) on point. (The documentary, *A Morning Sun*, 2003, directed by Carma Hinton and others, also offers a generous selection of good clips from the model works.)

Director Yan-Ting Yuen uses the revolutionary fervor of the Maoist decades to provide the contrast with the China of the era of globalization. In the obvious sense, Starbucks is on numerous urban corners, but the sense of a culture freed from traditional strictures while at the same time acknowledging its roots comes through her film. She interviews former actresses, dancers, and musicians associated with the model works, as well as contemporary dancers and musicians. The latter remark that the old revolutionary music still has power to move them, but when we see contemporary youth dancing in the streets they clearly have an international tilt to their jeans.

Besides a generous selection of clips from the model works—featuring what one person calls those sexy dancers in Red Army shorts—we hear a voice-over from an actress giving Madame Mao's self-congratulatory opinions about revolutionary art. When Madame Mao committed suicide in 1991, after many years in prison, the container ships had already established their presence on China's horizon, replacing the Red Sun that was Chairman Mao.

Recommended Readings

Chu Lan. "A Decade of Revolution in Peking Opera." *Chinese Literature* 9 (1974): 85–94. A propagandist for the model works concludes: "The revolution in Peking opera is the first great campaign in the socialist revolution in the superstructure [noneconomic arena] in the past ten years."

Dargis, Manohla. "*Yang Ban Xi*, a Documentary on Chinese Operas as Propaganda." *New York Times*, 29 March 2006. Agrees that for "some of the artists and musicians interviewed in the film, who were children during the Cultural Revolution, the model operas are not just a source of nostalgia, but also a sustained fount of inspiration."

Snow, Lois Wheeler. *China on Stage*. New York: Vintage Books, 1973. An American actress who was an enthusiast for the model works reports on her experiences in China. Includes scripts for a number of operas including *The Red Detachment of Women*.

▶◀▶◀▶◀

The Yes Men

ANTI-GLOBALIZATION

2004, 83 mins., United States
Directors: Chris Smith, Dan Ollman, and
Sarah Price
Postmodern Documentary

Even Wal-Mart was not amused when in 2003 a website (www.re-code.com) offered hundreds of bar codes with prices of one's own choice to print out and use at Wal-Mart. Such use would constitute theft, according to letters from the company when they learned of the latest exploit of the Yes Men, Andy Bichlbaum and Mike Bonanno, two merry anticorporate pranksters who know their way around websites and legitimate global conferences. (The bar code section of the website "is temporarily down while" the pranksters "decide how to deal with the latest threat from Wal-Mart attorneys"; see *Re-Code.com Commercial.*)

Taking their name from corporate lingo for compliant executives, the Yes Men began with an earlier phony website that resembled the site of the World Trade Organization. Soon they were receiving invites to give presentations at global conferences, such as a Finnish trade conference called "Textiles of the Future." Documented in this film, the visit to the conference included Bichlbaum wearing a gold lamé suit with a television attached to a giant inflatable penis, what he called an "Employee Visualization Appendage." Perhaps, the *New York Times* reviewers noted, Finnish executives are so polite—"the ultimate yes men and women"—that they were not fazed by the three-foot appendage or even the announcement that the World Trade Organization was going to disband and be replaced by a "new trade body whose charter will be to ensure that trade benefits the poor."

Although so many people fell for the Yes Men, the film includes one encouraging sequence. While posing as representatives from McDonald's the Yes Men tell a class of college students that the hamburgers provided them as samples is the company's latest initiative to help the Third World by providing them with products made from First World human waste. After a glance at the burgers in front of them, the students begin to pelt the Yes Men with them.

The website (www.yesmen.org) for the Yes Men provides their history and latest exploits. The film doesn't cover some of their earlier, wonderful pranks—swapping voice boxes of GI Joe and Barbie dolls and returning them to the shelves for sale or their interview broadcast on the BBC saying that Dow Chemical has finally agreed to compensate the Bhopal victims with $12 billion—but there is more than enough to make them the leading contenders for an award as anti-globalization pranksters of the new century.

Recommended Reading

Dargis, Manola. "There's a Lot Up the Sleeves of Two Political Jokesters." *New York Times,* 24 September 2004. Wanted the filmmakers to "work harder and assume less" about globalization. Otherwise the phony announcement about the WTO helping the poor will be appreciated only by ironists. "For free-trade absolutists, though, it will probably just sound like W.T.O. business as usual."

▸◂▸

Zoned for Slavery: The Child behind the Label

EXPORT PROCESSING ZONES
OUTSOURCING AND OFFSHORING

1995, 23 mins., United States, English and
  Spanish with English subtitles
Directors: David Belle, Katherine Kean, and
  Rudi Stern
Distributor: National Labor Committee (NLC)
Agit-Prop Documentary

One of the earliest exposés of the Central American offshore assembly plants, emphasizing the sweatshops in San Pedro Sula that make clothing for J.C. Penney's, Gitano, Eddie Bauer, Wal-Mart, and Oshkosh, this film remains quite powerful. Not only is the workforce, 95 percent of which consists of teenage girls, underpaid and overworked, but they are locked into the factories, harassed by armed guards, and are lectured on personal matters if they get pregnant. We actually see the discarded birth control packets the teenagers say they are forced to use, and one testifies that she was given an abortifacient (again we see syringes at the town dump). Mostly from rural homes, the young women and their families end up in shanty towns near the factories.

The film covers some familiar territory and adds some daring allegations. But its sponsor, the National Labor Committee (NLC), has been diligent over the years in exposing a less well-known feature of this system: American government support and subsidies for the companies that own the factories. It was well established that these plants constituted free trade zones, which, in practice meant no taxes for the corporations and no benefits for the workers. In some instances American funds promoted the locations and subsidized the creation of the zones. Charles Kernaghan, the tireless leader of the NLC, displays ads paid for by American agencies that boast of hiring a worker named Rosa Martinez for 57 cents an hour one year and then the following year an almost identical ad in which Rosa now makes just 33 cents an hour.

In this film the NLC crew manages to infiltrate a Korean factory and interview the workers making Gitano shirts until the owners discover them and throw them out. Before they leave they interview workers who complain of harassment. They are also not allowed to bring food that might stain the goods they are making but they can hardly afford to purchase meals from the company canteen.

The bottom line is that a worker in a typical Gap manufacturing maquiladora is paid 12 cents for a garment that sells for $20.

Recommended Reading

York, Suzanne. "Honduras And Resistance To Globalization." International Forum of Globalization (online at www.ifg.org/analysis/global ization/Honduras2.htm). History and analysis of the maquiladoras in Honduras.

▸◂▸

Zoolander

GLOBAL LABOR

2001, 85 mins., PG-13, United States
Director: Ben Stiller
Screenplay: Drake Slather, Ben Stiller, and
  John Hamburg

Hollywood actually did a remake of *The Manchurian Candidate* (1962), John Frankenheimer's classic political thriller, three years

Zoolander: Soul-searching fashion models, Zoolander (Ben Stiller) and Hansel (Owen Wilson).

before the release of Jonathan Demme's official remake (which changed Cold War paranoia into a petro-thriller and substituted a multinational corporation for the original film's communist conspirators).

It was called *Zoolander* and it was one of the first globalization comedies, a not very crowded subgenre. The film features a series of duels (frenzied moves on the catwalk, break dancing, underwear removal while fully clothed—you get the idea) between two incredibly vain male fashion models, Zoolander (played by Ben Stiller) and Hansel (played by Owen Wilson). Most of the satire, silliness, and genuine laughs are devoted to a send-up of the fashion industry. But the film has interest for us because Zoolander becomes a Manchurian candidate, that is, he is brainwashed (using methods closer in style to Alan J. Pakula's *The Parallax View*, 1974, than Frankenheimer's or Demme's films) to assassinate the new prime minister of Malaysia who campaigned—and won—an election on an antisweatshop platform: no child labor and higher wages for workers. Obviously the bad people at the top of the fashion industry cannot allow this because it will destroy their bottom line.

A number of critics worried when the film was released that somehow the satire, while picking on a worthy subject, was uncouth. To be sure, the send-up of the fashion industry is almost too easy, and one wearies occasionally of all the cameo appearances of the legends of New York's celebrity world (although Jon Voight as Zoolander's coal mining father from southern New Jersey is almost too good to be true). When Zoolander returns home and works for a day in the mine he complains of having contracted black lung disease. And when Zoolander and Hansel reprise the apes-and-plinth sequence from *2001—A Space Odyssey* (1968) the laughs come cheap but plentiful.

Recommended Readings

Ebert, Roger. "Zoolander." *Chicago Sun-Times,* 28 September 2001. Although he doubts that the World Trade Towers should have been airbrushed from the cinematic skyline, Ebert raises the central issue: "The back-to-school clothes of American kids are largely made by Third World kids who don't go to school."

Mitchell, Elvis. "A Lost Boy in a Plot to Keep Fashion Industry Afloat." *New York Times,* 28 September 2001. Sensitive to the recent World Trade attacks, Mitchell worries that "the assassination subplot" is "troubling" because "the central idea is that fashion has used models as assassins for centuries." He concludes that the film is "a reminder of the atmosphere in this country after the terrorist strikes into the heart of America."

Topical Index ≡≡≡≡

HISTORY OF GLOBALIZATION
The Bed You Sleep In
Betrayed
Congo
Controlling Interest
Death in the Garden
The Global Assembly Line
High and Low
It's All True
The Mattei Affair
Mine
MM
New Earth
Profit & Nothing But!
Red Desert
The Revolution Will Not be Televised
Savage Capitalism
Save the Tiger
Squaring the Circle
The Tank Man
El Valley Central
Water
Where the Rivers Flow North
The White Rose

IMMIGRANTS
Blue Collar and Buddha
Dirt
Dirty Pretty Things
Maid in America
My Journey Home
The New Americans
Valley of Tears

INDIA
American Daylight
A Darker Side of Fair
Diverted to Delhi
Fishing in the Sea of Greed
Nalini by Day, Nancy by Night

INTELLECTUAL PROPERTY RIGHTS
Big Bucks, Big Pharma
Blue Vinyl
The Constant Gardener
A Darker Side of Fair

The Future of Food
The Insider
The Island
McLibel
Mondovino
Net Loss
Winstanley

ITALY
Another World Is Possible
Bella Ciao
The Mattei Affair
Now or Never
Il Posto dell'anima
Red Desert

KOREA
Edit
Save the Green Planet
A Single Spark

LABOR HISTORY
Edit
How Yukong Moved the Mountains
It's All True
Mine
New Earth
Nightcleaners
The Phantom of the Operator
A Single Spark
Squaring the Circle
Winstanley
Workingman's Death

LATIN AMERICA (EXCLUDING
    MEXICO)
Argentina
Between Midnight and the Rooster's Crow
Choropampa
The Curse of Inca Gold
H-2 Worker
Life and Debt
The Revolution Will Not Be Televised
Savage Capitalism
Trinkets and Beads

Inch'Allah dimanche
The Jaguar Quartet
The Little Girl Who Sold the Sun
Mandabi
The New Rulers of the World
Rebellion in Patagonia
The Revolution Will Not Be Televised
Rouch in Reverse
Saaraba
Up in Smoke

OIL
Baked Alaska
Between Midnight and the Rooster's Crow
Blackout
Caribe
Commanding Heights
Enron
Extreme Oil
The Mattei Affair
The Oil Factor
Oil on Ice
Red Desert
The Revolution Will Not be Televised
State of Play
Syriana
Trinkets and Beads
The White Rose

ONLINE FILMS
The Diamond Life
EPIC 2014
Outsource This!
Re-Code.com Commercial
Where's Rosie?
Why Cybraceros?

OUTSOURCING AND OFFSHORING
American Daylight
American Jobs
Diverted to Delhi
Maquila
Nalini by Day, Nancy by Night
Outsource This!
Il Posto dell'anima

Save the Tiger
Where's Rosie?
Why Cybraceros?
Zoned for Slavery

POLITICAL THRILLERS
American Daylight
The Bank
The Constant Gardener
Edge of Darkness
Ghost in the Shell
Rollover
State of Play
Syriana

POSTMODERN FILMS
Czech Dream
Phantom of the Operator

REAGANOMICS
Blacklist of the Skies
Collision Course
Wall Street

SCARCE RESOURCES (EXCLUDING
   FISH)
Choropampa
Congo
The Curse of Inca Gold
The Diamond Life
Diamonds and Rust
Mine
Thirst
Unreported World
Where the Rivers Flow North

SCIENCE FICTION
EPIC 2014
Ghost in the Shell
The Island
Save the Green Planet
They Live

SEX WORK/TRAFFICKING
Dirty Pretty Things

Human Trafficking
The Island
Lilya 4–Ever
Live Nude Girls Unite!
Sex Slaves
Trading Women
The Wire
Women for Sale

STRIKES OR LOCKOUTS
The Battle of Orgreave
Edge of Darkness
Our Friends in the North
Where Do You Stand?

STRUCTURALIST FILMS
MM
Phantom of the Operator
Red Desert
Songs from the Second Floor
Under the Tower
Unknown Quantity
El Valley Central

SWEATSHOPS
Knock Off
No Sweat
Zoolander

TAXI DRIVERS
Dirty Pretty Things
Night on Earth
Taxi Dreams

TELEVISION SERIALS AND SERIES
The Apprentice
Commanding Heights
Deadliest Catch
Edge of Darkness
Our Friends in the North
Outrageous Fortunes
State of Play
Unreported World
A Very British Coup
The Wire

THATCHERISM
Auf Wiedersehen, Pet
The Battle of Orgreave
Dockers
Edge of Darkness
The Navigators
Our Friends in the North
The Ploughman's Lunch
Under the Tower
A Very British Coup
Water

TRANSNATIONAL MIGRATION
Auf Wiedersehen, Pet
Chain of Love
Maid in America
Mojados
My Journey Home
The New Americans
Los Trabajadores
Women for Sale

TRANSNATIONAL ORGANIZATIONS
Argentina
Life and Debt
The New Rulers of the World

UNIONS IN THE GLOBAL AGE
The Battle of Orgreave
Betrayed
Collision Course
Edge of Darkness
The Globalisation Tapes
Wal-Mart
Why Wal-Mart Works

WAL-MART
Chain
The Hidden Face of Globalization
The Human Cost behind Bargain Shopping
I Heart Huckabees
Is Wal-Mart Good for America?
Off the Clock
Outrageous Fortunes
Re-Code.com Commercial
Store Wars

Talking to the Wall
This is Nowhere
Wage Slaves
Wal-Mart
Wal-Mart's War on Workers
Where the Heart Is
Why Wal-Mart Works

WOMEN WORKERS AND CHILD
    LABOR
Chain of Love
The Globalisation Tapes
The Hidden Face of Globalization
Phantom of the Operator
Working Women of the World